This Time They Perceive

Volume XV

BY: TODD ANDREW ROHRER

iUniverse, Inc.
New York   Bloomington

This Time They Perceive

iUniverse books may be ordered through booksellers or by contacting:

iUniverse
1663 Liberty Drive
Bloomington, IN 47403
www.iuniverse.com
1-800-Authors (1-800-288-4677)

ISBN: 978-1-4502-2376-8 (sc)
ISBN: 978-1-4502-2377-5 (ebk)

Printed in the United States of America

iUniverse rev. date: 04/07/2010

The author is giving his testimony after negating the neurosis caused by written education and math that in spirit is the same testimony given by many human beings who negated said neurosis going back to the beginning of civilization itself and thus the beginning of written language and mathematics.

Happiness is achieved when one is free from worries because their mind can comprehend any situation that arises.
The concepts the details suggest is the most important detail.

Slander is simply saying something false or malicious that damages somebody's reputation. Somebody could be a group or organization. I am suggesting written education in fact veils right brain when taught improperly and that is the spirit of what I write about. If that is not true than anyone can apply the remedy or the negating method , the fear not remedy, and then nothing will happen to their perception and then it will be understood what I suggest is a slander against the "brand" of education civilization pushes on the children. The antonym to slander is glorification. Glorification is to praise something highly. So some may perceive I slander civilization but in reality I am glorifying right hemisphere traits and in turn I am speaking out against the ones who veil said traits which means they discriminate against said traits. I accidentally applied the ancient fear not remedy and negated the effects of written education and unveiled right brain and now I am a believer in right brain, the god image in man. I am pleased with the power of right brain when it is unveiled and I am unwilling to deny that understanding no matter how many beings spit on my understanding. It is not important how many people disagree with you, it is only important that you have the ability to convince them to agree with you. So although there are few beings in my country that see any value in right brain because they are all engaged in veiling it in the children, by way of their "brand" of education, I am convinced because I have right brain unveiled I eventually will come up with an argument they will be unable to argue with. This is relative to the concept of the one with the most convincing argument is the only vote that counts. Since this document is in diary format I officially have not started my argument yet, I am simply getting my notes in order for the argument. It is first important to understand what civilizations "brand" of education really is, not what it appears to be but what it is from a neurological stand point. The most important thing to perhaps understand about the two hemispheres of the brain relative to how traditional education affects them is that left brain is sequential based or linear based and right brain is random access based. These two aspects denote processing speed but they are also relative to how one perceives things. Random access denotes the ability to jump from one concept to another totally unrelated concept swiftly. Relative to a person who has right brain veiled this appears to be skipping round to many unrelated topics or what one might suggest is "babbling." This is a logical conclusion one with right brain veiled would come to when they hear a being with right brain unveiled speak so it is expected. A being with right brain veiled will hear a being with right brain unveiled speaking and suggest "This person is babbling" and that is an accurate description but it is not a symptom of mental illness it is a symptom of right brain random access traits in that person with right brain unveiled factoring into thought patterns and thus their speech. What this means is a being with right brain veiled will see right brain traits as alien or foreign and assume they are bad or a symptom of illness. That is logical and expected. One clarification is a being with right brain unveiled simply has negated the effects of the traditional education so their right brain is not at 90%, their right brain is back to 50% and this means their left brain is reduced to 50% influence relative to its impact on thought processes and perception. In this mental harmony state it is logical and expected a person will speak at times in sequential and also at times speak in random access concepts equally. Because of this it is important to understand which of the two hemispheres is more powerful when both are at fifty percent. In this mental harmony state is where random access and sequential access compete. A file system has either random access searching or sequential access searching. So there is a billion record file and in order to get from record one to record one billion sequential access takes a billion steps and in random access only one step is required. So in this determination of which hemisphere is more powerful in the sequential and random access contest right brain is clearly more powerful. So right brain is winning the contest one to zero against left brain when both are at 50%, mental harmony. Another aspect of the hemispheres is left brain has intellect which is book smarts and right brain has intuition which is street smarts. Intellect is relative to knowledge and intuition is relative to ignorance. This is an interesting reality so it requires clarification. A person lands on a desert island and they have no knowledge, intellect, relative to what kinds of plant life on that island are edible. So this person is looking at all these potential plants they may be able to eat but they have no knowledge if they are safe to eat or not. So in this case intellect will not serve them so they have to rely on intuition which is relative to ignorance which means they have to experiment in order to gain knowledge, intellect. What this means relative to traditional education is, an adult cannot just cram knowledge down a child's throat so to speak and expect that knowledge to take because knowledge is only gained through intuition and thus is a result of ignorance. A teacher will tell a student "This is how you spell dog, "DOG"". That teacher will perceive they have given that child knowledge but in reality that is not knowledge because it is simply telling that child what to think so that child never gets an opportunity to experiment with intuition and thus ignorance so that lesson is not learned it is just crammed down that students throat. The student is essentially being told what to think and is never getting a chance to think for their self. Thinking for one's self is what intuition is all about. This shows a fundamental flaw in the methods of traditional education. Traditional education is not so much about learning as it is about telling the student what to think and if the student doesn't think that, they are punished. If a teacher says to a class of students "The water flows swiftly in the shallows" and leaves that comment as it is and does not tell any of the students what it means to them, each student will experiment with their intuition by pondering that comment and they will come to their own personal understanding relative to what the comment means and thus will gain their own knowledge from that comment. Traditional education has a template of what is and what is not. For example "This is how to spell dog, "dog", and any other attempt to spell dog differently is wrong and bad and a symptom one is stupid." Did some supreme being tell us if you spell the word dog in any way but "dog" you are stupid or did some human being tell us that? If I suggest any human being that does not spell the word dog, "dawg" , that is proof they are not intelligent and thus they get discriminated against by getting poor grades and that eventually leads to that person getting a slave job later in life, then I am rather cruel and out of touch with reality but that is exactly what traditional education does. Since another person told you that you have to spell dog "dog" or you are stupid, and you believe that then you are a sheep and unable to even think for yourself because all beings are equal. People determined the word dog should be spelled "dog" so their opinion is no more valuable than any other humans opinion except everyone subscribes to allowing those "select" humans to determine exactly how everyone will be spelling "dog" in school or that person will be deemed not intelligent, given bad grades, and eventually end up with a slave job as a result. So the cerebral ideal is along the lines of "Who made you so intelligent you can tell every other human being how they will spell the word dog?". " Who the hell are you?", is another way to look at it. This concept is exactly what Moses was saying in this comment.

[Exodus 2:14 And he said, Who made thee a prince and a judge over us? intendest thou to kill me, as thou killedst the Egyptian? And Moses feared, and said, Surely this thing is known.]

[Who made thee a prince and a judge over us?] "Us" being human beings. Who told you that you are a prince over others and able to determine what is the proper thing to do and not do? I certainly did not tell you that you are a prince over "us" so I am curious why you have the delusion you are a prince over "us." I don't care what other beings suggest you are, you are not a prince and also not a prince over "us". All humans are equal so there cannot possibly be one human or group of humans telling another human what they should do, ever. When you prove to "us" you are a supreme being we will all gladly bow down to you but until then you are nothing but an equal no matter how many sheep say you are a prince. Moses went to the ruler of civilization and essentially said "Who made you God?". So I will attempt to emulate that and tell every single control freak, law maker, etiquette subscriber, ruler in civilization, "Who the hell made you God?, because your delusions of grandeur are quite obvious to me." Who told you that you are allowed to tell a child they are stupid if they do not spell the word "dog" like you suggest they should? Tell your child on the next spelling test to add an "E" at the end of every word on the spelling test and when they come home with an "F" you will understand school is just a place to tell children how to think and if they resist they are discriminated against. Now back to this intellect and intuition contest. If a person is dropped into the middle of a jungle with no food and no water and they their mind is blank with no previous experience in life at all and they can either have intellect or intuition which is better to have? In a utopia it is best to have equal parts of both but civilization has determined for you it is best you just have intellect and just a hint of intuition.

There is a recent news story and it is described in terms like this:

An incident in which punches were thrown triggered an accusation of brutality by police from the mother of the 18-year-old honor student who was involved.

Notice this comment "18-year-old honor student". Now because this student was an honor student somehow that is some sort of blanket reason that what happened to them is even more devastating. One can understand why the tribes such as the Africans and Native Americans were looked at as of little importance because they did not get the traditional education and that was relative to how they were treated in the span of relatively recent history. This is also why civilization looks down on the tribes in the Amazon and determines it is acceptable to try and take their land and resources from them using its "laws" under the guise of "progress". Society by way of education has been conditioned into a state of mind that does not accept all beings are created equal. For example:

An incident in which punches were thrown triggered an accusation of brutality by police from the mother of the 18-year-old high school dropout.

The ones that sense time, the left brain conditioned beings perceive the more education one gets the more valuable they are and that is not possible because all human beings are human beings. What the traditional education "grades" really show is that a human being can be told what to do and be given directions and then they follow them well and are rewarded with grades. The better grades a being gets the better lap dog they are and the less they think for their self.

[18-year-old honor student] This means this being follows directions when they are told what to do. Left hemisphere relies on directions because it has no intuition to think for itself.

[18-year-old high school dropout] This comment means this being prefers to think for their self. Right hemisphere does not like directions because it has intuition so it prefers to think for itself. Simply put I unveiled right brain so I will direct you since you cannot think for yourself and you will be pleased for me to direct you because you are pleased to be directed.

A right brain aspect has an aversion to following directions because right brain has very powerful intuition so no matter what it is told to do it will always think for itself firstly and that means if someone gives it a command, if it does not agree with that command it will not do it and then that person will appear to be "bucking" the establishment when in reality that being is simply thinking for their self. A cult is based on the reality a cult leader can get a cult member to do as they command and that requires the cult member to do as commanded without questioning the command. A right brain influenced being, which means a sound minded being, is not prone to ever be in a cult because they think for their self and so they are their own leader and although they can follow directions they are not going to go jump off a cliff because an authority tells them to, contrary to that, a being with right brain veiled, is prone to jump off a cliff without thinking at all because their intuitive right brain aspect is veiled. It really comes down to one thing, beings who get the traditional education and do not apply the fear not remedy are left brain dominate and they make excellent sheep and beings that apply the fear not remedy become excellent trap detectors and thus not only are not sheep they are a threat to any control structure because they can expose the control structures traps, so they often appear to be revolutionaries. Society is based on a group mentality and what that means is, it is dangerous to think for yourself and ironically societies education methods veil the right brain and that makes sure not many are going be even be able to think for their self because their right brain intuition is veiled. It all comes back to what Moses was saying to the control structure or Ruler. [Exodus 2:14 And he said, Who made thee a prince and a judge over us?] Children will often say, "You are not the boss of me." That is a right brain thought. Right brain wants to think for itself and come to its own understandings no matter what, but a left brain being is the opposite and they are prone to want to control or covet so they will perceive that child is "bucking" the establishment. A control freak will always have weapons or threats of punishment to enforce on beings that resist doing what that control freak suggests they better do. One that senses time, left brain influenced beings, are not really about laws and morals and rules they are just control freaks and they suggest laws and rules and morals so that if anyone does not do what they say, they can punish them and then boast about how evil a person is for not doing what they are told to do by control freaks. Of course a control freak is not prone to agree with that because that may lead to them losing their control. It is not against the law to misspell the word "dog" but if a child does misspell the word "dog" they get a bad grade and they eventually end up with a slave job because they got too many bad grades and all that means is, they did not do as they were told, and now they have a slave job. "You do as you are told or you will be punished." That is all traditional education is, conditioning human beings to stop thinking for their self and making them learn to follow directions or be punished. And Moses said to that [Exodus 2:14 And he said, Who made thee a prince and a judge over us?] and the Ruler or Taskmaster heard what Moses said and concluded [Exodus 2:15 Now when Pharaoh heard this thing, he sought to slay Moses.] This is what a control freak does to beings who do not want to be controlled. That is logical. If a taskmaster has slaves that do not want to listen to his directions then they are deemed evil and criminal and they must be eliminated or they may convince the other slaves to revolt and start thinking for their self. Right brain does not like directions it likes to think for itself and that is bad news for a control freak so the control freak has to have methods to punish those who do not follow its directions. Teachers give children "F's" when the child does not spell the word "dog" the way they are told to spell the word "dog." The core of all control structures are based on rewards for following directions and punishments for thinking for one's self. Left brain needs directions because right brain has intuition and can think for itself. Education favors left brain so society is simply children conditioned by education so that they cannot think for their self and must rely on directions to know what to do. Relative to a taskmaster, freedom is a frightening prospect.

1/24/2010 7:43:19 PM – [Psalms 34:11 Come, ye children, hearken unto me: I will teach you the fear of the LORD.] This comment is a riddle in a way. It is speaking to the children although everyone was a child, so it is speaking to everyone who ate of the tree of knowledge, written education. The right brain aspect when unveiled means one has no fear or this spirit of fear disappears. It is complex from the stand point fearlessness is required considering civilization goes out of its way to veil the right brain in all the children using its "brand" of education, written education. One can learn written education but then the details start coming into focus. The details are, if written education is taught to a child of six or seven then it will veil their right brain and then they have to apply the fear not remedy and that is essentially mental suicide and that's is very difficult to do as in nearly impossible, so that child is essentially mentally ruined by written education. So this comment [I will teach you the fear of the LORD.] is a riddle and the answer to the riddle is in this comment. [2 Timothy 1:7 For God hath not given us the spirit of fear; but of power, and of love, and of a sound mind.]

What is the fear of the Lord? [For God hath not given us the spirit of fear]. The god image in man, right brain has no fear. So this comment [I will teach you the fear of the LORD.] is saying "I will teach you the lord has no fear and being fearless is a symptom of [a sound mind.]" One is not fearless because they go to a spooky place alone at night with no flashlight or an abandoned house in the middle the woods at night all alone with no way to escape and no lights. Fearlessness is applying the fear not remedy and becoming mindful written education taught as it is taught in the world factually veils right brain, the god image in man, and not being afraid to explain that understanding on a world stage, because everyone one else who explained it on a world stage got butchered essentially. That is what fearlessness is. Fearlessness is being mindfully unable to fear what other beings may do to you for speaking facts. I am speaking the truth relative to what written education does to the mind, veils right brain, but because many beings have not applied the fear not remedy, they only see truth as lies. So all I can do is speak the truth and I can explain the truth so no being with even elementary understandings about the mind or brain can argue with them but when all is said and done it comes down to one

8

reality. If I convince you written education has veiled your right brain and then explain to you the remedy and you do not apply it then you are in denial of reality. I can convince you that you are on fire but this aspect that influences you, left brain, may prefer you remain on fire and in that case you are beyond my ability to assist. That is not an indication of my failing that is an indication of how powerful the curse is relative to [Genesis 3:14 And the LORD God said unto the serpent, Because thou hast done this(got the written education, tree of knowledge), thou art cursed...] You factually ate off the tree of knowledge, got the written education, the details for you doing that do not matter at all because you are here now, [thou art cursed]. You right brain is veiled and your sense of time is the proof because the right brain aspect paradox no longer factors into your perception, and in this case your perception of time, so the curse is you are mentally unsound. The only thing you should be asking since you are factually cursed is "What is the remedy to the curse." You are not able to determine the validity of the remedy because you are cursed so you can only ask what the remedy is and accept the remedy as the remedy. There is only one remedy to this particular curse you have although there are many variations of the remedy it is still one remedy. In some respects I prefer not to tell anyone about these mental effects caused by written education as a result of written education being taught to them at such a young age their right brain aspects have been veiled or reduced to a subconscious aspect and on the other hand I am fearless. Another way to look at it is, it does not please me to tell you that is fact, on one hand. So the paradox relative to telling you the things I tell you is: I do not want to tell you and I do want to tell you at the exact same time and that reality never changes and that is the paradox aspect of right brain factoring into my thought processes. I know for a fact you are cursed because I got cursed and we both got the same "brand" of education, written education and let me guess you started school at around the age of six or seven? Let me guess, you knew your ABC's before you were seven and perhaps even knew how to read a bit. You are under this weird impression I am so good because I negated the curse by applying the ancient fear not remedy. I am not good. I accidentally applied the ancient fear not remedy. I did not intend to apply the remedy so I am factually an accident. Because of that I am in a situation I have something on my plate I did not ask for. I do not recall before the accident asking to be in a position I have to explain to people how written education veiled my right brain and in turn made me mentally unsound. I can think of safer causes to be associated with, one might suggest. Because there are varying degree's the mind is bent to the left as a result of the education there is no uniformity. Physiologically the written education does not do anything to the brain relative to being able to detect it on a scan for example and that is infinitely bad news. One has to look at this brain and the mind as two separate things and at the same time one thing. Physiologically my brain scan is exactly like your brain scan. There is nothing that fall's outside of normal limits on my brain scan and there is nothing that falls outside of normal limits on my EEG, but then the mind aspect comes into play and in that area we are totally opposites. I do not sense time and you do. I do not sense hunger and you do. I do not have a sense of mental fatigue and you do. So because of this our perceptions are different, or another way to look at it is what you perceive I do not perceive. Perception is a big cup of tea and is relative to the cerebral cortex. If you travel too far, you are probably lost. The last thing you ever want to do is usually the first thing you should do.

1/25/2010 12:27:48 PM – There are no human beings with left brain traits being their dominate traits that are mentally within normal limits. What is means is every human being is born with left and right hemispheres at fifty percent. In this harmony state of mind right brain traits and left brain traits make up a whole mind but because right brain traits are contrary to left brain traits beings who get the written education and in turn have their right brain veiled see beings, children, in the mental harmony state as strange because right brain traits are random access, ambiguity and paradox. Some children appear hyper to adults but that is just a right brain traits known as "quick" in the ancient texts but an adult who is left brain influenced will see that hyperactivity as illness and force pills on that child to "fix" that child. The reality is the left brain influenced being see a sound minded beings behavior as a symptom of "illness" because they see right brain aspects as bad because they are a left brain influenced beings and left brain is contrary to right brain. The world is made up of beings that are right brain influenced, sound minded, which means they have right brain unveiled and beings who are left brain influenced which means they got written education and didn't apply the remedy to re-unveil right brain after written education veiled it in them as children. I did not know my right brain was veiled until after I accidentally applied the remedy. What that means is you cannot tell your right brain is veiled because it was veiled when you were still a young child and so all you know is what it is like to have right brain veiled. That is what you perceive is normal now. You do not know what it is like to have right brain unveiled so you have no experience mindfully with what right brain traits are when at full power, when right brain is at fifty percent in the mind. Your right brain was veiled by the time you were ten or twelve and because the mind itself is not fully matured until the age of twenty to twenty four there is no way you could possibly know what right brain at full power and unveiled is like. The ancient texts you know as the religious texts are simply suggesting two points. The first point is written education, the tree of knowledge has dangerous mental side effects and if not taught properly this invention veils right brain, the god image in man. The second point is, if one is taught the written education, the tree of knowledge improperly there is a remedy one has to apply to get their right brain unveiled, to break the curse of being mentally unsound. Because of this the ancient texts are not about rules and morals and codes of conduct relative to everyday life they are in fact explanations of how one can get the complex aspect of their mind back after it is veiled by written education, the tree of knowledge. It is not possible a person can live their life if the complex aspect of their mind is veiled to a subconscious state. With right brain veiled to a subconscious state the mind itself is built on sand and that means the mind is unsound and that means the fruits of that being with an unsound mind are rotten fruits. One can only get unsound fruits from an unsound mind. Another way to look at it is, a being is conditioned knowingly or unknowingly by written education and in getting this left brain favoring conditioning right brain is slowly silenced to a subconscious state and in turn all the thoughts that being has are a symptom that right brain has been veiled. Every human beings bottleneck is their mind and the mind is relative to their perception. Once right brain is veiled the show is over, that person's life is over unless they do something to unveil right brain. This is simple elementary logic. A being is born and their right brain is at fifty percent then they get years of left brain education and right brain is veiled then they have to do something to unveil right brain or they are mentally unsound for life. So this remedy is not about doing something to improve yourself, it is in fact a required exercise to get back to where you were before your right brain was veiled. The remedy is an exercise to get back to square zero and because of that it is not about self improvement it is about regaining what was taken from you. One cannot get any better than being in sound mind, right and left brain at fifty percent, and that is how everyone is born but since the written education was taught improperly one is less than sound minded, has right brain veiled, and so there is this ancient remedy to regain sound mind. So in that respect you have to go through this exercise and apply this remedy just to get back to where you started at birth. You perhaps are unable to mentally grasp that because that would mean someone did something harmful to you mentally, and you perhaps do not want to face that reality. I will just suggest you were factually mentally raped into hell, the place of suffering, because of the written education and you can get out of that place of suffering, but your chances are slim. That is an indication of the mental damage that all of that left brain education did to you as a child. Understanding the remedy takes no effort at all but applying the remedy will cost you every ounce of courage you have and that is an understatement and that is an indication of how much damage that traditional education did to your mind. This is the percentage you have to work with relative to your chances of applying the remedy and unveiling your right brain. Jesus spoke to five thousand. Out of five thousand twelve considered applying the remedy. Five thousand divided by twelve is .0024. .0024 percent multiplied by six billion is 14,400,000. The whole concept that beings who subscribe to these ancient texts, religion, have all applied this remedy is not even in the realm of possibility. Even if you dedicate your life to applying this remedy your chances are only .0024 percent and if you have any hesitation at all then your chances get even worse. If you start listening to people who have not applied the remedy, ones that sense time, to give you advice on the remedy your chances get even worse. One simply cannot negate years of left brain education just by having a positive attitude. I do not live in miracle world, fantasy world or hocus pocus world. The good news is you do not have to go through what I went through to apply the remedy and the bad news is you have to come very close though. As long as your answer to the question: "What are you willing to do to get your complex powerhouse, right brain back to a conscious state?" is "Anything and everything" then you are at least headed in the right direction. If you answer is anything less than "Anything and everything." then you are already defeated so it perhaps is best to give up so you do not harm yourself by reading further.

7:37:05 PM – Einstein dropped out of high school at the age of sixteen. This is why he worked a slave job at the patient office. There are a couple of accounts why we dropped out , one is that he was not pleased school limited his creativity, a right brain trait and another account was that his teacher kicked him out because he was rebellious, he broke the rules, another right brain trait. Left brain see's rules as safety and right brain see's rules as limiting. So when one has their right brain veiled they like lots of rules and regulations and when they follow all of them they feel safe and feel secure and when the rules and regulations are broken they feel bad or unsafe. Many of these rules are known as etiquette and so they are not even laws they are just society rules. Anyone who breaks these society rules are assumed to be uncivil so Einstein was breaking rules and the teacher decided he was uncivil and kicked him out of school. Breaking a rule has no bearing on intelligence and it never has and it never will, but a person who has right brain veiled naturally assumes it does because left brain believes the more rules the better. This is one of the reasons a person who has their right brain veiled is a self defeatist or a house divided against itself. They tend to create more and more rules to live up to feel safe and then they cannot live up to all those rules and so they see their self as a failure. Some people will say "You can't go into a building with a hat on or you are bad." but that has no basis in reality relative to being bad or uncouth so it is really just that person, left brain influenced, is pleased with many rules because it gives them the impression of safety in that extreme left brain state the written education conditioned them into. One cannot be very creative, a right brain trait, and have lots of rules, a left brain trait. The more rules you load yourself down with the less creative you become. This is in part the reason the ancient texts have so many rules. A person who has not applied the remedy and has a veiled right brain will seek to follow all the rules in ancient texts and they will become bogged down because they cannot live up to all those rules and so they will become depressed and in turn move closer to the 9th circle of hell, treason, which is the remedy itself which is required to be in a state of mind t apply the remedy.. Those who lose their life mindfully will preserve their mental life, is treason. Walking through the valley of the shadow of death and fearing not, is treason. Another way to look at it is, a person who applies the remedy unveils right brain and they understand the ancient texts and so they understand those rules are a snare set for the ones who have not applied the remedy, the ones that sense time, the left brain influenced. Because the remedy in the ancient texts unveils right brain, the god image in man, there are no rules after that. One cannot veil right brain after they unveil it so following rules or not following rules are not going to make any difference. This is relative to the comment seek the kingdom first. That means apply the remedy because it is understood you got the written education, tree of knowledge. So that is the only rule. Society makes sure you break the first rule, don't eat off the tree of knowledge so you are stuck at the second rule, apply the remedy to the tree of knowledge to unveil your right brain because the tree of knowledge veils right brain, the god image in man. You are prone to following rules and etiquette now because your right brain is veiled but after it is unveiled you are going to be prone to creativity and be a free thinker and many etiquette rules you will find only get in the way. You will become very cerebral contrary to how you are now. One has either applied the remedy and has become very cerebral or one has not applied the remedy and so they are left with seeking physical and material aspects to achieve pleasure or to be pleased. I have a lot of thinking to do now since I unveiled right because I am mindful I was not doing much thinking the thirty odd years right brain was veiled. I am mindful a person with right brain veiled can perhaps not even imagine that. I am pleased to write my thoughts down and that is the most important thing in the universe because without my thoughts I have no universe. Perhaps you are unable to understand how valuable right brain is because yours is veiled. I only require something to write my thoughts down on and I will give up everything for that and if worse comes to worse I will keep my thoughts to myself. That is an indication of how powerful right brain is. It changes a person from being materialistically pleased into a being that is pleased by the power of a sound mind and that is infinitely bad news to an economic system that is based on materialistic items to give beings pleasure. I do not need to be in the materialistic race any longer because I have this fountain that never dries up, and it is free, and that is enough for me.

9:41:23 PM - Written education veils the right brain, this is why Buddhism is an oral tradition. Once one gets written education the remedy is one has to defeat their perceived fear of death. This is suggested in Buddhism as one goes to a cemetery at night alone and meditates, of course one who has right brain veiled will not be meditating, so to speak. Neurologically speaking, the hypothalamus is sending many false signals after one gets education, so one has to get it to give them the death signal and then they ignore it and that unveils right brain and one returns to consciousness. So one has to seek, walk through, the valley of the shadow of death, to get the hypothalamus to give them the death signal, and then they fear not and that is the remedy. One knows they have applied the remedy properly when they lose their sense of time about thirty days after they apply the remedy. This no sense of time is relative to right brain paradox. One will think how much time has passed, and the paradox will say time has passed and no time has passed and that will be the minds final answer, so one has no sense of time, and that is the fountain of youth, the inability to sense time passing and that means the body also reacts or functions accordingly, one is not effected by stress caused by being able to sense time.

<rasmine> :)

1/27/2010 3:40:29 PM - There is no reason to panic about anything because impermanence is certain. Doubt encourages experimentation and certainty encourages stagnation. There are only two things in life that are certain and certainty is not one of them. Ambiguity certainly keeps one honest. Witt is not wisdom. Knowledge is taught but wisdom is terminal. It's not important how wise one is, it is only important how wise the ones they speak to are. Sound minds tend to have a purpose and the other minds tend to just have dreams of purpose. Nature and wisdom are in harmony. Sensing time is relative to foolishness and wisdom is understanding that. One key to wisdom is clarifying all of your clarifications. One with a full cup has no thirst.

[Pity not the blind man, for he is hindered not by the visions of this world, but rather pity yourselves, for he will see the light before you do.]

[Pity not the blind man] = ones with no sense of time are not very good judges because they see everything as one thing , a right brain holistic aspect, like a child trusts everyone so they are not good judges, so in that respect they are "blind men", they trust or give everyone the benefit of the doubt, ambiguity is a right brain trait. So this is saying to ones that sense time, do not pity that being you assume is "dumb" they are not dumb they are sane and you just assume sanity is insanity because you are mentally unsound and your sense of time proves it. Insanity always see's sanity as insanity, so there is no need to pity that "blind man" because he is sane, instead you should pity yourself because that blind man can see very well and you cannot see that.

[for he is hindered not by the visions of this world] = Ones that do not sense time are of sound mind so they are the wise, they are mindful exactly what is going on in this narrow, this world, their awareness is at maximum power because they have right brain unveiled, so their visions of this world are not hindered because their mind is not hindered because they applied the remedy to the tree of knowledge, written education, as the ancient texts suggested they should.

[but rather pity yourselves, for he will see the light before you do.] Pity yourself which means focus on the log in your eye and attempt with all of your might to apply the remedy to the tree of knowledge so you are not stuck for the rest of your life in this unsound state of mind caused by the tree of knowledge so you will stop idolizing that blind man, your pity of him shows you idolize him.

[In a time of need he spoke to a rock, not with his lips, but his mind, and the rock wept tears of fresh water until his thirst was quenched.]

[In a time of need] = ones that sense time have desire and cravings like greed and lust and envy.

[he spoke to a rock] = a being with no sense of time is speaking to one with a sense of time, a rock(the mentally dead or unsound minded, ones with

16

right brain veiled after they ate off the tree of knowledge and did not apply the fear not remedy).

[his lips] = he spoke to the rock, the ones that sense time , the mental rock as in dumb as a rock, with oral suggestions which is contrary to what written education does, it teaches with text books and is based on script, or written aspects and learning these aspect have a price, they veil right brain. His lips denote oral education.

[and the rock wept tears of fresh water until his thirst was quenched.] denotes sometimes one with a sense of time will hear the words of the wise and apply the remedy and they will unveil right brain and they will return to sound mind and their thirst for wisdom will be quenched because right hemisphere is as fountain of wisdom that never runs dry.

Relative to the parable of sower:

[he spoke to a rock] He told ones with a sense of time, the remedy to the tree of knowledge, he spread the seed, the remedy, the "word". The remedy falls on many rocks, the ones that sense time, and some rocks do not apply the remedy, so the seed, the remedy, is crushed by the rock, but sometimes a rock applies the remedy and they [wept tears of fresh water until his thirst was quenched] which means they unveil right brain and become wise and thus become a sower of the seed, the remedy.

[Make yourself one with the path, and the journey will lead you to eternity.]

[Make yourself one] right brain is holistic, it sees everything as one thing, so the path to being one is to apply the remedy to unveil right brain, [lead you to eternity.] denotes no sense of time. Right brain paradox always answers the question, how much time has passed with a contradiction so one can't sense time, and that is the fountain of youth.

[Make yourself one] This suggests once one applies the remedy they unveil right brain and they stop seeing everything as parts, a left brain trait, and start to see things holistically, a right brain sound minded characteristic.

[If you speak the language of the cosmos, the infinite mysteries shall be revealed within your words.]

[the infinite mysteries] once one applies the fear not remedy they unveil right brain and then they are in infinity, have no sense of time, and no sense of time is the eternal or infinite mystery. If one's mind does not sense time then relative to that person's perception how long do they live for? Infinity or eternally.

Right brain the god image in man is the key or the infinite mystery, so traditional written education veils the infinite mystery in the children, thus the paintings of the devil eating the children. The darkness, the ones that sense time see 's the mentally sound children and "kills the light" veils their right brain using written education, the tree of knowledge.

Thus the comment relative to education, "no child left behind" or we, the ones that sense time, get all the children, veil the light, right brain, in all the children.

[Guide us on the path that we may triumph over the enemy of our salvation and be with you in the end of ends on the planes of enlightenment.]

[that we may triumph over the enemy] = "we" are the ones with no sense of time, the ones who apply the remedy and unveil right brain , {enemy} is the ones with a sense of time, ones with right brain veiled, ones that veil the children's right brain with their "brand" of education. Relative to the ancient texts the serpent, the vipers, the darkness.

{planes of enlightenment} is when the mind is at 50/50 harmony, left and right brain at equal in power. Relative to the east this mental harmony is called the middle way, in Greece it is called the ideal plane and in the west it is called the kingdom or heaven which is simply consciousness or sound mind.

There is an article I read today that Pope John Paul II use to beat him self with a belt and slept naked on the floor to get closer to Jesus, so to speak relative to:

[Mark 8:34 And when he had called the people unto him with his disciples also, he said unto them, Whosoever will come after me, [let him deny himself], and take up his cross, and follow me.]

[let him deny himself] is relative to prostration and submission. If one seeks the shadow of death which means they are in a situation, like a dark spooky place, and their hypothalamus says "Run like the wind danger is coming." and one does not run, they deny their self. So avoid assuming one has to harm their self physically to achieve this remedy, but, relative to your perception you are going to feel like you are going to be killed, in that spooky place, alone at night, but be mindful that is what deny one's self is. Neurologically speaking all that is happening is your hypothalamus is giving lots of false positives in that extreme left brain state so the being is not really afraid it is just their hypothalamus is not acting properly , so the being just has to understand that and go to a place for the sole purpose of getting that hypothalamus to give one of its false "death is coming" signals, like a spooky place, and when it gives that signal one simply ignores it or tells the hypothalamus, "I no longer listen to your false signals." and that is the remedy, and right brain unveils about thirty days later and you are on your own after that,

[Psalms 121:7 The LORD shall preserve thee from all evil: he shall preserve thy soul.]

[Luke 17:33 …; and whosoever shall lose his life shall preserve it.]

The above two comments are the same spirit or same principle and relative to seeking the shadow of death and fearing not evil. Neurologically speaking the whole remedy is simply getting the hypothalamus to give you the death signal in a situation where actual death is not possible only the shadow of death is possible. Relative to your perception you will think something in a scary place will kill you literally but that is only because your hypothalamus is sending you lots of false signals because your mind was bent to the left as a result of written education. A ghost has never killed anyone ever in the history of the universe but your hypothalamus in that dark spooky location is going to suggest they have so you have to wait for it to tell you a spook is coming to kill you and then you ignore that signal and that memory is stored in the amygdala and never again will your hypothalamus give you prolonged false fear signals and that will unveil your right brain because the mind will be cleared of all those false signals from the hypothalamus. Since you are influenced by left brain, it likes to quit, so keep that in mind, and so it is best to go to a dark spooky place that you do not ever want to go to the first time and get it over with. This mental suicide as it where, is totally painless, it is all in your head, and it is simply a mental self control exercise. One needs nothing else but a spooky place to get that hypothalamus to give them that death signal and so one can watch a few scary movies or read a scary book to get their self a bit scared and then go to the scary place. Keep a mind of experimentation and no matter what, there is always a dark spooky place you do not want to go alone at night, so never assume you can't find that place because your hypothalamus is going to tell you, "Don't go to that place its probably dangerous." And that means that is exactly the place you want to go.

[1 Corinthians 3:18 Let no man deceive himself. If any man among you seemeth to be wise in this world, let him become a fool, that he may be wise.]

When you are thinking about that scary place to go to, and your mind says, "That place is scary so you would be wise not to go there." You, [, let him become a fool, that he may be wise.] ; become a fool and go there. Whatever spooky place your mind says do not go to is exactly the place you want to go to and that is what [let him deny himself] means. Don't ask other people if that is what you should do because they are all [If any man among you seemeth to be wise in this world,] " Wise in the world." They will say it is not wise to go to a spooky scary place at night alone to seek the shadow of death so you can fear not or deny yourself. They will go into infinity suggesting it is not wise to do that, and that is why you are going to be a fool and do the reverse of what they suggest and what "you" suggest. Be mindful the ones that sense time only have one purpose, to keep you from applying the remedy because misery loves company. They perhaps are not even mindful that is their only purpose but none the less that is their only purpose.

[Numbers 22:29 And Balaam said unto the ass, Because thou hast mocked me: I would there were a sword in mine hand, for now would I kill thee.]

[^{KJV} Numbers 22:29 And Balaam said unto the ass, Because thou hast mocked me: I would there were a sword in mine hand, for now would I kill thee.]

Ass in this comment is referring to ones that sense time.

[I would there were a sword in mine hand] This is an obvious error in grammar but it is none the less in the ancient texts. The ancient texts slipped one by on the left brain influenced who defend their demotic script grammar with everything they have, how unfortunate.

1/29/2010 9:19:33 AM-

Knowing is less important than understanding. A mind with fear only knows panic. What your brain tells you is not always what you should be told. Everyone has a brain but not everyone has a sound mind.

When a loss is perceived to be an understanding failure is not possible. Contests are for those who perceive loss. The only way to be certain of the outcome is to understand you are not certain of the outcome. Wisdom has more to do with memory than intellect. The last thing one should do is oft the first thing they won't do. Time only kills those who allow it. Illusions cannot be controlled only bent to the will. One with a full cup has no thirst. An empty cup is paramount to inspiration. One does well by doing good so leadership starts at home. If one is leading others they are being led. Relativity suggests one is only relevant if they perceive they are. Everything is for the taking so avoid that. Traditional Education allows a child to see parts they wish they never saw.

Failure is a certain way to avoid stagnation. Treason oft leads to freedom.

<Rohrer> <Rikstafer> Is that what you "think"?
<Rohrer> <Rikstafer> Inability to choose?
<Rikstafer> See a doc

<Rohrer> When one is six they start to get left brain sequential education and by the time they are 12 or 14 their right brain has been veiled to a subconscious state so their perception is altered so their ability to choose is robbed, so one has no choice because written education "must" be given to everyone

<Rohrer> in the book 1984, it talks about the thought police. That is what written education does, controls perception and thus thoughts, so education is a verb

<Rohrer> it alters ones perception to the point the being is hallucinating, so inability to choose is exactly what that suggests because written education is forced on the children.

<Rohrer> If one gets conditioning and it veils their right brain , ones perception is altered so ones thoughts are altered so ones thoughts are controlled.

* You were kicked from #mensa by March (Rohrer)

Never apply the fear not remedy unless you are pleased with the prospect of getting your teeth kicked down your throat into infinity.

7:57:44 PM – Right brain has a trait called intuition. In the ancient texts this aspect is what is known as soul which is conscience. If one is walking down the street and see's a child being beaten by a stranger it is not intuition that drives one to protect that child because it is a visible reality they are observing so it is left brain intellect, visual aspect that drives one to attempt to protect that child. After one gets the traditional education their right brain is veiled and so their intuition is veiled and so their soul or conscience is veiled. Because intuition is sensing things one cannot readily see a person with their right brain veiled does not have any reaction to what the written education does to the mind of a child, veils the child's right brain, because they cannot see it being done, it is a spiritual or mental damaging so they perceive nothing improper is happening and that is because their intuition is veiled and so they have no conscience about it because they no longer have a soul. In society there is now law against mentally harming children because society has their right brain intuition veiled as a result of the education. Once one applies the remedy and unveils right brain they will have their intuition back and they will be fully mindfully aware of the damage being done to a children as a result of written education being taught improperly to six year old children. Perhaps you should reread this small section over and over again into infinity.

1/30/2010 12:26:30 AM – The left brain see's parts and seeing parts is the same thing as seeing details. Contrary to that right brain see's holistic aspects. So relative to evolution, stop focusing on minor details because these minor details are not going to change the fact written education has veiled your right brain and is not going to change the fact you have to apply the remedy to unveil the god image in man, right brain. The understanding you are a lemur monkey is not going to apply the remedy for you, is another way to look at it.

1/30/2010 5:34:17 PM – In the Cistine Chapel there is a painting done by a being that one might suggest had lots of creativity, a right brain trait. In said painting there is the arm of God reaching out attempting to touch the finger of a man. The two fingers are very close to each other but they are not touching so there is a gap between those two fingers and they never touch but they very close to touching. The space between the two fingers is the disconnect between the ones that sense time, the left brain influenced containers and the ones that do not sense time, the right brain influenced containers. This suggests the contrary aspects between right brain, the god image in man and left brain, the Cain, the evil one, relative to the ancient texts. The only way a being who gets the written education, the tree of knowledge, can cross that bridge is to apply the fear not, deny one's self remedy. One has to deny that left brain influence they are under and every time they do they embrace the right brain influence, the god image in man. Because after one gets written education they are a left brain influence this transition of embracing the right brain appears to them to be suffering or harsh and that is relative to the submission or prostration aspects. One has to destroy the left brain influence reality they are use to, their temple, in order to find the right brain influence reality which is a subconscious aspect after one gets the written education. A left brain influenced container will perceive they are denying their self or destroying their self mindfully but in reality they are embracing the right brain influence and that appears to be dangerous to them, they will oft avoid doing it and that is exactly what fear not is relative to. One has to kill off that left brain influence that is in them and since it is the spirit of fear it is going to suggest danger and fear aspects to convince one not too kill it off, so to speak. A left brain influenced container will suggest to their self , "I have morals and class and I have pride in myself so I will not apply this remedy, I am pleased with myself." and that is not them at all, that is the left brain influence tricking them because it wants to stay in power. A left brain influenced container perhaps has no conscience because conscience is relative to right brain intuition and that is veiled so they have no conscience they only have delusions of pride and morals but those are not morals. If a left brain influenced container has any conscience that was worth mentioning, intuition, they would at least be able to be aware all the left brain education they give to a child veils that child's right brain, the god image in man and in turn leaves that child in a place of mental suffering but the ones that sense time have no intuition, conscience, so they perceive they are doing the children a favor by veiling the child's right brain. They know not what they do. They are not aware of that right brain veiling at all and that is devastating a child's mind or spirit but they do not even sense that at all as a being so they have no conscience or soul at all with the left brain influence aspect in control. They are sending children mindfully or spiritually to the place of suffering, hell, by veiling that's child's right brain and they do not even sense that at all. They could not be harming a child any more than they are harming a child by doing that but they do not even sense that at all, in fact they are proud of doing that. One way to look at it is something has taken their conscience or soul and there is only one way to get it back but they perceive that way is dangerous so they are afraid of that, and that is because the spirit of fear, which is what they are under the influence of and so in turn keeps them in its clutches. So this finger of God, a being with no sense of time, a right brain influenced container in the Cistine Chapel is attempting to touch the finger of a being that has a sense of time, a left brain influenced container but they can never touch them because they are separated from the image of god in man, the right brain. The ones that sense time are not of God, they have the right brain god image in man veiled so they are of the spirit of fear, the sinister.

[2 Timothy 1:7 For God hath not given us the spirit of fear; …..but,.. of a sound mind.]

So the remedy is fear not and what that means is one has to kill off that spirit of fear. If a being is afraid to say one single word they have the spirit of fear in them. If a being is afraid to listen to one single song they have a the spirit of fear in them, Now they may attempt to suggest they do not fear that word or that song they just have morals and a conscience but they do not have morals or a conscience they just have the spirit of fear and that spirit of fear is tricking that being into thinking their fear is morals or a conscience. The moment a being underestimates this spirit of fear, the "serpent" that is in them and thus the curse they have relative to [Genesis 3:14 And the LORD God said unto the serpent, Because thou hast done this, thou art cursed] they are doomed forever. You got the tree of knowledge, written education, and all the details for that mean nothing because that won't break the curse. If you doubt you have the curse that is proof of how powerful the curse is. You sense time so the paradox in your right brain no longer even figures into your perception and if you doubt that is truth you are cursed to a degree you are totally out of touch with reality. You have been placed in an alternate reality as a result of this perception altering written education tool. What that means is what you perceive is truth is not truth or fact. You perceive you have morals because you do not say cuss words but you do not even have a conscience, intuition a right brain trait, so you cannot possibly have morals. If you sense time the paradox of right brain is veiled from your conscious state and thus the intuition of right brain is veiled from your conscious state so you cannot have a conscience at all. A person with a conscience does not mentally hinder a child into the place of suffering, into an unsound state of mind, and then brag about it. You brag about it. You are proud you do that to a child. So you have no conscience. I write books explaining why it is improper to veil a child's right brain and you spit in my face and suggest that is not what you do, yet that is exactly what you do but you have no conscience, intuition, to "see" that is factually exactly what you do to the children. So never say the word conscience because you know nothing of that concept in your "sense of time" state of mind.

Another way to look at the Cistine Chapel extended fingers painting is the right brain, the image of god is attempting to bring left brain, man, the ones that sense time, back into the fold, mental harmony, but left brain wants nothing to do with that because when right and left brain are in harmony right brain traits rule and so left brain would only play second fiddle so it hates that prospect and will do anything in its power to avoid that reality.

This is the Rohrer version of the fear not remedy. Take ten to twenty pills. Within an hour your body will start showing symptoms of taking those pills. You may perhaps even convulse a bit and you will certainly feel a great sense of panic come over you. Soon your hypothalamus will say "If you do not call for you help you will certainly die." And that is when you respond with "I do not care if I die." And then you go to sleep and if you get lucky you will wake up the next day and in about thirty days right brain will unveil. So perhaps you can understand the Rohrer version of the fear not remedy perhaps makes the other versions of the fear not remedy look rather docile in contrast but in any case that is factually the Rohrer version of the fear not remedy. One might suggest my version of the fear not remedy scares the hell out of them on several different levels, so to speak. A judge told me "If you want to kill yourself there is nothing anyone can do about it.", so there is some sort of precedent apparently. The reality is, one does not have to risk their life to such a degree by using pills because the pills are simply a catalyst to encourage the hypothalamus to give the "death" signal. For example, the exact same results would have happen if I just went to a spooky place and when the hypothalamus said "If you do not call for you help you will certainly die." And then I responded with "I do not care if I die." Now since you sense time you are scared like a little dog so you are going to attempt to explain my version of the fear not remedy is dangerous or bad but that is only because you are in deep neurosis and thus afraid of a bad haircut. You put the children in the neurosis because you do not have the mental capacity to understand all the left brain education forced on a small child hinders their mind so it is important you attempt to speak as little as possible until you apply the remedy mentally.

9:18:31 PM – Plato wrote a book called Apology of Socrates. Apology in the context of this book means defense. This is the very first comment in that text.

"I do not know, men of Athens, how my accusers affected you; as for me, I was almost carried away in spite of myself, so persuasively did they speak."

This initial line in the proves Plato had right brain unveiled and that proves he listened to Socrates and took Socrates advice and Socrates advice was "No true philosopher fears death" which is what the remedy is. This comment [so persuasively did they speak.] is out of sequence and only a person with right brain unveiled would be typing out of sequence because it appears bad or improper to one who has right brain veiled. It should be [so persuasively they did speak.] relative to proper sequence. Perhaps it is relative to the observer, after all the ones that sense time just killed Plato's teacher and I am certain he was not pleased about that. The second comment in his Apology text is. "And yet, hardly anything of what they said is true." That of course is because the ones that sense time are anti-truth. I detect a bit of humor in that comment also. This is the third line "Of the many lies they (the ones that sense time) told, one in particular surprised me, namely that you should be careful and not be deceived by such an accomplished speaker like me." The humor in this line is the ones that sense time are anti-truth so Plato applied the remedy and unveiled right brain and the ones that sense time were saying "Although you cannot find argument with anything Plato says you should still not believe it." It has never been that ones that sense time are born with broken minds it is simply all that left brain favoring written education has broken their mind and the remedy appears dangerous to them and unwise to apply because their mind is broken and it tells them lies. An insane person is not aware they are insane and in this case, insane is mentally unsound, their right brain has been veiled to a subconscious state as a result of all that left brain favoring written education pushed on them as children so they are not insane, mentally unsound, by nature they are simply the fruits of a cause and effect relationship relative to written education being pushed on them as children. Buddha called the ones that sense time, the sane. The ancient texts called them the devil. There is no difference between those labels because at the end of the day a mind divided is an unsound mind and so the fruits of that mind are unsound. Since the ones that sense time are unsound mentally the only possible way for them to escape that unsound state of mind is to have a good accident. If they attempt to do something they perceive is wise they will never escape their insanity so they have to do things they perceive are unwise and in doing that they may have a good accident and that is what the concepts of submission, prostration and thus deny one's self is relates to. This is an indication of how much mental damage all that left brain written education has done to them. If human beings were born mentally like the ones that sense time behave then the species would have died off thousands of years ago. There are no lemur monkeys in the wild that become depressed and kill their self is another way to look at it.

Let's look at this whole situation relative to written education from two different perspectives, firstly the supernatural perspective. So right brain is the god image in man and so God gave man his image and that is right brain and this written education, the tree of knowledge, veils or silences the God image in man. So the written education is simply a method to attack the God image in man and in turn encourages the serpent image in man, left brain. In that case it is justified to fight anyone who is veiling the God image in man and thus attacking God. This is more along the militant point of view and is why some militants attack the traditional education school system. This is why some militants kill anyone who messes around with written education. So this point of view is why Abraham and Lot burned down the cities and this is why scribes are suggested to be bad in the ancient texts and also why the pen of the scribes is in vain and in vein so to speak, as suggested by the ancient texts.

[Genesis 19:13 For we will destroy this place, because the cry of them is waxen great before the face of the LORD; and the LORD hath sent us to destroy it.]

[Luke 20:46 Beware of the scribes, which desire to walk in long robes, and love greetings in the markets, and the highest seats in the synagogues, and the chief rooms at feasts;]

28

[Jeremiah 8:8 How do ye say, We are wise, and the law of the LORD is with us? Lo, certainly in vain made he it; the pen of the scribes is in vain.]

[certainly in vain made he it] This comment is out of sequence so it is a sign post of authenticity meaning the being who wrote this comment had right brain unveiled and right brains random access aspects are evident in this beings comments. This comment should be [certainly in vain he made it] relative to proper sequence.

One thing is for certain, written education does not favor right brain because it is sequenced based, a left brain trait and right brain is random access based. So this supernatural take on this left and right, Cain and Abel type battle is why the violence is happening or why this war that has been going on for thousands of years, the ones with no sense time attempting to stop the ones that sense time from veiling the god image, right brain, in children.

Now let's look at it from a no supernatural point of view. Human beings invented a tool and this tool favors left brain and in turn every time the left brain traits are favored a bit the right brain traits are veiled a bit and at the end of a child's education the right brain is veiled to a subconscious aspect. So even in this situation the child is being harmed mentally. So the only way a human being could allow this to happen to children is if they have no morals because harming the children insures the future of the species is harmed. Ones with no sense of time and have unveiled right brain have to turn to stone or salt so to speak because if they try to hold onto pride and morals they will implode as a beings because they cannot stop written education, cannot stop the ones that sense time who push it on young children, and cannot stop mental harm being brought to the children as a result. So all of the concepts of morals and rules and righteousness cannot be allowed in a being who has applied the remedy because they would implode at the levels of awareness one reaches when right brain is unveiled, in the sound mind state. Pride is one of the sins, and the sins are simply mental side effects one exhibits after they get the tree of knowledge, written education. Simply put if you apply this fear not remedy and attempt to have pride in this situation we are in as a species, relative to this written education, you will implode. These concepts of personal rules and morals one lives by are symptoms of pride and an indication one never has applied the remedy after getting the education. The bottom line rule of thumb is our species invented something that altered our perception and now we are a species divided and so we are prone to destroy ourselves. There are only two kinds of human beings on this planet, ones who got the education and did not apply the remedy, ones that sense time, and ones who never got the education or ones who did and did apply the remedy after the education, ones with no sense of time and these two factions are against each other whether they know it or not and so we are a species divided against itself and a species divided cannot stand which means sustain itself. So this whole idea that one person is better than another person, is on a species level false because we are all in the subset of the species and we are a species divided against itself, so we are all screwed, so to speak.

The fundamental problem with written education, math and writing, is that it favors left brain. So if one wants to get written education at such a young age they have to give up their right brain as a sacrifice. Because all of civilization is based on written education and math one is expected to sacrifice their right brain and even when they do, that does not mean they will become some wealthy rich person in civilization it just goes without saying one is expected to sacrifice right brain. Math for example is all parts. The number one is not like the number two, so both are parts and right brain is holistic so it simply does not do well in math at all because it see's everything as one thing and math is strictly parts, a left brain trait. There is nothing holistic about math.

X = written education, math and written language
Y = sound mind
Z = money and luxury
A = poverty
B = unsound mind, left brain powerful right brain veiled.
C = oral education, inability to use written language and math proficiently

$X + B = Z$
$C + Y = A$

Written language and math is what civilization is based on. Your job and thus your pay is determined by how much written language and math you get and that is what is called education and that is under the subset "required in this narrow". That is the way of the world so to speak. So this comment is referring to that.

[1 John 2:15 Love not the world(education or the methods of education the world uses), neither the things that are in the world(written language and math and money and material aspects associated with that education). If any man love the world, the love of the Father(right brain) is not in him(right brain in veiled).]

This is relative to the great trade off. You either get the written education or you get your right brain but you will never get both. You will not be lukewarm. You are either going to be a good scribe and mathematician or you are going to have a right brain in your conscious state of mind. So if you are very good at writing or good at math or both you factually have your right brain reduced to a subconscious state. The beings in the ancient texts sounded very strange to some because they were saying avoid that written education and thus avoid education, it veils the god image in man and so they sounded exactly like the militants sound today. The militants say "Don't give people education." And they mean written education because it veils the god image in man, right brain when taught to seven year old children. This written education has to be taught by a Master that is fully conscious and aware of its mental side effects and that is a fact. And then the ones that sense time suggest that is a bad thing. I am not suggesting do not give people education I am suggesting give a child oral education and then when the child is older start on the written education but in reality one cannot have both right brain unveiled and have written education so it's all just crap. So the ancient texts came up with a solution, after you get the tree of knowledge, apply this fear not, deny one's self remedy.

2010-02-01 12:28:54 AM – I attended a community college and I was rather good in computer classes. I was good at hardware and understanding the concepts relative to building a computer system. What is interesting is I passed every single class to get my associate degree except for accounting. I took the class twice and I could not pass it, I thought I was stupid and so

I accepted the reality I would be working slave jobs the rest of my life. But now I understand my mind would not let me veil right brain any more. It would not allow me to subscribe to these left brain conditioning classes, math is left brain focused, and veil my right any more than the classes already had. Accounting is very "seeing parts" and making judgments heavy and those are left brain traits. Your education is nothing at all except a right brain hindering invention and has nothing at all to do with wisdom or intelligence it is factually just mentally hindering insanity. This exact reality is playing out on a world scale every single day. Children assuming they are stupid because they cannot pass all of this left brain traditional education, written language and mathematics. This is why the ancient texts suggest the ones that sense of time, the scribes are demonic and of the darkness and the serpent. The darkness seeks to do the maximum damage it can do and that is damage against innocent children and that is why the ancient paintings show the devil eating children. I am suggesting civilization itself is of the darkness and the darkness makes sure it damages all the children and turns them into what it is, which is diabolical. There is not much else happening here on this plane of existence but an unsound beast tricking children into becoming unsound beasts by using trinkets of luxury and safety with a nice measure of fear tactics and punishment attached for not "following directions.". I feel no need to mask that reality because the darkness would never admit to it anyway. The darkness, civilization or society will deny its brand of written education veils the god image in children, right brain even when neurologists who they award Nobel prizes to agree with what I suggest:

["What it comes down to is that modern society discriminates against the right hemisphere." - Roger Sperry (1973) - neuropsychologist, neurobiologist and Nobel laureate]

This being made this comment one year before I started school. I was five years old when this being made this comment. Civilization, the cult, the beast, does not even listen to ones it suggests are wise. All this comment is saying "What it comes down to is that modern society discriminates against the right hemisphere." is: Written education favors left brain and in turn anyone who gets it becomes a left brain influenced container and in turn makes all their offspring left brain influenced containers using the same "brand" of education.

No other sound minded human being could ever convince the abominations of the dangers of all that written education on the minds of children so I find no reason to edit my thoughts from them because they can't do anything about it anyway relative to burning my books or their head will be hung on a stake by the common people. I already accidentally applied the fear not remedy so I certainly am not very stressed out whether you apply the remedy or not. I am at the stage since the accident I laugh oft. I laugh about many things that perhaps I should be taking seriously but I do not see any solution to the problem relative to what traditional education has done to our minds so I just laugh at it. I am no longer a beast of burden. I do not become a nervous wreck over spilt milk from a leaking container. Because you sense time you cannot think clearly and so you assume something bad is going to happen to us but in reality that sensation is your slight right brain intuition that you have left is letting you know something horrible is happening to us right now and has already happened to us. You are getting signals of danger but you do not have the mental clarity to translate them properly so the signals are coming out of your mouth garbled. We as a species fell from grace over 5400 years ago as the result of the invention written education and math because in learning those inventions we veiled the right hemisphere aspects and so we are mentally unsound and thus fallen from mental grace. What exactly am I supposed to care about since I am fully aware we fell from grace 5400 years ago? That is why you and six billion of your minions are not capable of ever making me afraid or making me censor my thoughts because the show is already over. For me to die and you to live, which is better God only knows.

2:41:59 AM – I came to be reminded of the reality once one applies the remedy they cannot speak in depth with ones who have not applied the remedy for long periods because the "curse" bleeds into them. I do not know how to put it any better than that. One who applies the remedy has heightened awareness and one of these aspects is the intuition of right brain and so the longer one talks with someone who has not applied the remedy the more the "curse" bleeds into them and they became "possessed" by the curse also. I imagine if you sense time that is perhaps the craziest thing you have ever heard in your life and I will humbly remind you I am an accident and just an experimenter and I report what I understand. I will chat with beings who have applied the remedy and no such thing will happen but then I chat with those who have not applied the remedy and after even a few comments about the situation and the reality of the situation relative to this written education, they will start to just mock the whole thing. They will crack jokes and then start suggesting I am a liar or I am mentally unsound and then I will ask them questions about what do they think will happened to a child's mind if that child is given extensive left brain education starting at the age of six and then they crack jokes and they cannot keep up and it all falls back to the one reality the Catholic church suggests: "Never reason with the darkness." I don't understand how it can be a joke when we are talking about the minds of children but they seem to think it is a joke. I will show you an example in the ancient texts of the wise beings attempting to reason with the ones that sense time and then the wise beings become angry and this is the "bleeding" of the curse into them.

[Matthew 12:34 O generation of vipers, how can ye, being evil, speak good things? for out of the abundance of the heart the mouth speaketh.]

This being is speaking to the ones that sense time, the scribes, and after a few moments this being is starting to "spit blood" because he is attempting to reason with the darkness and the darkness is bleeding into him.

[O generation of vipers, how can ye, being evil, speak good things?] Asking the darkness questions is reasoning with the darkness. One should avoid asking the ones that sense time questions, one should only tell the ones that sense time how it is, and how it going to be, and no matter how they respond it should never be considered anything but an attempt by the darkness to get you to reason with it.

I saw this text while searching so I am compelled to explain it.

[1 John 3:12 Not as Cain, who was of that wicked one, and slew his brother. And wherefore slew he him? Because his own works were evil, and his brother's righteous.]

[And wherefore slew he him?] is out of sequence so it is a signpost of authenticity. Should be [And wherefore he slew him?] Again this is question and an attempt of this being trying to reason with the darkness. That is why the answer to every question I ask you is "perhaps".

This comment is saying left brain, Cain, revolted against right brain, Abel, and did this using written education which favors left brain, and in turn "slew", which means veiled right brain to a subconscious state, and because left brain alone cannot run a human mind, its revolt was evil as in it harms the being, and [his brothers works are righteous], because right brain just wants to be at 50/50 is harmony with left brain but in that situation left brain is weaker and takes second fiddle which is why left brain revolted against right brain to begin with. Simply put Cain, left brain, cannot stand to be in harmony with right brain because in that scenario left brain is always the lesser of the two hemispheres and that makes left brain jealous and it will not tolerate that ever. Simply put , you sense time so you are under the influence of left brain so you are your own worst enemy and so you have to deny yourself , because yourself is not your true self, it is the left brain influenced self, Cain, the evil one. One can understand it properly if they consider this equation.

X = Cain state of mind, left brain influenced.

Y = the core being.

Z = sound minded state of mind left and right hemisphere are equal in influence.

Y has to trick X into thinking they (Y) has let go of life and literally died, and then X lets go of one and then one (Y) returns to (Z) as they were as a child, so one returns to being a child of God. So this is achieved by one (Y) seeking willingly the shadow of death and when the shadow of death approaches, the hypothalamus says "A spooky thing is coming to kill you(Y)" and one (Y) fears not and that tricks (X) into believing (Y)

35

has literally died, let go, and then (Z) state of mind returns. This is why it is very important you (Y) do not seek advice from beings that sense time because they are influenced by (X) relative to whether you should apply this remedy or not because they will always suggest it is bad or evil or improper because misery(X) loves company.

[Matthew 13:19 When any one heareth the word of the kingdom, and understandeth it not, then cometh the wicked one, and catcheth away that which was sown in his heart. This is he which received seed by the way side.]

This comment is saying sometimes after you apply the remedy you will speak about the remedy and why it is important, and sometimes one that sense time will not understand it and maybe another left brain influenced being will come around and say "This guy is crazy and on drugs" and so that initial person you were talking to will be drawn away.

[then cometh the wicked one[(X), Cain, one that senses time], and catcheth away that which was sown in his heart.]

Simply put (X) will deny written education is the tree of knowledge and will also deny fear not or deny one's self is the remedy. This is universal because if one has not applied the remedy they only see fact or truth as lies. The darkness cannot admit the tree of knowledge is written education because if it does it destroys itself, it reveals to itself its own nature and that nature is to mentally/spiritually harm children. Simply put before the accident I had no idea written education mentally harmed me but since the accident I fully understand that it did, but since I am not use to this reality of heighten awareness I write books attempting to disprove what I fully understand is fact. What that means is I doubt what I understand and that is healthy because as I attempt to disprove what I understand I in fact prove it more thoroughly. The right brain ambiguity is valuable because if I had absolutely no reservations about the mentally hindering aspects of written education on the mind then the only logical conclusion would be to go to war against the ones who push said education on children and thus veil the children's right hemisphere aspects and leave the children mentally unsound and in the place of suffering. Of course I speak in paradox, a right

36

brain trait, because the fact I publish these texts indicates I have no doubt and I am at war with the ones that sense time and these texts are my battle cries. Perhaps you should put me on your terrorist watch list now and perhaps that will apply the remedy for you, perhaps.

[Malachi 4:3 And ye shall tread down the wicked; for they shall be ashes under the soles of your feet in the day that I shall do this, saith the LORD of hosts.]

This comment is not as much about ego as it is just simple logic. A person who unveils right brain is light years beyond the mental ability of a person who gets the education and does not apply the remedy to unveil right brain. It is just simple, who is wiser a person with both hemispheres working in the conscious state of mind or a person with only one hemispheres and the lesser of the two hemispheres to boot, working in the conscious state of mind? This is not relative to ones genes or intelligence this is relative to one person got written education and applied the ancient fear not remedy to unveil right brain and one that did not, so there is no possible way the one who did not apply the remedy can compete with one who did on a cerebral level ever into infinity. This comment is attempting to explain contrast. I have not come across the word brain in any of these ancient texts yet so they had to use other methods to explain the brain and thus the mind. That should be elementary that they would have to use parables and contrast statements to explain this situation.

[Malachi 4:3 And ye shall tread down the wicked(the ones that sense time, the ones who got the education and did not unveil right brain); for they shall be ashes under the soles of your feet(not mentally sound so they in turn are not mentally playing with a full deck so they cannot compete mentally with ones with a sound mind) in the day that I shall do this(apply the remedy to unveil right brain), saith the LORD of hosts.]

So when you apply the remedy there will be no human being on earth that has not applied the remedy than can even compare to your cerebral abilities but that is not because you have good genes that is because right brain is very powerful when unveiled which leads one to ponder why the ones that sense time would veil it to begin with. Please be mindful I am pleased with these ancient texts and find no flaws with them at all but that does not mean I agree with your ways and your days.

[Luke 6:39 And he spake a parable unto them, Can the blind lead the blind? shall they not both fall into the ditch?]

I detect humor in this comment. How can a person who has their right brain veiled show a person who has their right brain veiled the way to unveil the right brain? How can a person with a sense of time explain to another person with a sense of time what no sense of time is like? The point of this parable is the only way one can ever get out of the curse caused by written education is if someone breaks the curse and tells them how to break the curse. The being who said this comment was saying " I broke the curse and only I can explain to you how to break it because someone who has not broken the curse is not even aware of the curse." Simply put I had no idea I was applying the fear not remedy in that last suicide attempt, I had no idea, so it was simply dumb luck or an accident relative to my perception at the time. That is an indication that there is no possible way you can determine you have the "curse" unless someone who breaks the curse explains to you the symptoms of the curse. It is all relative to contrast. I once was blind but now I see. I once was lost but now I am found. I once was cursed but now I am not. I once had right brain veiled but now I don't. Of course this is not fantasy land. You certainly can apply the remedy if you decide to and then you will be compelled to explain how you were once blind but now you can see, and that is where the teeth getting kicked down your throat celebration kicks in because the ones that sense time only see truth as lies. Simply put , I am saying it is fact written education veils the right hemisphere and so written education hinders the mind and the ones that sense time will say "That is just your opinion or that is a lie." But in reality what I suggest is fact and truth.

[Luke 18:32 For he shall be delivered unto the Gentiles, and shall be mocked, and spitefully entreated, and spitted on:]

Gentiles are ones that sense time, the scribes. You will be saying "I applied this fear not remedy and unveiled my right brain and it is truth." And the ones that sense time will mock you, and spit on you every time you say that because no matter how well you explain it and speak convincingly if they do not apply the remedy in the end everything you say is in vain. This is where no morals or rules comes in handy. It is strange but if you say everything perfectly and fail it's much more grief than if you just go with the flow and suggest what you are compelled to suggest and then fail to convince them to apply the remedy. They will attempt to say you are bad and a liar and a fool for telling them what you tell them so if you start looking at them as anything but illusions you are in for one long eternity and eventually you will give up and perhaps go hide. They are human beings but they had their mind bent to the left and so they are factually mentally unsound so you have to just take everything they say with a grain of salt at all times and that is very difficult to get use to. They are not mentally capable of complexity because that is a right brain trait and since they sense time their right brain is in a subconscious state totally. You are only going to be able to speak in a complex manner so there is a huge disconnect. The deeper reality is, you have to piss them off and make them angry and slowly drive them to the 9th circle of hell, treason, because that is where the door out of hell is. It is like the concept of tough love. You will drive them to the 9th circle of hell, treason with the understanding once they are there they very well may end up killing their self literally as opposed to just mindfully, which is what the deny one's self reality is. That reality is what is known as paying the piper. Human beings have their mind bent all the way to the left as a result of written education and the remedy is they have to deny their self and they are not going to deny their self if they are happy about everything, so they have to get to a mental state they can deny their self, and many never come out of that place and end up in a body bag, but that is not important at all. Civilization put them in that situation, all you are trying to do is find some wheat in the pile of chaff. Civilization does not understand the importance of oral education until the child is older so obviously civilization does not care if beings kill their self, so you cannot do anything about that, so put it out of your mind. Is it proper to explain to a human being of your species who have had their right brain turned off how to turn it back on. It is proper or is that improper? I believe it is proper so I do not care about any rules or morals or laws that may suggest it is improper no matter how many beings that sense time vote on it. I will not allow the beings that knowingly or unknowingly veil the right brain in other beings tell me what is proper or improper. I may pretend to follow their ways but I certainly will not subscribe to their ways. When in Rome and such. Don't take advice from beings that can't understand you.

[Education is an ornament in prosperity and a refuge in adversity – Aristotle]

When a child is born their mind is sound so they are in cerebral prosperity, they are of sound mind and have no problems so written education is meaningless. If you leave that child's mind alone until they are a bit older, perhaps sixteen to eighteen, and just give them oral education they will be brilliant but you just do not get that because you are the darkness. After that child gets the education their right brain is veiled and so they are in refuge, in trouble and so then all they have is education, because they no longer have their right brain. Leave well enough alone. Why are you in such a rush to push all that left brain education on a child? Because you perceive that child is bad because when you see a child of sound mind in your unsound mind state you see them as bad and in need of "fixing". You want to mentally abuse that child like you got mentally abused and that is one reality you perhaps are mentally unable to face. Socrates was killed for corrupting the minds of the youth and one of those youth was Plato and ones of Plato's students was Aristotle and Socrates version of the fear not remedy was "No true philosopher fears death".

Traditional education is an enchantment to fools and an obstacle to wisdom. Writing and Math has as much to do with wisdom as mental confusion has to do with clarity.

[Luke 6:39 And he spake a parable unto them, Can the blind lead the blind? shall they not both fall into the ditch?]

Relative to organized religion this comment is saying if the Minister of a church or worship group has not applied the fear not remedy there is no possible way ever a person could be assisted in that worship group. If a "minister" does not understand what exactly the tree of knowledge is and exactly what the remedy is to unveil right brain is that proves they have not applied the remedy. If they sense time they have not applied the remedy.

The interesting thing about this is if a being does apply the remedy the full measure they will understand exactly what the tree of knowledge is and they will attempt to suggest it to others and they will be spit on and mocked and they never will have a worship service or church or organized religious place because they will be a flock of one. The early churches in the New Testament were not as much as places to assist ones to apply the remedy as they were places for ones who have applied the remedy to hide. There are places on this planet right now that are places of refuge for beings that have applied the fear not remedy. They are not places of worship as much as they are places to hide. Simply put after you apply the fear not remedy, you unveil right brain, the god image and you are filled with that spirit so what on earth are you worshiping? You are not worshiping you are telling the world of the light you have found, attempting to convince your friends of the remedy, and so worshiping is really proof that beings never applied the remedy. I do not hesitate or ask questions or ask for things because right brain provides me with everything I need so there is no need for asking for assistance. I am mindful of the task and I do the task and there is no need to ask for anything else. I do not need anything from anyone of this world because I have the only thing that matters on my side, right brain, the god image in man. I cannot understand what I would ask for greater than that.

If one must ask for something more they never really found the door.

[Psalms 9:17 The wicked shall be turned into hell, and all the nations that forget God.]

This comment is saying, the ones that sense time have right brain veiled, so they ate off the tree of knowledge and did not apply the remedy so they are in hell, mentally unsound, and so any nation that teaches the tree of knowledge and does not suggest the fear not remedy in turn is also in hell, mentally unsound, because their right brain is left veiled, because everyone in that nation will end up with their right brain veiled and that nation will be of hell, mentally unsound, and not of God because a nation that teaches written education and does not suggest the fear not remedy forgets about God, the right hemisphere, the God image in man. Simply put, you teach a child written education and then never even suggest the fear not remedy or assist that child to apply that fear not remedy to restore their right brain, you forget about God and when you do that you are doomed because every human being needs right brain in the conscious state of mind or their mind is built on the sand and so they are doomed to crumble and that goes for an entire nation and the entire species.

This conversation is interesting because at first the being with a sense of time understood what I was saying but then because I apparently was going to fast and he assumed I was a robot and stopped listening. It is difficult to determine how fast or slow one goes when they do not sense time because patience or impatience is relative to time.

<Rohrer> Written language is the tree of knowledge, it favor lefts brain and in turn veils the god image in man, right brain. Any being that teaches it to a child veils the god image in that child and leaves that child in the place of suffering, hell.
<Rohrer> The remedy to this is the fear not remedy
<Rohrer> one has to seek the valley of the shadow of death and then fear not
<Rohrer> this in reality means one has to defeat their fear of death mindfully and this shocks teh mind and unveils right brain, the god image in man
<Rohrer> unless this is done one is forever under the influence of the seprent
<Rohrer> Neurologically speaking, after one gets teh written edcuatin their hypothalamus starts sending many false signals so they have to get that hypopthalamus to give them the shaodw of death , signal and then they fear not and that shocks it back into working porperly
<hichiban> hehe
<hichiban> that actually makes alot of sense
<Rohrer> A scribe is a person who gets taught written language and after one applies teh fear not reemdy they can no longer use the written language well, because written language uses parts, judgement, and right brain is holistic thus this comment about scribes

<Rohrer> Jeremiah 8:8 How do ye say, We are wise, and the law of the LORD is with us? Lo, certainly in vain made he it; the pen of the scribes is in vain.

<Rohrer> the pen of the scribes is in vain.

<Rohrer> this means one is far wiser with the god image in man unveiled than if they can write

<Rohrer> if one can write well they cannot think well, it is a trade off, one can write well in the world but its costs them the god image in man, their soul, right brain

[<hichiban> flooder

<hichiban> i have no time for that

<hichiban> im off]

This being Hichiban see's me as a robot because I am very fast relative to sloth. He assumes I must be a robot and not real because I spit out information so swiftly but relative to me I am just saying things at normal speed so he see's quick as false or not real because he is accustomed to sloth. So because he assumes I am a robot and fake he talked himself out of listening any further. But the deepest reality is he is a left brain influence and left brain cannot stand the traits of right brain, it hates the traits of right brain so I convinced this being to assume these traits were symptoms of a bad thing, a robot, and in turn convinced this being to leave. So initially this being saw what I was saying as in the realm of possibility [<hichiban> that actually makes alot of sense] but then a few moments later he determined I am a robot and fake [[<hichiban> flooder

<hichiban> i have no time for that

<hichiban> im off] and so he was deceived by the left brain influence and he left. Left brain always see's right brain as bad because it is jealous of right brain because it knows in a 50/50 mental harmony situation right brain traits always rule. So any being who senses time is a left brain influenced and they will assume right brain traits are bad unless they understand that is what is happening, then once they understand right brain traits they will slowly start to see what is happening when they see hyperactivity as something bad, they are really just seeing quick relative to their perception

of quick relative to the fact they are slothful. A parent will see their child as hyper and determine their child is mentally unsound but in reality that child is showing symptoms of right brain and that adult got the education and is simply seeing right brain traits as symptoms of illness. Darkness see's light as darkness because darkness sees itself as light. Left brain sloth, sequential simple minded aspects, see's quick random access right brain traits as bad because left brain sloth see's sloth as good so it is logical sloth would see quick as bad or a symptom of illness so this being assumed I was not even a real human being because I was quick so he assumed I was a robot. A flooder [<hichiban> flooder] is a robot program.

I am a robot. I talk like a robot.

I am astonished by the ones that sense time vast desire for their emotions and I am even more astonished I found out a way they can turn them off.

Another chatroom:

<Rohrer> Luke 22:63 And the men(the scribes, the ones who could use written language and had not applied the fear not remedy) mocked him, and smote him. = <Spazette> bye :) = You were kicked from #christian by sheela (I can't make you stop, but I can make sure you don't stay here!)

[Luke 22:63 And the men (ones that sense time)... mocked him, and smote him] = You were kicked from #christian by sheela (I can't make you stop, but I can make sure you don't stay here!)

Smote = [but I can make sure you don't stay here!]

My translation or perspective of the ancient texts are unlike anything sheela has ever heard and so if she believes my translation of the ancient texts she has to first submit all the teachers of these ancient texts she has listened to in her entire life were false teachers. Other words, none of the teachers she has ever listened to have suggested the tree of knowledge is written education so she has determined what I suggest must be lies because if they are not lies she has been hood winked so greatly by her teachers of the ancient texts she has to start her whole life over from scratch. That is what denying one's self or eating crow is all about and ones that sense time have this thing called pride and that is relative to ego. I am mindful what I suggest is telling ones that sense time everything they thought they knew about the history of mankind relative to civilization is factually wrong so it is understandable they would smite me because their pride is so great which means their cup is full, they have no more room in their narrow mind for reality, anymore. This is an indication left brain influenced beings do not do well with change because pattern detection, intuition and the ability to adapt swiftly are absent from their thoughts and those are all right brain traits. I hope my whole premise relative to written educations effects on the mind of young children is in error but I am mindful my hope will not erase my understanding that my premise is not in error and my hope will not erase my understanding that I am not suggesting a premise relative to written educations damaging effects on the mind but a fact. Simply put I am the proof. Perhaps you do not know proof when you see proof.

I am a robot. I talk like a robot.

[Matthew 7:15 Beware of false prophets, which come to you in sheep's clothing, but inwardly they are ravening wolves.]

False prophets are the scribes, the ones who got the written education and never applied the fear not remedy, so they are inwardly mentally unsound, under the influence of the left brain and have the right brain, the god image in man, veiled. It is not possible to be under the influence of left brain and be mentally sound because when right brain is at 50/50 those right brain traits are the dominate traits because right brain is the more powerful of the two hemispheres. So when right brain is at 50%, paradox plays a role in ones perception and so one no longer senses hunger or senses time so sense of hunger and sense of time is proof one is under the influence of left brain and thus mentally unsound and thus a [ravening wolves.]

[, which come to you in sheep's clothing] This comment is relative to seeing. After one applies the remedy they see everything as one thing or see's everything as pleasing. So this means one is not able to judge a book by the cover any longer, everyone simply looks pleasing so one has to deny what their eyes are telling them and this means one has to use their right brain intuition and that will assist one in understanding by the fruits and deeds and comments of others to be able to tell who has not applied the remedy. I just ask people if they sense time and many openly admit they do, because they do, so that is one fast way to determine who has applied the remedy and who has not. My eyes tell me everyone is perfect but my right brain intuition suggests that is not possible. So my eyes see everyone as [which come to you in sheep's clothing] but right brain intuition suggest many are [but inwardly(mentally) they are ravening wolves(mentally unsound, have the right brain aspects veiled).]

So a prophet is simply a human being that got written education, had right brain veiled, then applied the deny one's self, those who lose their life mindfully will preserve it, fear not remedy, and then unveiled right brain, then they go around and attempt to explain to beings who have not applied the remedy, firstly why they need to apply the remedy to the tree of knowledge, written education, and then explain the remedy itself so they can unveil right brain, the god image in man. Of course explaining to beings who have not applied the remedy that written education, the tree of knowledge, mentally hindered them, or spiritually hindered them does not go over very well so one can look at it like after they apply the remedy they have infinite job security.

[Matthew 7:29 For he taught them as one having authority, and not as the scribes.]

I taught someone today that I cannot be taught.

There is a concept called the ends justify the means. When one separate's people out of this concept and simply looks at a the reality left brain influenced container will see a right brain influenced container and seek to make that containers like itself that concept is easier understood. One reality is the situation works both ways. A right brain influenced container will attempt to make a left brain influenced container like itself. In a true vacuum which is normal, is a person a right brain influenced container or

46

a left brain influenced container? A right brain influenced container is how everyone is born relative to a being born with no physiological defects. A right brain influenced container is a being with their mind in the middle relative to the middle way, so that is the norm in all human beings, so a left brain container can only be created by another left brain container but that is not an absolute because just before the first person started learning written language they were a right brain container and in learning written language they became a left brain influenced container. So relative to a left brain influenced container relative to the concept the ends justify the means, simply means a left brain influenced container will see a child, a right brain influenced container, and push the left brain favoring education on that child and also influence that that child into a left brain influenced container even though it makes that child mentally unsound and thus leaves that child in a mental state of suffering and thus in a physiological state of suffering. So the state of suffering that child is put in is justified as long as that child in the end becomes a left brain influenced container. Another way to look at it is, the end is to bend all the children's minds to the left and in turn veil right brain, and the means to do that is written education and that harms the child but that is proper to do as long as all the children become left brain influenced containers like their parents are and thus like society is. This appears like a conspiracy on a human being level but in reality left brain always see's right brain as bad and determines it is improper and so it seeks to fix a right brain influenced container and make it like it is. Another way to look at is this left brain influence wants to make everything a left brain influence, misery loves company and so from a right brain influence perspective harmony seeks harmony. Left brain influenced beings perceive they are harmony and the see a child, a right brain influenced, and seeks to make that child left brain influenced so they see a child in mental harmony as disharmony and thus they want to fix that child. In reality they are harming that child but relative to the left brain influenced they are making that child harmonious. The darkness always sees itself as light and always see's the light as darkness. You do not give a child education to make them dumb you perceive you give them education to make them wise, so you have determined how that child was born, was dumb, but that is impossible so you are out of touch with reality. A child is born mentally in perfect harmony so if you attempt to

47

make them into mental harmony you will only ruin their mental harmony. A left brain influenced container is not possible unless the mind is in disharmony so it seeks to make other minds into this disharmony state, and right brain is a symptom of mental harmony so it seeks to make a left brain influenced container into itself, or bring that disharmony container back into harmony. If one judges their scale of intelligence based on one's ability to use a manmade invention, written education and math, then the fear not remedy makes one less intelligent. If ones scale of intelligence is cerebral complexity and vast pattern detection and heightened awareness then the fear not remedy makes one greatly more intelligent but not from a point of view it gives one something, as much as it simply turns on the switch, right brain, the written language turned off. I am suggesting intelligence is a bit more complex than being able to arrange letters in sequential order but that perhaps is infinitely beyond your understanding.

<Rohrer> The middle way is relative to the mind. This is simply mental harmony, relative to left and right hemispheres have an equal say in ones thoughts.

<Rohrer> Every human being is born in mental harmony or every human being is born conscious.

<Rohrer> The written education favors left brain and in a short time their right brain aspects are veiled so they are in the place of suffering.

<Rohrer> Another way to look at it is, a human being is suffering if one aspect of their mind is veiled.

<Rohrer> So the remedy to what this written education does to the mind is for one to be in a situation where they sense death is coming and then they ignore that signal.

<Rohrer> In Buddhism this concept is known as going to a cemetery at night alone and then meditating.

<Rohrer> Neurologically speaking in this unsound state of mind, the hypothalamus starts sending many false signals relative to death and fear so this cemetery mediation is simply being in a situation that hypothalamus

<Rohrer> gives one a signal that a shadow of death is coming to kill one and then by ignoring that signal the hypothalamus starts working properly again

<Rohrer> because the amygdala remembers that event and no longer will allow the hypothalamus to send false signals , so then right brain unviels and one returns to mental harmony, and this is known as nirvana or consciousness.

<Rohrer> This cemetery concept is in principle the exact same principle in the west as "going through the valley of the shadow of death and fearing not" as in "go to cemetery at night alone and when your mind says a shadow is coming to kill you, fear not"

2/2/2010 2:42:29 AM – [Proverbs 23:27 For a whore is a deep ditch; and a strange woman is a narrow pit.]

Deep ditch is relative to the place of suffering, hell and this is from the perspective of mindfully and that is apparent because a narrow pit relates to a narrow mind. A mind with right brain veiled as the result of written education is a narrow mind. A narrow is small, as in simple minded, or limited in size as in hindered, left hemisphere is simple in contrast to right brain which deals with complexity. So one gets written education, it veils their right brain because it favors left brain so one's mind is hindered and thus narrowed. The whore is a contrast statement, the whore is a human being that gets written education and does not apply the fear not remedy and thus their mind is simple minded because left brain is simple minded in contrast to right brain , and compared to a sound mind , one with both aspect in harmony. This whore has nothing to do with literal females. Cursed is cursed regardless of gender.

[Job 27:14 If his children be multiplied, it is for the sword: and his offspring shall not be satisfied with bread.]

This means the ones that sense time have lots of children because they are mentally unsound and have no foresight to understand one cannot just have billions of offspring on this tiny planet without destroying the planet. [it is for the sword] means the ones that sense time are violent and so their offspring are used to fight battles for land and resources because they see value in material things over cerebral thing because they have no cerebral power. [his offspring shall not be satisfied with bread.] This means ones with a sense of time have a huge sense of hunger because their

49

right brain paradox aspect is veiled so they in fact need way more food than a sound minded being needs just to maintain their left brain sequential simple minded state of mind. Simply put once the right brain is veiled by the education the entire being starts showing symptoms of this mentally unsound state of mind and strong sense of hunger is one of those symptoms. If one wishes to cure food shortages they should stop mentally hindering children and then the children will not have such a huge craving for food. If you want to have food shortages then keep veiling the right hemisphere in the children and we will continue to kill each other and take advantage of each other over money for food. This is why Moses burned the crops of the ones that sense time in Exodus , because he knew the ones that sense time need lots of food just to maintain simpleminded mental function, so that is their greatest weakness. So this is relative to [Genesis 3:16 Unto the woman(the whore) he said, I will greatly multiply thy sorrow…] This means a being that senses time, is a being that got the written education and their right brain is veiled so they need a great amount of resources just to remain alive, and even then they are never satisfied, [his offspring shall not be satisfied with bread.] A being that senses time eats, and in about four or five hours they need to eat again and then in four hours they need to eat again or their body starts to stop functioning and they cannot concentrate and they cannot think and they get irritable but when right brain is unveiled one can eat one small meal a day and still outthink a being that senses time on every level. So this curse caused by written education is a multipronged cursed but a simple way to look at it is when right brain is veiled the being falls apart and is no longer viable until the fear not remedy is applied and there are no exceptions to that reality. There are many stories in the ancient texts attempting to explain how powerful right brain, the god image in man is. So I can suggest a person with right veiled is a person with a mind unsound and thus built on the sand and when a storm comes they collapse and then I can explain a being with right brain veiled finds their self in troubled stormy seas and then their boat sinks, but a being with a sound mind can calm the rough sea's or withstand them because their mind is sound and thus built on the rock because they have mental clarity. I can just say right brain is unnamable in power. I can say a person with right brain veiled cannot handle the adversity a person with right brain unveiled can, and that is what the story of Job is suggesting. But even if a person that senses time understands all these concepts it does not mean they unveiled right brain because the only way to unveil right brain after one gets the education is to apply the fear not remedy in one way or another and that is factual mental suicide and they will simply avoid ever doing that but not because they are stupid it is because they are under the influence of the left brain, Cain, the evil one, and left brain hates right brain and it knows if it allows that being to apply the remedy that being will unveil right brain and right brain is the dominate aspect when the mind is in harmony and that is relative to the Cain and Abel story. You are not like me just because you understand what I suggest and you never will be like me because I applied the remedy and you will not apply the remedy because you perceive it is dangerous or foolish. So never ever assume you are like me because as a being I accidentally applied the remedy to the tree of knowledge and you as a being do not have what it takes to break the curse caused by the tree of knowledge. I did have what it takes and you do not, and that is an indication how devastating all that left brain education has on the mind. Perhaps you should give up on the remedy all together and use your time to send me letters to tell me how great I am. I have spoken to enough beings with a sense of time to understand they do not have what it takes to break the curse and they never will. If beings that sense time felt right brain at full power for one second they would rush out to apply the remedy but since they do not have that perspective they are doomed forever by their own perception, relative to how powerful right brain is. I can only demonstrate how powerful right brain is by telling you everything I can and writing one book a month into infinity and perhaps before I finish the thought will enter your head, what is this guys secret and I will tell you, I applied the fear not remedy accidentally and unveiled right brain, and you still will not apply the remedy because that is beyond your understanding. In one way I do not care about people who have the curse because my main purpose is to stop those people from giving the curse to the children. All the left brain traditional education is just to devastating on the mind for the vast, vast majority of people to ever undo the damage mentally speaking. If you doubt that even for a second that proves your mind is gone. I was in a chat room and I told a room what I suggest in my books and a person said "Where did you hear that junk?" So you see they are relying on intellect, which means if someone doesn't tell them what

51

to think, they cannot think because they have no right brain intuition any longer, the education killed it all totally. They have been reduced from genius wise beings to slave dogs that must be told what to do as a result of all the left brain education and the ones who teach it without question g its potential mental side effects are slave dogs, and the ones who suggest they should teach it are slave dogs and the ones who pay money to make sure all the children get it and never question is mental side effects on the minds of children are slave dog whores. I break every grammar rule you can invent and I get away with it and that drives you mad.

[Luke 18:25 For it is easier for a camel to go through a needle's eye, than for a rich man to enter into the kingdom of God.]

[a rich man] A rich man is a human being that senses time and thus got the written education and is a scribe, and does everything but hates their life and everything about it. If you sense time and you got written education and you do not hate your life to the point you wish you were dead, you are a rich man and your chances of applying the remedy are less than the chances of a camel going through the eye of a needle and that is an indication of how much that traditional education broke your mind. I am not here to give you a pep talk because I do not speak to ones who mentally rape innocent children. Do you perceive I would speak to ones who mentally rapes innocent children? My only purpose is to convince you to kill yourself mindfully because you are nonviable mentally in every definition of the word nonviable. If you do not understand that is fact you in fact prove to yourself you are mentally nonviable. Jesus convinced 12 out of 5000 and even one of those 12 ended up succumbing to the 9th circle of hell, treason, and he hung himself. You are factually mentally unviable so I have no reason to encourage you. You factually mentally rape innocent children or support it knowingly or unknowingly so I certainly am not going to encourage you in any way shape or form except to encourage you to kill yourself mindfully. Perhaps you assume I am kidding even when I say I am factually not kidding. I tear down the temple and kick around the dust and see if any signs of life arise from the ashes and that is as good as it will ever get and that is why your ways are not my ways. I perhaps would do much better with my methods in the submissive bondage chat rooms. Perhaps I need to experiment with that epiphany. Perhaps you are still wondering what the tree of knowledge is.

The complexity in the Judas story is Judas turned Jesus in to the ones that sense time, civilization, and then Judas realized what he had done and he went straight to the 9th circle of hell, treason and so in turning Jesus in, Jesus indirectly assisted Judas to go to the 9th circle of hell, treason but once a person is there, they perceive intense depression and can oft end up literally killing their self. So Judas did not fully believe in the deny one's self concept Jesus spoke of, so he turned Jesus in to the ruler scribes and in doing so Judas realized he turned in the "truth" over to the "darkness" and he went straight to the 9th circle of hell treason and so he had a chance to escape hell, apply the remedy, but it did not pan out for him and he literally killed himself instead of "lose his life mindfully to preserve it."

5:54:21 AM - [Genesis 1:1 In the beginning God created the heaven(right brain) and the earth(left brain).]

The right hemisphere has vast complexity and vast cerebral aspects and is the powerhouse of the two aspects and it is cerebral in focus or spiritually focused. The left hemisphere is simple minded, in contrast to right brain, and sequential based and so it is not a great thinker and so must rely on physical aspects.

Every human being is born with left and right brain aspects at 50% which means the mind is in harmony and in that situation right brain traits dominate. Left brain see's part and right brain see's holistically.

[Genesis 1:10 And God called the dry land Earth; and the gathering together of the waters called he Seas: and God saw that it was good.]

[and God saw that it was good.] means God saw everything he created as good and this is a holistic view and a right brain trait.

[Genesis 1:26 And God said, Let us make man in our image, after our likeness:] = God gave man a right hemisphere and that is right brain and that is the image of god in man and its trait is to see holistically, and it has complexity and vast processing or spiritual power.

So God made man in his image and that means God gave man right hemisphere, which is the God image in man.

[Genesis 2:17 But of the tree of the knowledge of good and evil, thou shalt not eat of it: for in the day that thou eatest thereof thou shalt surely die.]

Then along came written language and math and these aspects are left brain heavy and they deal with parts.[good and evil] is seeing things as parts but God , the god image in man see's [and God saw that it was good.] which is holistically, a right brain trait.

So mankind started to teach everyone written language and math and it favored left brain, and in turn it veiled the God image in man, and so mans mind became unsound. And so after man got this tree of knowledge education God said,.[Genesis 3:14 And the LORD God said unto the serpent, Because thou hast done this, thou art cursed]

[said unto the serpent, Because thou hast done this, thou art cursed } serpent means one is mentally unsound because the God image in their mind is veiled. Cursed denotes contrast, so they went from being a child of God with a sound mind and now after the education they are mentally unsound, but with every curse there is a remedy to that curse.

[Luke 17:33 ....; and whosoever shall lose his life shall preserve it.]

So after one gets the tree of knowledge, education they are the serpent and cursed, they can tell because they mindfully sense time, and that is a symptom their right brain paradox has been veiled to a subconscious state. What that means is when a person thinks "how much time is passed" the paradox in right brain when unveiled says "No time has passed and some time has passed" and that is its final answer, so the person has no sense of time. So if you can tell time is passing mindfully you are factually cursed and factually the serpent, so you have to trick that serpent to leave you. Thus the remedy:

[Luke 17:33 ....; and whosoever shall lose his life shall preserve it.]

One has to find the shadow of death, a spooky situation, and when their mind, the serpent state of mind, says "run and save yourself" one has to not save their self, and that tricks the serpent to let loose of one, and so they preserve their right brain or it unveils because the curse is broken. Thus:

Luke 17:33 ....; and whosoever(that got the education, tree of knowledge, and sense time as a result, and is thus cursed) shall lose his life(find the shadow of death and fear not) shall preserve it(unveil right brain, the god image in man).]

[Luke 18:25 For it is easier for a camel to go through a needle's eye, than for a rich man to enter into the kingdom of God.]

[than for a rich man to enter into the kingdom of God.]

Kingdom is the right brain. So one gets the education and it favors left brain, and in turn veils right brain, and so one is of the serpent. One will never ever apply this remedy if they like anything about their self.

Look at it this way.

Jesus spoke to a crowd of 5000 and out of 5000, 12 people considered applying his version of the fear not remedy, so,

5000 divided by 12 is .0024

Six billion people on earth multiplied by .0024 is 14,400,000 relative to 144,000.

This is an indication of how difficult it is to get rid of that "serpent" once it is in a person. You are not mocking the spirit of what I am suggesting that serpent in you is. You are not you at all anymore, because you factually got the education and so did I but the only difference is I accidentally applied the remedy and you factually did not. I took a handful of pills in a suicide attempt, and when I started to get very ill, my mind said "go save yourself or you will die" and I said "No I want to die" and so I accidentally

"Lost my life (mindfully) and thus preserved it" and about a month later right brain unveiled and I do not even relate to what I was like before , my past life, my life when I was cursed, or dead, or under the influence of the serpent, so I was lost but now I am found, and I was dead but now I am transformed or I once was blind but now I see. So before you spirit on the spirit of what I suggesting you better make sure you know what you are spitting on because I am just an accident.

"No man knows the hour or day (of an accident) but the father(of that accident)." Oct 31 2008 1:38 PM

6:05:57 AM – Now, who are you again?

Cain is the jealous brother of Abel. He was so jealous of Abel he killed Abel. Focus on that concept and relate it to what is happening relative to the tree of knowledge, written education. Written education favors left brain, and in turn veils right brain, the god image in man. So it turns a person into a left brain influenced being. All of left brain traits are opposite of right brain traits so a being in the left brain influenced state of mind will see a being that has unveiled right brain by applying the fear not remedy as bad. This is what the antichrist concept is, it is a reverse thing, So a person who applies the remedy after getting written education, unveils right brain and returns to sound mind 50/50 left and right brain and in that position right brain traits dominate.

So this means it has nothing to do with the person as much as it has to do with what influence that person is under. For example, I unveiled right brain so I have sequential left brain traits and also random access right brain traits at the same time so I can understand any left brain influenced being who has not applied the remedy after getting written education, which favors left brain and thus veils right brain, but a left brain influenced person cannot understand me because they have right brain veiled, and sequential aspects cannot understand random access aspects and determines it is a symptom of mental illness because left brain see's right brain as bad because it is contrary.

So left brain revolted against right brain and took over the mind of beings, and when a being applies the fear not remedy and unveils right brain, the majority which are now left brain influenced, because they all get the written education, see that person as bad or ill or sick or stupid, because left brain, Cain, hates right brain, Abel, because when the mind or spirit of a person has right and left brain equal 50/50, right brain always dominates and left brain, Cain, hates that and is jealous of that and so It kills that, firstly in the children by pushing the education on children and then in the disciples and Jesus' case, killed those beings . It's not the people it is what they are influenced by and left brain hates right brain because when right brain is at 50% in the mind or spirit, it rules. You perhaps should consider that everything you have done in your life has happened so you could read these texts and so this is your one chance you have been seeking and your one chance is upon you.

You are factually not who you were born as, you got the written education, tree of knowledge so you now are under the influence of left brain, and so if you want to get yourself back you have to apply the fear not remedy. The influence your are factually under is going to tell you that is not true and that is crazy talk, because it knows if you apply the remedy it goes back to 50% power in harmony with right brain and right brain rules in a 50/50 contest. You may never have heard this explanation in your life, and that is because all the beings you listen to also are under the influence of left brain because they got the education and never applied the fear not remedy.

[1 Corinthians 3:18 Let no man deceive himself. If any man among you seemeth to be wise in this world, let him become a fool, that he may be wise.}

What this comment means is, you are going to think it is stupid to seek the shadow of death and then fear not, when you mind says to run. You are going to think it is foolish to go to a spooky place alone at night and when your mind says to run the shadow of death is coming, you don't run. You are going to think it is foolish when your mind says a spooky thing is coming to kill you and then you have to mindfully lose your life to preserve it.

[you seemeth to be wise in this world, let him become a fool, that he may be wise.]

You better start being infinitely foolish. You better make it your sole mission on earth to be foolish relative to this remedy [let him become a fool, that he may be wise.] because I am mindful you are way to wise in the ways of the world. Do not ask anyone that sense time if what I suggest is truth because they have not applied the remedy so they do not know truth. You think for yourself about the spirit of what I suggest, do not ask for opinions because you are only going to get opinions of people who are [wise in this world,], = the anti-christ = ones that sense time and thus have not even applied the remedy = ones that [Galatians 4:10 observe days, and months, and times, and years.} = sense of time is the mark of the beast and is proof right brain is veiled and thus right brain paradox is veiled. You do not know anyone with no sense of time so you have to think for yourself and that is the one thing you cannot do because your right brain intuition is veiled.

Abel, as in the one "able" to withstand the storms and problems because it is the rock, right brain, the god image in man.

When you were a small child perhaps two to three and maybe even four you do not remember that time period well because your right brain was unveiled and when right brain is unveiled one is like an absent minded professor. Sometimes a child says wisdom far beyond their years. Because right brain is contrary to left brain it does not like rules because rules get in the way of its complexity and paradox and also pattern detection and creativity. So a child is young and then a parent starts to tell that child the rules. They say "Pick up your room so you are not a pig" and "Don't do this and don't do that" Left brain influenced perceives the more rulers the better and right brain see's rules hinder it's options.

Since the parent got the education and did not apply the remedy that parent perceives they are "raising" their child but in reality that parent is simply a left brain influenced container and they are seeking to make the perfect mentally sound child a left brain influenced container, relative to misery loves company.

Traditional education is based on one premise only. When a child is born they are mentally bad or stupid and unwise and so they need to be educated so they become wise and that is exactly what this comment is saying:

[Genesis 3:6 And when the woman saw that the tree was good for food, and that it was pleasant to the eyes, and a tree to be desired to make one wise, she took of the fruit thereof, and did eat, and gave also unto her husband with her; and he did eat.}

[and a tree to be desired to make one wise]

The principle of a Trojan horse is it looks really good to the eyes [pleasant to the eyes,]

And it is thought to be something only a fool would pass up on [tree was good for food,]

I am mindful the main disconnect in this whole situation comes down to one thing only. Once a person gets this education their right brain is veiled so they are mentally so simple minded relative to: [Proverbs 23:27 For a whore is a deep ditch; and a strange woman is a narrow pit.]

Deep ditch denotes deep neurosis and narrow pit denotes simple minded, a left brain trait is sequential based and simple minded and a right brain trait is random access based and complexity, these traits are all contrary. You have to think about one thing only. Is it possible out of all of man kinds inventions only written education , writing, script, math has no flaws or possible bad side effects? Mankind has invented millions of things that have bad side effects, like penicillin, asbestoses, agent orange, but you never heard that written language has any bad side effects because you get the sinisters take on reality because you are the under the influence of the sinister because you ate off the tree of knowledge and never applied the fear not remedy, and that is fact.

There are two versions of history relative to mankind.

One version is: Mankind invented written language and that ushered in math and also civilization and everything has been fantastic since then.

Then the ancient texts version of history is: Mankind invented written language and became scribes and fell from grace because it was of the tree of knowledge and favored Cain, the evil one left brain, and veiled Abel, right brain, the God image in man.

Relative to the sinister, the ones that sense time, you got educated and became wise and relative to the ancient texts you became [Genesis 3:14 ... the serpent, (and became)...cursed above all cattle(mentally unsound),]

So since you believe written education made you wise you perhaps need to stop reading the ancient texts because you deny their truth and you mock anyone who attempts to explain the dangers of written education so you so pray to your whore written education, everything I say is wrong because I am judging the world's great whore, which is written education and you perhaps will not be surviving that judgment.

[Revelation 19:2 For true and righteous are his judgments: for he hath judged the great whore, which did corrupt the earth with her fornication, and hath avenged the blood of his servants at her hand.]

[which did corrupt the earth with her fornication] Corrupt means written education favors left brain and in turn veils right brain, the god image in man, and so it takes a mentally perfect child and turns them into a mental abomination, mentally unsound.

You think very hard about this comment. This being perhaps dedicated his life to studying the effects of written education on the mind and he said exactly what I am saying.

["What it comes down to is that modern society discriminates against the right hemisphere." - Roger Sperry (1973) - neuropsychologist, neurobiologist and Nobel laureate

I am saying civilization, modern society, veils the right brain, god image in man, with it education and in turn, sins against God, veils the God image in man. and even if you believe that your chances of breaking the curse, applying the remedy, is still .0024%. You got tricked by the whore and you cannot admit that because your pride is so great.

[Genesis 3:13 ...., The serpent beguiled(charmed) me, and I did eat.]

Society said, get our education and you will make a lot of money, so perhaps you should take all that money you made from selling your soul and rub it on that mark on your head and see if that breaks the curse. There is a part in the Lord's Prayer and a Lord is a Master of the house, which means they have both hemispheres active. They are of sound mind because they applied the fear not remedy. In the Lord's prayer is say's:

"Lead me not into temptation but deliver us from evil"

So there are only two kinds of people, ones who applied the remedy after the education , and in turn have no sense of time, and ones who have not applied the remedy and thus sense time. So if you have a sense of time it means you have not applied the remedy, and so when you read this line it is a hex against you.

X = one that has applied the remedy, one with no sense of time.
Y = one that has not applied the remedy, one with a sense of time.

Lead me(X) not into temptation(Y) but deliver us (X) from evil (Y)

If said by a person who has not applied the remedy

Lead me(Y) not into temptation(Y) but deliver us(Y) from evil(Y)

So it is simply one is denying their self which is a hex which is an indication these texts are against the ones with a sense of time and if they read them they harm their self because the darkness, the ones that sense time, harm their self in the presence of the light. I didn't know any of this a year ago, before the accident, but somehow one might suggest I have grown quite fond of the ancient texts. I am pleased with their strategies in dealing with the ones that sense time. These ancient texts are battle plans to be used against the ones that sense time, the cursed, so it is logical the ones that sense time would continue to publish them because the ones that sense time are mentally unsound and thus are a house divided and so the ones that sense time are self defeatist by their very nature. So they publish these ancient texts and in doing so defeat their self and they are factually not even aware of that because disharmony see's its own destruction as harmony. A being with a sense of time will see killing their self is the right thing to do when in reality it is disharmony to destroy yourself. A being with a sense of time will see's destroying a forest to build a condo no one will live in is proper when in reality it is disharmony. A being with a sense of time perceives eating three meals a day is totally normal when in reality it is abnormal and harmful but that is because disharmony only see's disharmony as harmony. Disharmony see's a perfectly mentally sound child as "bad" and so it must swiftly "fix" that child with its wisdom education. This is why modern society says "We will make sure all the children get written education and we will leave no child left behind" because disharmony see's destruction as harmony. This is the reverse things, or the "anti-christ" or "anti-truth

reality. Modern society, the ones that sense time, suggests they are wise and kind to make sure all the young children get the written education and math and the ancient texts suggest that is proof they are the serpent.

[The heart is like a garden. It can grow compassion, fear, resentment or love. Which seeds will you plant? – Buddha]

Which seeds will you plant? is a riddle, the answer is society plants fear seeds in the children using written education because it veils the child's right brain and in turn makes their hypothalamus start sending greatly increased false fear signals, and that is why people fear their own body, words, certain music, of course they perceive they have morals or taste in music or words but that's just the neurosis caused by having their right brain veiled and so they see parts, a left brain trait. I assure you if you sense time you are not capable of judgment in any meaningful way.

[Do not take the word of a blind man ask questions. – Buddha], = society teaches you written language (words) and makes you mentally "blind", veils your right brain.

[1 Samuel 12:21 And turn ye not aside: for then should ye go after vain things, which cannot profit nor deliver; for they are vain.]

What is vain? [Jeremiah 8:8 ….; the pen of the scribes is in vain.] Why is the pen of the scribes in vain, written language? Because to learn it you veil your right brain so you end up mentally hindered or retarded so you actually harm yourself so that is vanity. You take perfection, mentally, and you make it abomination so you harm yourself and once you do that you have to apply the remedy which you cannot do readily so you are doomed so you are separated from God because the god image, right brain is veiled, separated from you, and you do that just to learn to write some words, and for the promise of a good job, money, so you sell your soul for the promise of a few silver pieces, and thus the pen of the scribes is in vain because all the money in the universe is not worth giving up your sound mind.

You were a small child and trusted everyone around you and so you trusted the ones who got the education and they made you just like them. Misery loves company. The darkness only sees itself as light so it saw you, a perfect mentally sound child, and made you just like it, a mental abomination. Another way to look at it is, the mentally unsound only seek to make the mentally sound (children), mentally unsound. Another way to look at it is the light of a child drives the darkness mad so it has to kill the light in the child, right brain, because it cannot stand that light. You can look at it any way you want to , but that will not apply the remedy. You have to deny yourself , and lose your life(mindfully) to preserve your real life, unveil right brain, and that will never change so you need to wake up to reality swiftly. Perhaps you should tell me why you give your money to cult leaders that never tell you what the tree of knowledge is, and never tell you the remedy to the tree of knowledge? Perhaps they are more interested in profits than Prophets.

Never ask questions you don't want answered.

8:01:50 PM – If you take a human being and alter their perception mentally they are no longer considered a human being because their perception is not that of a normal human being so they are in fact a hybrid human being and this is what written education does to a human being. It alters their perception over the period of the education and when they are finished their perception is altered in a nearly permanent way and so they are no longer human beings mentally they are human being hybrids. It is one thing to make a human being hybrid more intelligent and wiser than a normal human being by altering their perception but it is another thing to make a human being hybrid far less intelligent and wise than a normal human being but that is exactly what written education does to a human being because it favors the simple minded, sequential based left brain instead of the complex powerhouse right brain. So the concept of making a hybrid is to make the being better than they are normally but in this case it actually makes the being mentally hindered so it is not really making a human being hybrid as much as putting a curse on a human being which suggest it is making a human being suffer so it is simply torture and abuse. So once in a while one of these human being hybrids, the cursed, in one way or another breaks the curse and revert back to how they were before the curse and they attempt to explain it to the ones still cursed and the ones still cursed mock that being because they cannot imagine any longer that that being is simply telling the truth about the curse written education causes. The ones cursed are no longer mentally viable enough to understand truth relative to what causes the curse. I would pleased if I could tell you there is a group of humans and they have a conspiracy to veil everyone's right brains using education but the truth is, human beings invented something that had subtle yet devastating effects on the mind and it's so subtle one cannot even tell it is happening and because it is pushed on children when they are six or seven, the child never even knows it is happening.

A little child will walk up to a fat person and say "You are fat", and that child is telling the truth and feels no shame, but the adult will feel shame for that child telling the truth and apologize for that child telling the truth.

10:29:49 PM – There is a study I came across on the net. I found it on this site. http://www.eric.ed.gov
The title of the study is : A Study of Suicide-Related Behaviors among Colombian Youth: Reflections on Prevention and Implications for Health Education.
Now, this is the result of the study.

"Surveyed 10th graders from 32 Colombian public schools to examine risk behaviors related to depression and suicide. About 21 percent of respondents expressed suicidal feelings. This transcended to actual plans in 19 percent of respondents, while 16 percent reported at least one attempt in the previous 30 days. Suicidal thoughts and attempts differed by gender, perceived academic performance, and type of school."

These children were all in school getting written education and they are already showing symptoms of their mind being bent to the left, depression and suicidal thoughts. It is very simple to understand if one can grasp when right brain is unveiled or not veiled the thought processes are very fast and also random access so a thought like depression cannot be maintained so one is mentally always in a state of neutral in general. The thought processes when right brain is unveiled are so fast and also random so maintaining any one state of mind, like, lust, greed, depression, envy, jealously is not possible so one simply has no sloth in their thought patterns.

[About 21 percent of respondents expressed suicidal feelings.]Twenty one percent of these children are suicidal and then you sit there and boast about how proud you are you make sure all the kids gets your "brand" of education. That is why you no longer have a conscience, right brain intuition, because you are factually killing children with your "brand" of education and you totally believe you are not so you are without a soul or a conscience at all in your "state of mind". You mentally kill and thus literally kill your own offspring and then blame it on them or suggest "I don't know what went wrong." I know what went wrong. The beings in the ancient texts understood this [About 21 percent of respondents expressed suicidal feelings.] and they attempted to explain it:

[Genesis 2:17 But of the tree of the knowledge of good and evil, thou shalt not eat of it: for in the day that thou eatest thereof thou shalt surely die. Genesis 3:3 But of the fruit of the tree which is in the midst of the garden, God hath said, Ye shall not eat of it, neither shall ye touch it, lest ye die.]

[About 21 percent of respondents expressed suicidal feelings.] = [neither shall ye touch it, lest ye die.] = [for in the day that thou eatest thereof thou shalt surely die.] So these young children are in the tenth grade and it's not important they are in Columbia, it is universal with written education and math because it is all sequential based and favors left brain and thus veils right brain, and these children are already thinking about killing their self.

A being that has their right brain veiled is an unsound minded being and thus a nonviable being and a house divided, a mind divided, cannot stand. It is elementary cause and effect and it is universal. It does not matter what country it is or what language it is, if you teach written education to a young child it will veil their right brain and kill that child mentally and potentially literally but killing a child mentally is killing a child literally. You do not even consider oral education for the children because you got written education and you turned out just fine as long as your definition of fine is a complete mentally nonviable being. I am one of the children you voted to have their mind bent to the left and it almost killed me but I worked my way out of that neurosis you put me in and my only purpose is to expose you for what you are and what you do. I had my first suicidal thoughts in about seventh or sixth grade and I was trooper and somehow woke up after many years but I am mindful I should be dead because I was very depressed and I am factually certain before this is all over, you will wish I died and you will wish you could hide. Now, back to the study.

[Suicidal thoughts and attempts differed by gender, perceived academic performance, and type of school.]
[perceived academic performance] What this means is some children do not take well to having their right brain veiled no matter how much you punish them and beat them and insult them for poor grades eventually they start to perceive they are just stupid because they trusted you are not a mental abomination because they trusted that their own parents would not mentally rape them into hell. These young children, your children, want to kill their self as opposed to allow you to veil their right brain and that is fact and a deeper reality is right brain will at times make that being kill their self to avoid being veiled and that is really all that is happening in suicides. Right brain knows what it has to do after it is veiled and that is fight back to get into mental harmony as it was when the child was born and that tends to end up with a being that kills their self because right brain is fighting back and it is veiled so those signals are veiled and not taken properly and so that being starts to become suicidal.

The definition of religion is: mental exercises and mental methods used to negate the mental side effects caused by written education, written language and mathematics, in order to restore the mind to a sound state; namely methods used to unveil right brain after said education veils it.

A poor man with lots of money is a very poor man. A sound minded being in prison is better than a mentally troubled ruler.

2/3/2010 3:42:43 AM - Suicide: a: a human being that during or shortly after the traditional education, which veils their right brain and in turn heightens all their emotions, mentally and emotionally collapses and this collapse results in said being terminating their self.

b: a human being, over the age of thirty, who after getting the education has a delayed emotional collapse as a result of their right brain being veiled by traditional education and terminates their self.

c: a human being who gets the written education and thus has their right brain veiled that slowly over time self destructs by way of addictions to food, drugs, material gains, or various compulsions and obsessions and determines to terminate their self when these "Band-Aids" no longer relieve their mental suffering, caused by right brain being veiled by the traditional education.

Because the traditional education is left brain favoring the amount of left mind leaning a person experiences varies from person to person. Oft a young person who does very well at the traditional education becomes very depressed very swiftly and oft a person who does not do well at the education does not become depressed as swiftly. The general age that a being begins to show symptoms of these emotions being turned up as a result of right brain being veiled is between twelve and fourteen. At the age of twelve to fourteen the being begins to use drugs to relieve the mental suffering and the being begins to exhibit mentally unsound behaviors such as violence, vandalism, self harm and generalized disorderly conduct against society as a whole relative to society's rules. The more education these beings get the more veiled their right brain becomes and the more they attempt to fight that by breaking perceived rules or order and organization, a right brain trait, it dislikes rules. Some beings will speed in their cars because they are attempting to break society's rules and breaking these rules gives the being a right brain sensation or rush because breaking perceived rules encourages right brain. On one level suicide is universally looked at as a bad thing to do and that rule is what attracts some younger beings to break that rule just to show society it does not subscribe to its rules but on a deeper subconscious, right brain level that being is attempting to negate the many years of left brain education by subconsciously defeating their fear of death and this oft leads to the beings literally terminating their self. The very young, twelve to sixteen year old suicides are simply beings who did not take well to all the left brain education and it turned their emotions to such a high level they tend to terminate their self over trivial matters that appear meaningless to an observer. These young beings perception of value and of worth has been altered as a result of their right brain being veiled and so their own self worth is perceived to be low so they terminate their self. This low self esteem aspect is prevalent in any being that gets the traditional education and does not take measures to unveil right brain but it is a large area and so there are many classifications of this low self esteem that play out in various ways.

A: low self esteem caused by personal outlook about the future. These beings perceive their minds are not on par and so they perceive life will be very difficult for them and so they see their future will be rough and so they determine there is no point and they terminate their self. This is a classic left brain trait to give up easily and is not a bearing on the being as much as it is a symptom their right brain has been veiled by traditional education. Because their right brain has been veiled their mind and thus outlook is build on sand and thus they cannot withstand life itself.

B: low self esteem caused by how one perceives their physical self. This being may perceive they are not attractive or are obese or too thin relative to weight, and this perception encourages thoughts that life is not going to work out for them or they are going to have a rough life as a result of their appearance so they determine to terminate their self. This low self esteem view is strictly relative to the fact at the education has favored their left brain and left brain see's parts so they see's their self as many parts and they see good parts and bad parts and if they see more bad parts than good parts they determine to terminate their self when in reality there are just good parts but they perceive these good parts as bad parts because their perception is altered.

These two low self esteem aspects above are a kind of umbrella that covers many others. Most who have their right brain veiled either perceive they are not mentally able to deal with life or they perceive they are not physically "up to par" to deal with life. The traditional education system judges them as intelligent or not intelligent based on sequential based tests and these young beings believe the results of those test indicate their physical self worth and mental self worth when in reality the beings who test young children solely on sequential, a left brain trait, based testing should not be allowed around children ever.

Depression: A mental state that is a symptom the written education has veiled the right brain and so thoughts of sadness, desires and cravings linger in the mind for prolonged periods creating a mentally depressed state as a direct result of the right brain random access thought patterns being reduced to a subconscious state.

Prolonged Depression in any form is a symptom a person has had their right brain veiled and some type of experience has encouraged a sad emotion in their mind and since their right brain is veiled the emotion is very strong relative to the hypothalamus is sending out very strong abnormal signals and also their cerebral cortex is giving abnormal perceptions of events and so that "sad" thought stays in the mind because left brain sequential thoughts cannot get rid of it and so that thought festers and in time increases. One example would be a girl breaks up with a guy and the guy becomes very sad in a short period of time even over the period of an hour, relative to a clock, but if right brain was not veiled that thought of sadness would not be able to linger more than a few minutes relative to a clock because right brain random access thoughts would "shift gears" so to speak to another thought totally unrelated to that sad thought, so the being would never be able to maintain a mental state of depression and so a being would simply be mentally unable to become depressed.

One example would be a traumatic event. If a person is on a battle field and see's five of their buddies killed in a horrific way, if that being has right brain unveiled within minutes their thoughts would be in a totally different place and within an hour, that traumatic event would be essentially forgotten about relative to time stamps and emotional stamps and the next day that being wakes up and that event would be completely erased relative to it traumatic effects because right brain is an absent minded professor. It has a vast memory but not great at very short term memory so in a sound minded being, they are capable of some short term memory aspects, a left brain trait, but right brain traits rule when the mind is at 50/50 harmony. What this means is when right brain is unveiled the image of that traumatic event is saved as a concept instead of a memory with a time stamp and emotional stamp on it. Left brain see's parts and details, right brain see's holistically as in one concept. So a being with right brain veiled see's a traumatic event and stores all those details relative to that traumatic event in their memory and when right brain is unveiled all that is stored is one concept with no emotional or time stamps so the traumatic event swiftly is perceived as a dream or an event that the person did not experience at all. Right brain is not a judge left brain is a judge. So when right brain is unveiled the memory of a show is the same concept as the memory of a traumatic event and they are not different or are not sorted or judged to be good or bad. This absence of emotions and time stamps is relative to the concept nothingness but nothingness is not as accurate as neutral. A person with right brain unveiled in fact is more sensitive to events but the sensitivity is fractional in duration relative to a person who has right brain veiled. So what this means is the mind is always jumping around from concept to concept and no one concept or traumatic memory can be maintained so one's mind cannot fester that thought and so that thought cannot create or turn into a mental state of depression or sadness. In contrast to how one is with their right brain veiled, the emotional level is nearly zero but that is an indication of how high the emotional capacity is turned up as a result of all that left brain favoring conditioning called traditional education. The emotions in a being that unveils right brain are fractional in duration in contrast to a being with right brain veiled, a being that senses time. This has a great deal to do with the concentration level or the processing power of right brain is so great it has to turn down many aspects in order to function but this is not abnormal this is how a sane human being should be that has not had their right brain veiled. A reduced emotional capacity is relative to an increased concentration and heightened awareness capacity.

Drug Addiction: A symptom that a human being who had their right brain veiled as a result of written education is attempting to ease the mental suffering; the being takes drugs and the drugs unveil right brain for the duration the drug lasts and this eases their mental suffering but leads to addiction to the drug.

Deep Neurosis: A human being who has had their right brain veiled as a result of the written education and shows no obvious symptoms of depression or drug addiction but subscribes to many unfounded rules and regulations and is liable to snap mentally if they perceive their rules are not followed or if any unexpected events arise. Ones that sense time that show no outward symptom of depression are in fact in the deepest neurosis caused by written education . They are known as the "rich" in the ancient texts. It is very difficult for these beings to escape the neurosis because they are in such deep neurosis.

Memory is completely different when right brain is veiled and when right brain is unveiled. A depressed person will have long term right brain memories that come to the surface, conscious, but because they have right brain veiled these memories come with lots of emotional baggage attached and time stamps, details a left brain trait, and so they are painful memories emotionally speaking.

X = right brain long term memories stored as a concept
Y = person with right brain veiled and thus is left brain conscious
Z = strong emotional response to long term memories
A = person with right brain unveiled, both hemispheres working at 50%
B = slight emotional effects to longer term memories

$X + Y = Z$
$A + X = B$

What a person with right brain veiled, a person that senses time, perceives is long term memory is not long term memory at all it is only short term memory. Another way to look at it is, it is long term memory as long as your definition of long term memory is short term memory. Another way to look at it is, when right brain is unveiled and a person is asked a trivia question or a question about a fact their entire memory for their entire life is in their conscious state so facts and concepts are all right there so there is no, "I can't remember what the answer is." because the answer is right there. Think about the subconscious and the fact is never misses a beat and records everything and then imagine that in your conscious state and then imagine what kind of memory you would have and that is long term memory and so this memory in beings with a sense of time is nothing but short term memory. The point of the saying, those who forget the past are doomed to repeat it, is referring to the ones with a sense of time. I can talk with beings in chat that sense time and two days later we talk again and I say "Remember when you said this?" and they say 'I didn't say that." And I show them the chat log and they say "I don't remember saying that." But I remember it like it just happened because my mind does not sense time so everything is now but the complexity with this extreme long term memory is, one can only remember concepts. Short term memory has time stamps, emotions, details and that is why it is short term memory because in long term memory all those aspects would clutter the long term memory. A detail is a part and that is left brain trait so left brain stores parts and details in its memory. Right brain is holistic so it stores concepts. So this book has many details and parts which are words and sentences and I do not remember them at all essentially but I remember the concept of the entire book. So this entire book in my memory is stored as one concept and so I remember this book as one concept and the details don't really matter as long as the concept is remembered. This is the magic of right brain because it can take one concept and create a million details from that one concept. Now those million details appear like many different things to the ones that sense time and thus only see details so it gives the illusion that there is lots of different stuff happening when in reality there is just that one concept being repeated in different ways over and over. I recall I went into repeat mode after about the sixth book. Like in the ancient texts after the tree of knowledge story everything is repeating either the effects of that tree of knowledge or the remedy to that tree of knowledge and that is just repeating over and over. This is how right brain operates though because it does not see an ending or a start because that is left brain trait. It appears that one day I was left brain influenced, had a sense of time, sense of hunger and strong emotions and then my hypothalamus gave me the death signal and I ignored it and all the sudden I went right brain dominate but that does not make any sense. The one thing that does make sense is I had lots of left brain traits one day and my hypothalamus gave the death signal and I ignored it and then right brain unveiled and when right brain is at 50% with left brain right brain traits dominate. Because there is no physiological trauma involved at all it is not even considered. I did not get my head bashed in, I simply made a mental decision when my hypothalamus gave me a death signal and that is what totally altered my perception and perception is relative to the cerebral cortex. So I totally altered my mental perception permanently because of a mental decision I made when the hypothalamus said "You are going to die from taking those pills." and then I said "I don't care." and this was all on a mental level and took one second. So the mind is so powerful that in a situation of perceived death I made a decision mentally and the mind totally altered its perception but in reality it simply undid what years of left brain education did to it. The whole talk about facing the shadow of death has nothing to do with death because ones with a sense of time is afraid of a bad haircut. Another way to look at it is their hypothalamus is giving them death signals on just about everything, it just comes out as stress, shame, embarrassment, shyness, envy and perhaps many other emotions. You might be in a room of your peers and someone asks a question and you do not answer it because you are afraid of being wrong and ridiculed and that is your hypothalamus saying "Danger may happen if you try to answer that question ". Not that I ever get off topic but, think about a young child before they even start school and they are very shy. The reason they are very shy is because their parents cram rules down their throat and that is left brain trait. There is a concept that when a child is born they are totally mentally retarded and must be raised to be "good" and that is total insanity. This is relative to the curse and to exactly what Jung was saying, " Children are educated by what the grown-up is and not by his talk."- Carl Jung

Simply put a left brain influenced container will make a child, a right brain influenced container, a left brain influenced container. "What the grown up is" What are the only two possibilities that a grown up can be? Left brain influenced or right brain influenced and it is impossible for a being to be a left brain influenced being unless their mind is bent so far to the left by education their right brain is nearly gone relative to it factoring into that beings conscious perception. Even if the mind was bent 10% to the left so the mind was like 60% left and 40% right, right brain is so powerful its traits would perhaps still dominate so the only way a person can be left brain influenced is if their right brain is veiled to a subconscious state and all one has to do to accomplish that is give a six or seven year old child lots of rules and sequential conditioning and punish them if they break rules or do poorly at the sequencing and do that for about three or four years That all school is except they do it for twelve years.

Of course some graduate early:

L. W. (14) allegedly took her own life
S. M. (14) allegedly committed suicide by hanging
S. O. (14) allegedly committed suicide by hanging
K. O. (14) took her own life by an unknown method

Perhaps neurosis is perhaps the inability perhaps to tolerate ambiguity, perhaps.

Once you defeat your fear of death you defeat your fear of life. Fear of words is as devastating as fear of thoughts. The established norms are seldom established or normal. When you stop understanding you start repeating. Coming to an understanding is always worth the risk. If you are hesitant about a decision you probably should rethink it. The water in a pool only flows up and down. It's as lonely in the depths as it is in the heights. Wisdom is required to make sense of knowledge. Sense of time is a symptom not a benefit. One that can be embarrassed can be controlled. The effects of your deeds are not as important as the cause of your effects. Grief is a fruit of wisdom and understanding. Anger can consume you or inspire you but it can never do both.

2/4/2010 1:07:33 AM - Happiness is when one is free from worries because their mind can comprehend any situation that arises.

2:33:59 AM – At this point our species is a rotten tree. This means any fruits that come off that tree as in expected fruits are rotten. This means the core of the species it rotten. Everything that is happening is a symptom of this rot at the core of the species. This rot transcends all nationalities, because it is the species, the tree, that is rotten. Attempting to fix any of fruits, symptoms, of the rotten tree will not fix the rotten tree. Written education and mathematics is the reason for the rot at the core of the tree, the species. That is a fact. One has to ponder what sacrifice means relative to fixing this rot at the core of the species. If a being alive today determines nothing should be adjusted relative to written education and the methods in which it is administered then they are in fact determining every human being that comes after them will be rotten. A being is born and they are born into this rotten species and so they become rotten and so until the reason for the rot at the core of the species is addressed every being born into the species is going to be rotten. Is the species being rotten less important than written education and mathematics? If the species is rotten it does not matter if you can write and it does not matter if you can add. As the species is now, everything revolves around the fact a person can write and add. This is why the entire tree of the species is rotten. At the center piece of our species is a man made invention that alters our perception and so we are a rotten species. Every parent in the universe will tell their child "If you get a good education, written language and math, you will be somebody and you will make money and have luxury." and that is the rot. What that parent is really saying is "You can have luxury and money and all it will cost you is your right hemisphere and thus your soul, intuition, and your complexity in thoughts and thus your life." and that is the rot. Forget about all of your infinite delusions about supernatural, you factually do not have the mental capacity in your neurotic state of mind to even come within a billion light years of pondering supernatural. I do not detect any ghosts in classrooms teaching young children written language and math I detect beings who have had their perception altered to the point they can no longer even mentally detect when they are harming innocent children because their right brain intuition is all but gone because they were taught said written language and math as innocent children also. I only detect mentally unstable adults creating mentally unstable children on an industrial scale using written language and math. If that is all I detect that is factually all you detect. It is important to look at mathematics because it is a huge factor relative to this species rot.

1,2,3,4,5. Mathematics is based totally on sequencing. Mathematics is based solely on parts. When you are doing a math problem in your head you are counting numbers in sequence over and over. Some people even as adults count with their fingers and some do the math in the air. This is because math itself is not a natural mental process. A being in sound mind is horrible in math and at math because in sound mind the right brain holistic aspects make mathematics ability greatly hindered. Einstein was horrible in math and that is why in part he left school at the age of sixteen or was kicked out of school. There is nothing random about math and right brain is random access. What that means is mathematics by itself is enough to bend your mind to the left and then when it is factored in that a child is punished with bad grades if they do poorly at it, math becomes nothing but left brain mental conditioning. One must understand in order to be proficient at math they have to sacrifice their right brain hemisphere aspects. This is not a maybe and there is no half way. There is a trade off a human being must make in order to be proficient at mathematics and that means it is personal choice and it is a choice that will affect their perception for the rest of their life and so any government or authority that makes that choice for them robs that being of their life, liberty and freedom of choice. That is why education is not mentioned in the constitution or declaration of independence or the bill of rights. A child does not know mathematics is strictly left brain favoring and thus over time it will bend their mind to the left and in turn alter their perception. A child trusts the adults around them will not harm them, but that is a delusion on that child's part because in this location every child gets the education and in turn gets their perception altered starting at the age of six or seven and there is nothing in the universe that will stop that. You have been watching too many happy ending movies. I do not detect any happy endings on this planet and so you do not detect any happy endings on this planet. In mathematics there are aspects that symbolize greater and less than and equal to. These symbols look like this $<, >, =$. That is judgment and that is also detecting parts, it goes against right brain holistic traits.

The number one is less than the number ten. 1< 10. That is a judgment and so that is seeing things as parts and so that is a left brain exercise. Right brain see's holistically, what that means is relative to right brain every number in the universe is equal to every number in the universe. 1 = 10, 5 = 8 , 99 = - 66. Zero equals zero is another way to look at it. Since mathematics costs one their right hemisphere it has to be the individual's choice to get mathematics or not get mathematics but because this narrow is not fantasy land that is not reality. A being's worth is judged in part by how much mathematics they get. That is called "Get your right brain veiled or get a slave job." That is tyranny over the mind and grounds for revolution just relative to math being forced on beings at the age of six or seven. You are free as long as you get your right brain veiled and submit to going through your life with sequential simple minded thoughts. If you do not understand that is reality it only proves you are out of touch with reality as a result of your perception being altered by mathematics and written education. The equation is very simple so even in your conditioned simple minded state of mind you should be able to grasp the equation, but I doubt it.

X = written language
Y = mathematics
Z = sound mind, both hemispheres in equal harmony in the conscious state
A = unsound mind, right brain veiled to a subconscious state
B = money, luxury, comfort
C = poverty, struggle, discomfort, outcast in society
D = Oral education only, no written or math education

If the equation was this X + Y = Z(B) Then civilization would be full of sound minded beings.

This is the reality :
X+Y = A(B)
D + Z = C

What these equations mean is, in society or civilization you are given a choice. You can trade your complex right brain for the promise of some luxury and money or you can keep your complex right brain but you will live in poverty and discomfort and be an outcast. You can sell your soul, right brain, for a few silver pieces or you can keep your soul and suffer in poverty. This reality is what making a deal with the devil is about except in this narrow you do not get a choice, the choice is made for you at the age of six or seven by your parents or guardians and ultimately your government and your fellow citizens. So that is fact and that is reality and that is what has happened to you. The wise beings in the ancient texts understood that is exactly what was happening to people and so they came up with a solution to the fact a child's soul, right brain, is sold to the devil without hesitation by civilization when that child is at very young age. You were sold down the river as a child and nothing in this universe is going to take that back so it is the past and so past is past, so you must focus on the now. What are your options now that you have been sold down the river? Doing nothing will not get your soul, right brain, back. You are not ever going to get your soul back for free ever so avoid assuming you can get your soul, right brain, back because you just want it back. Because I am mindful I am speaking to mentally unsound beings I have to keep reminding them of aspects they should know on their own if they were mentally sound. Please be mindful none of my books are in the fiction section. I will explain symptoms you can test yourself for so you can determine you did get sold down the river as child but you must avoid assuming just because you have these symptoms I am not talking about you. You got traditional education so I am talking to you because beings that have applied the remedy and regained their soul, right brain, only read my books to laugh at the fact I am mocking you, ones that sense time, on a worldwide scale in plain sight for all to see. Because you got the written education your perception has been altered and so what you perceive is not reality but only abnormal perception caused by the fact your perception was altered starting at the age of six or seven.

Some of the obvious symptoms are strong sense of taste, sense of time and sense of hunger, strong sense of fatigue, mental and physical. So if you detect any of these symptoms it is proof you were sold down the river, had your soul, right brain, sold as a child.

5:57:52 AM – Not that I ever get off topic. No matter what I ever say, you are not going to hell if you do not apply this remedy because the state of mind you are in after getting all that tree of knowledge, written education, is hell. The ancient texts talk about hell and damnation and that is a place a person mindfully is in when their right brain, the god image in man, is veiled to a subconscious state. Hell is the place of suffering and what that means is you are mentally only able to use the left brain simple minded sequential based aspect of your brain and thus mind when you are conscious or awake unless you take drugs that unveil your right brain just a bit while the drugs last. Your concept of going to hell when you die is flawed because you cannot grasp the fact you ate off the tree of knowledge, written education, and it veiled the right aspect of your mind to a subconscious state and that means you are mindfully in hell so you cannot do anything right now except try to get out of hell before you die. You need to avoid topics that require complexity because as a child and as a result of getting traditional education the aspect of your mind that deals in complexity, right brain, was essentially turned off. There is a concept in the ancient texts relative to the quick and the dead and raising the dead to life. Because your right brain is veiled you take everyone on face value which means you use your left brain intellect because your right brain intuition is veiled to a subconscious state. I will explain the concept to negate the neurosis cause by traditional education to you but I do not raise people from the dead and that means I tell you the remedy and if you apply it you will raise yourself from the dead. My only purpose is to write infinite books and I am mindful raising the dead is not a part of that package so you are going to have to raise yourself from the dead. Raising the dead is similar to herding cats into cold water and quite frankly my video game is more important to me than raising the dead. I am not totally convinced you should be raised from the dead, would be another way to look at it. I write my books, poorly disguised thick pamphlet diaries, in diary format because there is a bit of ambiguity in my being that suggest I should not be telling anyone any of these things and I should just allow sleeping dogs to sleep, so to speak. The complexity in that is I am fully aware your chances of applying this remedy the full measure is .0024 percent. That is an indication of what all those years of left brain favoring traditional education did to your mind. If I allowed myself to try to assist a being who only has .0024 percent chance to raise their self from the dead I would destroy myself. I am not pleased with .0024 percent so I don't try. I don't look at it like I am forcing you to do anything because even if you listened to everything I told you to do, your chances are still .0024 percent. Because of that I look at you as too far gone and that way there is no point in me trying and no point in me stressing out because you are too far gone no matter what I say. You perceive a few choice psychological drugs are going to negate years of left brain favoring education and so you are not even in the ballpark of understanding how mentally devastated you are.

Let's look at one simple concept and this is very simple but it is complex for you. When you go without food for a few hours your body starts to act strange and as time passes you start to get a bit weak and you start to get a bit hungry and you start to be unable to concentrate and after a few more hours you are in desperate need to eat something. That is all false and a hallucination and your mind believes its own hallucinations and is acting them out on your body. Another way to look at it is, because your right brain is veiled your mind needs lots of nourishment all the time just to maintain ten percent mental capacity. If you flatten all the tries in your car and drive fifty miles and take note of how much gas you used and then fill the tires and drive fifty miles and take note of how much gas you used, you will be able to understand the concept of why your body starts feeling great fatigue and your concentration suffers even after you have gone without food for ten hours or five hours even. Your mind in its current state as the result of all that written education is similar to a plane that has such extreme drag it can barely make it off the ground and certainly cannot reach a height above fifty feet and even at that it consumes tenfold the amount of fuel a plane with slight drag consumes. The mind is relative to the body but the body is not relative to the mind. Your body is not telling you that you are hungry, your mind is telling your body to tell you that you are hungry. So because your right brain is veiled your entire perception of everything is out of whack or abnormal. Not some things, everything. Your perception of everything was altered as a result of your right brain being veiled by written education, so your sense of hunger is abnormal which means your sense of hunger is normal relative to a hallucinating mentally unsound freak of nature. That is not how you were born but that is how you are after years of left brain favoring traditional education. The psychology of your hallucinations is not as important as the neurological reasons for your hallucinations. It is not as important why you act the way you do psychologically it is more important to understand what this traditional education did to your brain function, because that understanding helps you understand why you act psychologically the way you do. I am not suggesting you were born hallucinating I am suggesting the traditional education altered your perception and that is why you are hallucinating now. Your cerebral cortex is relative to perception and because your mind favored left brain so much during the education it has affected your perception, cerebral cortex, on a mental level not a physiological level. Your cerebral cortex look exactly like mine does on an MRI scan for example but I am not hallucinating and you are so the "damage" is on a mental level not a physiological level. If you could just scan your brain and the physiological damage caused by written education showed up certainly civilization would have to at least consider that written education alters the brain in unfavorable ways, but this is not fantasy land and there is no way you can prove it even after you apply the remedy except by your fruits, by what you say. So you will apply this remedy and run around and say "I once was blind but now I see' and "I once was lost but now am found" and "I once was dead but now am quick" and the beings who have not applied the remedy will make quick witted comments like "That guy is insane " or "What kind of drugs are you on?" So get it out of your head you are going to apply this remedy and unveil right brain and then you are going to go prove it to someone, because the dead cannot see and cannot understand and you are surrounded by them. Not that I ever get off track.

Thursday, February 04, 2010 – Here is a good example of anti-truth in action. Perhaps you should first determine whose words are anti-truth. His comment:

"You speak many words but they show your ignorance as to how the brain functions. You are wrong in everything that you say. There is no religious or scientific evidence to back up your wrong beliefs and they are contrary to known science on the functions of the brain. It is normal for one hemisphere to have domaince over the other just as one person may be right-handed and another left-handed. Best to get your facts correct before you speak of something you know nothing about."

My response:

I prefer not to reason with what I own. What you are doing is basing everything you understand on intellect a left brain trait, what you have been told.
[There is no religious or scientific evidence] That comment is a total lie. This being is a scientists and he agrees with the ancient texts

"What it comes down to is that modern society discriminates against the right hemisphere." - Roger Sperry (1973) - neuropsychologist, neurobiologist and Nobel laureate

What is society? Civilization.

How does civilization discriminate against right hemisphere? Using written education . How is that done?

[If you reflect back upon our own educational training, we have been traditionally taught to master the 3 R's: reading, writing and arithmetic -- the domain and strength of the left brain.]
The Pitek Group, LLC.
Michael P. Pitek, III

What does the ancient texts say relative to these scientific facts ?

[Genesis 2:17 But of the tree of the knowledge of good and evil, thou shalt not eat of it: for in the day that thou eatest thereof thou shalt surely die.]

[tree of the knowledge of good and evil] = parts , good and evil is seeing parts, which is called judgment
What is the scientific fact relative to left brain relative to judgment or seeing parts?

[It excels in naming and categorizing things, symbolic abstraction, speech, reading, writing, arithmetic.]

[It excels in naming and categorizing things,] Categorizing things is seeing parts and that is contrary to right brain that see's holistically.

[1 Timothy 5:8 But if any provide not for his own, and specially for those of his own house, he hath denied the faith, and is worse than an infidel.]

You are worse than an infidel because you speak lies and steer ones who have a chance to apply the "deny one's self" remedy so you run along little serpent because you spit on the truth and assume you do not , so you know not what you do or what you say , so all I can tell you boy, is [Luke 9:23 - let him deny himself,]

[Best to get your facts correct before you speak of something you know nothing about.]

You are completely anti truth on every scale. If you understood one single sentence of the ancient texts I will remind you, boy.

END
I am pleased to toy with the mice.

Sometimes some of the ones that sense time are bent mentally so far to the left they are unable to grasp reality at all. They perceive they are "wise" but that is not possible considering their right brain is veiled but they perceive they are just fine because the mental damage that happened to them happened at such a young age they simply do not even recall or they are far removed from when they were seven, eight, nine, ten. This being is attempting to use intellect because he has no right brain, intuition. He is no longer mentally able to think for himself. What that means is, my intuition has lead me to where I am at in my understandings and I am at where I am at in my understanding because the ambiguity in right brain allows me to doubt everything I think, so I end up having to prove everything I assume using intuition. What this means is I am pleased to be wrong because then I can correct that misunderstanding and in turn come to further understandings. So this being assumes I do not do that. This being assumes I am pushing this as if I have not thoroughly pondered everything I suggest, the core of what I suggest. He perceives if written education veils the right brain society would have obviously have told everyone by now, but he is not at the level of awareness to understand society had the same thing done to it that was does to him. Other words society invented written language and math and it has major mental side effects but no one is at the mental level to understand that because they all got it, they all have the "curse", their right brain veiled. Subconsciously, right brain, he is detecting how vast the armies of goliath are but he is not consciously aware of it and so he cannot believe that is truth because if everyone around him got the written education and that means they all have the curse, veiled right brain, the god image in man, his entire world is shattered so then nothing he has thought his entire life is true, if what I suggest is true, so he assumes I lie because his simple minded left brain, cannot grasp such a complex problem, complexity is a right brain trait. The important thing to remember is Jesus had only twelve people who believed what he was saying, out of thousands only twelve believed him. The reason it is hard for one to believe the tree of knowledge is written education is because one has to scrap everything they know and start all over again and before they do that they have to swallow so much crow, which means they have to deny their self and everything they have learned in their life, and that is only possible when a being is meek, and a meek beings is a depressed being and a suicidal being. A suicidal being does not perceive their life is worth living, so they are ready to start a "real" life, escape mental death, or start over and that is required as a mindset to apply the remedy. A suicidal person is ready to try something else because they realize they want nothing to do with this life they know now. All one can do with beings who "love the world" , which means they are pleased with the world after they get the curse, is make them angry and that may make them think, and that may make them get closer to the 9th circle of hell, treason, because treason is what "those who lose their life(mindfully) will preserve it(unveil right brain)" is.

These are the only two kinds of beings that have the curse.

84

[Ecclesiastes 10:12 The words of a wise man's mouth are gracious; but the lips of a fool will swallow up himself.]

Some of the ones that sense time understand the spirit of what I suggest and they are pleased and it all clicks but that does not mean they apply the remedy but they are at least at a stage they understand truth when they hear it and they are gracious, and then there are fools, they just deny everything I suggest flat out, their minds are totally closed, the education killed them mindfully. One who applies the remedy cannot be wise or foolish because they revert back to the mental state of a child, so they just tell it like it is, but they have no sensation of thinking, I am wise, or I am foolish, because if they felt any shame or embarrassment, they would not be able to explain , written education veils the god image in man, because there are few beings on this planet that would believe that, so they are in a machine state where they just do with no mental impact on them mentally because they get spit on 99% of the time. One might suggest civilization spit on the disciples and Jesus and all the other beings that suggested this truth and that goes with the narrow, so to speak, that is par for the course so if anyone of them had any pride or ego, they would be annihilated swiftly and had hide or given up. Jesus and the disciples and many others did not give up until they were butchered by the ones that sense time. Sound minded beings do not give up on their species even if it costs them their life because being worried about dying is a symptom of ego. Young children that have a fatal illness are not afraid of death but often their parents say thing's that makes that child afraid of death.

6:28:10 PM – The only thing that is absolute is that there are perhaps no absolutes. There is a concept called absolute zero and this is essentially 0 K on the Kelvin scale. It is not possible to ever reach absolute zero because in order to do that one cannot be in the universe. This is similar to a true vacuum. One cannot create a true vacuum in the universe. This is complex because that perhaps shows this universe is absolute zero and a true vacuum. One is unable to prove they are in a bubble because only one outside the bubble is able to observe a person is in a bubble.

Here is an example. In the last few books maybe even more than the last few books I have suggested relative to the remedy, one wants to seek the shadow of death but avoid jumping in shark frenzies.

Yesterday in my town, Stuart, a surfer was out in the water and he was attacked by several sharks and killed . "A man was killed by sharks in a rare fatal attack this afternoon in the waters off Stuart, authorities said." Today they reported that there were thousands of sharks right off the beach feeding and so in reality that person unknowingly went suffering in a shark frenzy. I am fully aware now why I kept saying over the course of that last few books "seek the shadow of death but don't jump into any shark frenzies." No one has ever been killed by a shark in Stuart in Stuart's recorded history. I have said shark frenzy for that last few books and I do not perceive I said that because I was aware a being would be killed by a shark in my town, I perceived I said that because I was making the point one does not want to face actual death just face a situation that hypothalamus gives them the death signal, so seek the shadow of death. The reason I said shark frenzy is because right brain intuition is so powerful it is even beyond my ability to understand exactly what it tells me often. You may perceive I am some hocus pocus sorcerer but that is only because you have your right brain veiled and so you see right brain traits as bad because you were conditioned to dislike right brain traits. Anytime someone misspells a word you assume it is because they are stupid when in reality that is a symptom right brain threw in its random access version of the word. You were told you were stupid by your teacher when you misspelled words in your "schooling" and now you tell people they are stupid when they misspell words so you have been conditioned well. I am in a bubble and so all I can perceive is what I see through this bubble but you are not in this bubble so you perceive different things than I perceive. Before I wrote the first book I decided to write infinite books. I was fully aware what this accident meant on a cerebral level but I had no idea at that time what the accident really was, relative to I just negated the mental effects written education induced in me. So I was mentally aware on a cerebral level the concept of how large this "can of worms" was which is why I decided to write infinite book, showing how large the can is, so to speak, but I had no idea it was written language that veils right brain. This is what I suggest is going with the flow because right brain only communicates in concepts not words or pictures and that is what intuition is, a right brain trait. I can suggest right brain is unnamable in power but your chances of applying the remedy will still be .0024 percent. I can tell you human beings will never be able to determine how powerful right brain is based on its intuition power when it is unveiled, alone. Fourteen months ago or so, I decided to write infinite books explain this accident that happened to me but I had no idea it was related to written education but now here I am and I understand now fully why I decided to write infinite books, because all of civilization got the written education and so they are in fact mentally in a deep neurosis as a result and it will take infinite books to explain that to them because it is beyond their ability to believe, but I did not know that fourteen months ago I got just an intuition sensation and it was understood it will take infinite books to explain. The reason I always go with the flow relative to what I write is because it is beyond my own understanding relative to how powerful right brain is. What that means is I am in a bubble and I am writing down things that catch up to me far down the road and make sense to me far down the road. I in one way write the books blindly and far down the road why I write the things I write catches up to me and I understand why I wrote the things I wrote. Because of this, you may perceive things I write are wrong or false or not true, but in reality you have not looked at the whole picture yet. You are conditioned to assume when you read a non-fiction book everything is absolute. The Government has never told you written education favor's left brain and so education in turn will veil right brain because the mind is like a scale and if you favor one side the other side gets weaker or veiled so you assume since they never said that it cannot possibly be true. Certainly your parents would not mentally harm their own child and certainly the government would not mentally harm you as a child so what I suggest must be lies, relative to your perception. If your own parents allowed you to be mentally harmed to a gargantuan degree then who can you trust on this planet? If the society you live in and trust and will fight to defend mentally ruined you as a child using education who on this planet can you trust? Because you sense time , which proves your right brain is veiled, your mind cannot grasp such complexities so you think about them and come to a conclusion based on going one step down that logical tree and then you cannot mentally go any further so you give up and assume I am lying or wrong. You assume that I would write books telling you that written education veiled my right brain and it took me 30 failed suicide attempts to undo that damage because I am looking for friends or looking to make money. One does not try to kill their self 30 times because they love friends and love money. Attempting to kill yourself means you don't want friends and you don't want anything to do with this world. When one kills their self it means one is denying the world. A being that kills their self see's the world and then determines they want nothing to do with it or anything in it so they leave it. I didn't take a handful of pills to make money or make friends. I told the world, I have seen your ways and I want nothing to do with any of your ways, any of your groups, any of your laws, any of your morals or any of your methods.

I completely and absolutely denied the world because when I was very ill from taking those pills a voice said to me "You will die if you do not call for help and if you die you no longer get any of the perks that go with the world." And I said "I do not care I want to leave this world." That complexity is perhaps simply beyond your mental ability to grasp in the state of mind the education has conditioned you into. Right brain has paradox and complexity and so right brain deals with complex paradox. A paradox is two contradictions that reach one truth. Here is an example of complex paradox.

[I don't want to tell you about what written education did to your mind.
I have to tell you what written education did to your mind.
I will be awarded for telling you what I tell you.
I will be killed for telling you what I tell you.
I want to assist you to wake up.
I cannot assist you to wake up.
I hate you for doing this to me.
I don't blame you for doing this to me.
I won't write one more sentence.
I will write infinite sentences.
You will understand what I say and avoid mentally harming children with the education.
You will never stop mentally harming children with the education.
I want to wage all out war to stop you from mentally harming children.
I want to peacefully convince you to stop harming children.
I am certain you will understand what I say and change your education methods.
I am certain you will never change your education methods.]

This entire complex paradox is translated into one concept in right brain and it is a true concept. Because you hate right brain it seems like I must be very confused but I assure you I pray for ignorance and those prayers are never answered. Left brain simply cannot grasp complex paradox because it is not left brains nature or a left brain trait. It has nothing to do with genes or intelligence it is simply left brain traits are simple, sequential, linear and so that means right brain is complex, random access and intuition. They are totally opposites and there is no common ground relative to the two hemispheres and right brain is the powerhouse of the two. In the Cistine Chapel there is the arm of god, right brain and it is trying to touch the finger of man, left brain, and they never touch because they are not of each other. Society tells the children that honesty is the best policy and always tell the truth. The beings in the ancient texts were telling the truth relative to written education veiling the god image in man, right brain and society butchered many of them horrifically for being honest. You do not believe telling the truth is the best policy because you factually don't even know what the truth is. If you knew what the truth was you would hide like a little dog to avoid telling anyone it.

This is what you do to people who tell the truth:

Peter was crucified head down in Rome, 66 A.D.

Andrew was bound to death. He preached until his death in 74 A.D.

James, son of Zebedee, was beheaded in Jerusalem (Acts 12:1-9).

John was banished to the Isle of Patmos, 96 A.D. (Rev. 1- 9).

Phillip was crucified at Heirapole, Phryga, 52 A.D.

Bartholomew was beaten, crucified, then beheaded, 52 A.D.

Thomas was run through by a lance at Corehandal, East Indies, 52 A.D.

Matthew was slain by the sword, Ethiopia, 60 A.D.

James, son of Alphaeus, was thrown from a pinnacle, then beaten to death, 60 A.D.

Thaddeus was shot to death by arrows, 72 A.D.

Simon was crucified in Persia, 74 A.D.

You need to avoid every saying "always tell the truth" because if you knew what the truth was you certainly would not be telling it. I tell the truth because I see the truth as more valuable than I am and you deny the truth because you see yourself as more valuable than the truth. You sell the children to the sinister for the promise of a few silver pieces so you obviously have no morals or conscience and so you obviously have no ability to detect truth. The disciples were walking around saying "written education, the tree of knowledge veils the god image in man" and the anti truth, the ones that sense time said "Shut up we are tired of hearing your lies" and the apostles said "No we speak truth as a child speaking truth without reservations speaks truth" and the ones that sense time, you, became upset because the darkness cannot stand the light or the truth so they butchered these children of god, ones that unveiled the god image, right brain. That is all you do and that is your nature in the state of mind you are in. And that is truth and you hate truth. So I just keep telling you truth in hopes you go to ninth 9th circle of hell, treason and either kill yourself literally or wake up and the chances you will wake up are .0024 percent. I can convince you to mindfully kill yourself with my words so I do not need to raise a sword to you because you might get the impression I have to try. I am mindful of what you did to the other ones that tried to tell the truth so if you ever get the impression I am here to be your friend you are infinitely mistaken. There is nothing in this universe you could offer me that would do anything but insult me.

[34 Jesus said, "If a blind person leads a bind person, both of them will fall into a hole."]
This comment is out of the Gospel of Thomas and this is the definition of civilization. Civilization is simply human beings that got the written education as children, pushed on them by the adults and so their right brain is veiled and then they have children and push the written education on their children and then their children get the education pushed on them and so the entire species, civilization, is nothing but mentally blind, hindered abominations making their own offspring mentally blind abominations and so civilization is simply in this huge mental hole.
["If a blind person leads a bind person, both of them will fall into a hole."]
The only chance in this universe you have is if one of those children that were made blind by civilization wakes up and tells you the truth and the way out of that hole and once in a while they do, and this is what you do to them:

90

Peter was crucified head down in Rome, 66 A.D.

Andrew was bound to death. He preached until his death in 74 A.D.

James, son of Zebedee, was beheaded in Jerusalem (Acts 12:1-9).

John was banished to the Isle of Patmos, 96 A.D. (Rev. 1- 9).

Phillip was crucified at Heirapole, Phryga, 52 A.D.

Bartholomew was beaten, crucified, then beheaded, 52 A.D.

Thomas was run through by a lance at Corehandal, East Indies, 52 A.D.

Matthew was slain by the sword, Ethiopia, 60 A.D.

James, son of Alphaeus, was thrown from a pinnacle, then beaten to death, 60 A.D.

Thaddeus was shot to death by arrows, 72 A.D.

Simon was crucified in Persia, 74 A.D.

That is why your chances are .0024%. You kill the truth and you love the lies because the darkness sees itself as light and in turn see's the light as darkness.

[27 "If you do not fast from the world, you will not find the kingdom. If you do not observe the Sabbath as a Sabbath you will not see the Father."]

This comment is saying the exact same thing twice. You perceive it is saying two separate things because your definitions of every word is false truth. [fast from the world]

Your definition of fast from the world is every definition in this universe but the true definition. Fast from the world means you go to the one spooky place in the world you are certain a shadow of death will factually kill you and then fear not. Fast from the world means you seek the shadow of death like that is your sole purpose for being born and when you find it do not run like a scared dog but submit to it. A person that kill's their self mindfully or otherwise "fasts from the world". A person that kill's their self mindfully or otherwise, is what the Sabbath is, a sacrifice. You sense time so you have never ever observed the Sabbath. You sense time so you have never ever "fasted from the world". You assume showing up at building and giving a cult leader some money is going to get that mark off your head. You infinitely underestimate what .0024% means. You assume Jesus spoke to five thousand people and five thousand people applied the remedy and so you assume Jesus had five thousand disciples. If you go to a spooky place at night alone and the shadow of death shows up and you fear not but somehow that shadow kills you that is the same as you are now, dead and thus mentally dead. Even if that shadow literally kills you, you are still right where you are at now, but you have a .0024 chance to return to life so it is worth it. Observing the Sabbath is one time exercise and fasting from the world is a onetime exercise. You have either done it or you have not done it. Next time you hear someone say they observe the Sabbath you ask them how they mindfully killed their self and you will understand the definition of the word anti-truth when they say "What are you talking about?". The ones that sense time, the anti-truth, turn these texts into money making opportunities because money is the only thing they have of value because their right brain, the god image in man, was veiled in them as children. They only have material things now. They have no cerebral wealth so they attempt to make up for it in material wealth. They make billions of dollars off of these texts because they have no idea what these texts are even about. These texts are spitting in their face and they are totally oblivious to that fact. You get the mark as a child as the result of the ones with the mark determining its best to veil the light, right brain, in you, and then you spend the rest of your life attempting to get that mark off of your head and there is no other purpose in life until you do that. Where do you think you are at?

9:42:28 PM – I went out to eat and everyone looked perfect so I am doomed. In the human species the men defend the women. The deeper question is who defends the men? Before written education bent our minds to the left we saw holistically. What that means before written education we had no gender separation. A woman was not different than a man because they were both human beings. But because our minds were bent to the left we started seeing parts. This comment proves even the men who got written education were wise enough not to give it to the women. [Genesis 6:2 That the sons of God saw the daughters of men that they were fair; and they took them wives of all which they chose.]
The ones who applied the remedy, sons of God, ones who returned to sound mind they were as a child, relative to children of God. saw the men, the cursed, the ones that sense time, who did not apply the remedy and noticed they did not give the "curse" to the women so the ones who did apply the remedy saw it was okay to breed with those women because they did not

have the "curse". All through history the women tended not to get the written education. A person with a sense of time will assume that is a bad thing because they see the truth as lies. They are in the alternate perception reality. They assume the women not getting the written education means women were treated unfairly because they assume written education is the greatest thing ever invented by mankind and cannot possibly have any flaws and one who gets written education can be nothing but wise. The reality is because the women are the dominate of the species if you give them the curse the species is doomed. That is why women did not get the written education all through history and that is why women all through history appeared "dumb" to men who did get written education because the darkness see's the light as darkness. In our history relative to after written education was invented the women were the last of the species to get the curse. So after they started to get the written education the species downfall was ensured because they are the dominate of the species, they have the offspring and are keepers of the offspring and thus keepers of the species. Because civilization, the men with a sense of time, put this monetary system in place and made it so a person could never get money to get food the ones with a sense of time gained a monopoly over food. One is forced to get the written education to get the money, to get the food civilization has a monopoly over. Even in early American history you can see the concept "Women were not allowed to vote because they didn't have education and they were stupid." This is because left brain influenced containers always see right brain influenced containers as bad or evil or dumb. A child is born in mental harmony so they are a right brain influenced containers because right brain at 50% right brain dominates over left brain traits. So the only left brain influenced containers , ones that sense time because right brain paradox is veiled, are beings that got the written education and had not applied the fear not remedy. All this is saying[Genesis 6:2 That the sons of God saw the daughters of men that they were fair,] is : Well at least the ones that sense time were not so totally mentally ruined they also mentally ruined the women also with the written education. So civilization's version of history is women were once stupid and now they get written education they are wise, but the ancient t texts suggest exactly the opposite. Once women were the last vestiges of sanity among the group of humans that fell from grace, ate off the tree of knowledge. Now the women have all fallen from grace also and since the women are the ones that have children the species is doomed. Over thousands of years civilization has charmed the women with all its trinkets and material delusions of success and now all the women have eaten from the tree. So because civilization put women in a situation that if they wanted to have money and trinkets they had to get written education now families are secondary to everything. Civilization, the ones that sense time, have put women in a situation where it is saying to them "Raising your offspring is something best avoided." "Getting our brand of education is more important than raising offspring because you won't make any money off raising offspring." As a species we have completely sold our soul in the name of this tree of knowledge. We have given up everything for the tree of knowledge so to even suggest rules and morals at this stage is a symptom one is totally out of their mind. There are beings that have applied the remedy today that attack the traditional education school that teach women and you assume they are evil and bad and crazy because you are so crazy you would not know truth if it was writing books talking to you. If they do not attack the school it does not matter because we are doomed already, and if they do attack the school it does not matter because we are doomed already. The word hope was invented by a being in infinite denial and ignorance. There is a concept in the east that suggests "Nothing matters". Its relative on one hand to being in nothingness and that is simply a being who has applied the fear not remedy. On the other hand it means our species sold its soul to the tree of knowledge and so no matter what you do, our species cannot take that back.

2:40:42 AM – The world education web site: worlded.org has a motto: engage, educate, inspire.

A = No child left behind(give all the children written education)
X = engage, educate, inspire.
Y =[If you reflect back upon our own educational training, we have been traditionally taught to master the 3 R's: reading, writing and arithmetic -- the domain and strength of the left brain.]["What it comes down to is that modern society discriminates against the right hemisphere." - Roger Sperry (1973) - neuropsychologist, neurobiologist and Nobel laureate]}

If Y is false then X and A is righteous

If Y is truth then X and A is diabolical

The ancient texts say Y is truth and civilization says Y is false. This is a distinct adversarial reality which means there is no middle ground and there is no lukewarm. If civilization says our written education bends the mind 5 percent to the left and thus veils right brain 5 percent then everything relative to traditional education collapses. Because of this civilization has to maintain at all times Y is a total lie and totally false and thus the ancient texts are a total lie and totally false. One is either hot or cold. One either understands Y means right brain is veiled by traditional education or one totally denies right brain is veiled at all by traditional education, the tree of knowledge. Civilization maintains it is impossible this: [If you reflect back upon our own educational training, we have been traditionally taught to master the 3 R's: reading, writing and arithmetic -- the domain and strength of the left brain.] could veil right brain at all, even one percent. Would a human being with a conscience allow a child to have their right brain veiled five percent for promise of some money? Civilization looked at me when I was a child and determined it is best to veil my right brain and it nearly killed me and so no matter what I ever say ever, I am strictly on a vengeance mission. I am not here to make friends and I am not here to make money. You are not brave now that I am. Suffering leads to either change or more suffering. - 3:10:57 AM

6:13:28 AM – Those who let go of their life mindfully will find the light literally. Those who lose their life mindfully will regain their light literally. I follow my own rules as long as they keep changing.

2/5/2010 4:23:37 PM – There is an article about a Paleolithic tribes in India. The last remaining member of this tribe died today and she was 85. Her name was Boa Sr. This tribe is thought to be 65,000 years old. In the article it said and I paraphrase "The Bo perhaps are very hostile perhaps so they never leave their island." Perhaps what that being meant is, the Bo do not want any of the ones that sense time to ruin their culture so they are hostile towards the ones that sense time that attempt to invade their island, of course now they are extinct. It is one thing to be hostile which is protective and another thing to be aggressively hostile. The Bo language was a spoken language obviously so it died out when she died. She was the last speaker of the language. One has to at least understand from this story that Adam and Eve did not arrive on the planet 5400 years ago so it has to be that Adam and Eve represents the first human beings to eat off the tree of knowledge 5400 years ago and ironically that is when written language was invented relative to that area of the world. One could argue Adam and Eve represent's the first man on earth as long as ones definition of man is a being that ate off the tree of knowledge and did not apply the remedy to that so they were left with their right brain veiled. Another way to look at it is, before 5400 years ago relative to that area of the world there were human beings and then written language came along and beings started learning it and then they were men. Being in "human being" denotes a person in the now, relative to no sense of time. What is interesting about these cultures that don't have written language is they are so wise they appear strange or savage to ones who got the written education which is a nice way to say left brain influenced containers always see sound minded right brain influenced containers as bad or evil. The Bo may have been violent but they never killed 50 million people over grains of dirt. The Bo never had world wars in fact they may not have had had any wars relative to the size of the wars the ones that sense time had. Nearly every single war in recorded history relative to ones that sense time is an aggressive war over land and resources and that is a symptom of coveting. One exception is the American Revolution and that was not over land and resources it was over escaping the grips of a tyrant and that is a war over freedom or escaping bondage from a superior controlling force. A left brain trait is control because a right brain trait is freedom. Left brain perceives control and rules and organization is safety and right brain perceives freedom and free spirit and open mindedness is safety. Left brain hates open mindedness because that breaks rules and so it perceives it is unsafe or dangerous. So this Bo tribes lived for 65,000 years without written language and so that means they lived without math. The whole concept of civilization is one cannot live without written education but that understanding is based on the principle if you do not get written education you will not be able to make lots of money. So this means written education has a carrot on the end of a stick, money, and that is a charm because money suggests luxury.

In actual reality written education is just fine as long as one observes the Sabbath which means one gets the education and then applies the fear not remedy but if one does not do that written education is a mental death sentence. Other words everything would be just fine as it is as long as after one gets the education they are assisted with applying the remedy so their right brain would not be veiled or if one gives a child strictly oral education until later, perhaps the age of 15 to 18. Of course this makes it seems like the remedy is no big deal or does not take any effort to apply when in reality some beings who attempt to apply the remedy can spend their whole life trying to. That is an indication of the mental damage written education causes. Written education is the trade off of all trade off's. I am mindful some attempt to mask the remedy as self help or religion or unlocking the power of your mind and various other suggestions. No matter what one calls it, at the end of the day it is simply a way to negate the mental effects of learning written education. All of these ancient religions are nothing but mental exercises to negate the mental side effects of learning written language and accomplishing that may take the rest of your life but that is not because the remedy is difficult to apply relative to an absolute it is just the mind of a being after the education is essentially that beings greatest enemy. That being is trapped by their own altered perception so they must deny that perception to apply the remedy. Religion is more about damage control and containment of the damaging mental effects of learning written education than anything else. I see people with a sense of time and I can sense they are trying as hard as they can to deal with the fact their minds have been turned down to 10 percent and they cannot do anything but suffer from day to day. They see others as smarter than them because some 10 percent retard told them they were not smart. The 10 percent retard rulers telling people to apply their self after they have turned that beings mind down to 10 percent. 'Now that we have turned your mind down to 10 percent go out and apply yourself." Civilization is the mentally blind rulers leading the mentally blind sheep. I look at reality like this, I was born and some abomination turned my mind down to 10 percent and then I did all these things to undo that and from here on out I will remind the rulers I look at you as nothing but an abomination from here on out. I am not concerned with how many minions you have on your side. I am not concerned about your pinprick bullshit attempts at logic and reason because you are not capable of logic or reason. So you rulers go ahead and keep mentally hindering the people and I will keep reminding the people what you do to them and we will see who is left standing in the end because as far as I am concerned there is nothing but war now. I will use your rotten fruits as a mental conditioning aspect to achieve a level of concentration so that I can form the perfect sentence that will destroy the ruler scribes. That is my only goal in life, I have no other purpose. You ruler scribes are either too mentally ruined to tell the children about the remedy or you are too cruel to tell the children about the remedy after they get the education and I am going to find out which it is. I am going to find out if you are infinitely mentally nonviable or infinitely cruel, and once I understand that I can determine your punishment.

[Matthew 7:29 For he taught them as one having authority, and not as the scribes.]

I will explain the reality of this situation to the common people relative to these ancient texts. These ancient texts contain the remedy so you are able to free your mind from the mental cage the written education has put your mind in. The goal of the ruler scribes is to make these ancient texts unattractive because the ruler scribes are aware if these ancient texts are ignored the common people will never be able to free their minds and so the absolute tyranny over the common people's minds will be achieved. This of course is done on a subconscious level relative to the ruler scribes, simply put the ruler scribes got the education so they are lunatics. The fear not remedy is the key to get out of the mental cage the rulers scribes have put you in. The ruler scribes have hijacked the ancient texts and have over time made them appear as stupidity so people will not read them and not listen to them. The ruler scribes have contorted the spirit of the ancient texts to serve their purpose of tyranny over the mind. You have to understand these ancient texts are not about putting you in cages of isolation but they are methods to free you from the mental cages of isolation the ruler scribes have put you in using the written education. The ruler scribes will never mention the fear not remedy and they will never mention what the tree of knowledge really is. They never have told you what the fear not remedy is and what the tree of knowledge really is and that is because they desire to keep you in your mental cage knowingly or unknowingly. Do not allow the ruler scribes to tell you what these texts mean because they will tell you everything except the truth. Do not listen to any person on this planet that does not understand exactly what the tree of knowledge literally is and what the fear not remedy is in relation to that. The tree of knowledge is written language and the remedy to that to free one's mind is the fear not remedy. Any being on this planet that cannot explain that in detail has not applied the remedy because they will only see the truth as lies so they will never submit that is the truth. If any being on this planet cannot explain what the tree of knowledge is then they cannot possibly understand the ancient texts at all. That is the sign post to determine if a being is a scribe or the genuine article. A scribe will not be able to mentally grasp nor explain what the tree of knowledge is and in turn will not be able to explain what the fear not remedy is so that is the sign post they are a false teacher of the ancient texts.

[Matthew 23:15 Woe unto you, [scribes] and Pharisees, hypocrites! for ye compass sea and land to make one proselyte, and when he is made, ye make him twofold more the child of hell than yourselves.
Matthew 23:25 Woe unto you, [scribes] and Pharisees, hypocrites! for ye make clean the outside of the cup and of the platter, but within they are full of extortion and excess.
[Luke 23:10 And the chief priests and scribes stood and vehemently accused him.]

[scribes stood and vehemently accused him.] Who killed Jesus and the disciples?
The scribes.
Who are scribes. Anyone who gets the written education and then does not apply the fear not, deny one's self remedy, the ones that sense time. If one does not apply that remedy after the written education they have right brain, the god image in man veiled so they are opposed to right brain, the god image in man because left brain is anti or contrary to the god image in man, right brain. Any human being on the planet that got written education is a scribe until they apply the fear not remedy.

What is keeping the Sabbath? The Sabbath is a sacrifice and that is what the remedy is.

One who gets the written education must keep the Sabbath, apply the fear not remedy.

"Those who lose their life (mindfully) will preserve it"

Seek the shadow of death and then fear not. Relative to seek and ye shall find. It is a onetime thing. If one does not observe the Sabbath they have right brain veiled so they are a scribe.

10:25:20 PM - Maybe your child is still intelligent even if all of civilization judges your child not to be intelligent based on your child's ability to master civilizations left brain sequential based inventions called written education and math. You do not believe that because you punish your own child if they come home from school with bad grades. You will beat your child and send your child to bed without food if they come home with bad grades. If your child cannot veil their right brain fast enough, you beat your own child so that the ones who want your child's right brain veiled will like you. You will harm your own child mentally and permanently so you will be accepted by the herd.

A slave breaking even one rule reminds the tyrant his control is fleeting,

2/7/2010 3:27:32 AM –

Who is the man upstairs? Right Brain

What is the land of milk and honey? – A mind that has right brain in a sound state 50%, not a mind that has right brain veiled.

What is hell? A mind that has right brain veiled to a subconscious state as a result of written education.

What is the concept of the story of Medusa? For one to seek to find the shadow of death, Medusa head, and then fear not, which is the remedy to unveil right brain after written education veils right brain.

What is the ideal plane? The state of mind where one applies one of the various remedies to unveil right brain after written education veils it and returns to sound mind, consciousness.

What is heaven? The state of mind where right brain has been restored to 50% power after written education veils it.

100

What is the tree of knowledge? Written education, script, and mathematics.

What is the holy war? A battle on physical and verbal scales which includes several aspects.

A.) Beings who negate the right brain veiling that attempt to convince ones verbally who still have their right brain veiled by traditional education to apply the remedy to unveil right brain.

B.) Beings who wage literal war against the ones who push the traditional education which in turns veils the right brain in the children.

C.) Beings who were taught oral education and never had right brain veiled who participate in A or B.

D.) The holy war is also happening on an individual level. The war on this level is a being is born and given the written education and then they attempt to return to a sound mind, unveil right brain, but this personal holy war is not always perceived by the person with right brain veiled. They may perceive they are in a struggle or suffering but in reality it is the battle mentally they are going though to unveil right brain after the written education veils it.

This holy war relative to the west has continued for the last 5400 years and perhaps the first documented start of the war was when Abraham and Lot burned down the cities of the ones who encourage the written education on children and thus veil the right brain and never suggest the remedy that ensures right brain does not remain veiled. This documented story is known as Sodom and Gomorrah and later the story of Exodus, the Red Sea battle, is another major battle between the ones that that do not sense time, ones with right brain unveiled, against the ones with right brain veiled, the ones that sense time, known as civilization. Although there have been many wars between the ones that sense time over land and resources there has perhaps never been a war among the ones that do not sense time against eachother because the ones that do not sense time are solidly outnumbered in the holy war by the ones that do sense time. One of the underlying factors of this holy war is once a person gets the written education and their right brain has been veiled the remedy relative to their perspective is extremely difficult to apply. One has to essentially deny what they perceive and also deny what they think is proper or improper and because of this many are never able to restore their right brain. This is not an indication of a beings intelligence it is an indication how devastating the written education is on the mind of that being. Even if every human being who got the written education wanted to apply the remedy and unveil right brain the process is so difficult to accomplish only a small fraction would be able to go the full measure and fully restore their right brain to mental harmony with left brain This is an indication of how immoral it is to veil a child's right brain because that child even as a an adult may never be able to restore to sound mind and it also an indication that mankind has invented a tool, written education, and even after 5400 years civilization has yet to understand it has massively devastating mental side effects on a child when taught to them as such as young age. The mental side effects are so devastating the beings who get the education are no longer mentally able to even determine how devastating the side effects are so they in turn give the same education to their own offspring. This is a situation where an adult goes down into a pit and in that pit are poison gases and that adult calls their child to help them out and then that child goes down and then they are both overcome by the gases and then another family member see's that and goes down to help them and that being is doomed, and then another friend shows up and see's the three in the pit and goes down to help them and they all are over taken by the poison gas, so to speak. This has more to do with the fact the invention written education is very charming and is in fact a very good invention and appears to be flawless and that is the reason it is never questioned and because its unwanted side effects, favors left brain and in turn veils right brain, are never questioned by all of the beings who got the education because if they do, they must first submit to their self, they perhaps have been mentally ruined by the invention. The ones that sense time have right brain veiled so they are essentially only capable of simple minded logic tree's mentally. They determine, certainly their parents would not allow them to be mentally harmed so therefore written education could not have mentally hindered them.

X = inability to question if one has been mentally harmed by education

Y = Assumption an adult would never mentally harm a child knowingly or unknowingly

Z = inability to sense one has been mentally hindered because right brain intuition has been veiled

A = scale of the mentally hindered, written education is taught in every country on the planet.

These variables require one to be very open minded and essentially void of emotions because one with strong emotions and in turn has right brain veiled cannot comprehend the amount of destruction because it transcends all of their labels. Ones that sense time wants to look at their self as good or not a party of this problem and this situation requires one to look directly at their self and question if they are in fact not involved in mentally hindering children knowingly or unknowingly. Because the complexity of right brain has been veiled in the ones that sense time they cannot mentally see the huge picture they can only see small parts and thus are they are trapped in this tiny area of the picture and mentally cannot grasp the scale that is required to see the entire picture relative to the mental effects this invention written education has had on the entire species not just one select country. The ones that sense time minds will not allow them to face the reality that if written education does veil the right brain then they not only have been mentally hindered they may have mentally hindered innocent children and also their own parents may have allowed them to be mentally hindered. The ones that sense time emotions are turned up so high because of the fact their right brain is veiled they would emotionally collapse if this reality hit them in their state of mind because they would not be able to process all of that suffering without their strong emotions destroying them in the process. If the ones that sense time were simply told point blank the written education did veil their right brain by what they perceive are "authorities" and that means they may have also hindered their own children or were responsible for the mentally hindering of innocent, they would become suicidal and even homicidal because in their unsound state of mind they cannot mentally handle such a large scale of devastation. That's unfortunate. The ones that sense time cannot mentally handle they are knowingly or unknowingly responsible for the death of untold millions of beings as a direct result of their written education veiling the right brain in beings, adults and children alike so they discount it right out of hand because they would implode mentally and determine it is best for them to terminate their self. If being that has right brain veiled was convinced beyond a reasonable doubt of the harm that written education causes their simple minded left brain state would be unable to deal with the complexity and they perhaps would mentally self destruct because their emotions are so abnormally high in that veiled right brain state of mind. This is relative to ignorance is bliss. There are no beings on the planet with a sense of time, and thus right brain veiled that are happy or joyous for any other reason other than they are ignorant to what this written education does to the mind of innocent children and in turn did to their mind. Wisdom and awareness is relative to grief and so ignorance and unawareness is relative to joy. Simply put any of the ones who sense time who are happy are only happy because they are so mentally blind to what is going on relative to what written education does to the mind. The deeper reality is, no being that senses time is happy at all, they are just in various stages of well disguised suffering and sorrow that sometimes appears like happiness.

10:53:18 AM – There is a web site I went to that was for people who are right and left brain dominate or some such and there was one user on there and he explained "If I misspell a word it is not because I am stupid it is because I am careless." and what I understood from that comment is that he was apologizing for right brain, then I realized every time I type in a sentence and use the spell checker to fix it I am apologizing for right brain and then I realized this whole written language is nothing but a right brain biased piece of crap. If you can spell well you factually cannot think well. The only reason I use the spell checker is for the benefit of the ones who cannot think well, the ones that sense time. I have to write my books and keep in mind the mentally hindered may be attempting reading them.

2/7/2010 1:28:42 PM – The ideals in the following declaration are concepts and may be adjusted at the discretion of the adherent.

Declaration of Free Minds:

A.) Written language and Mathematics known as written education favor left brain and in turn hinders the mind; veils the right hemisphere aspects; if not taught properly; taught to children improperly or taught to any human being improperly.

B.) Because of the reality suggested in (A) it is improper to teach written education to ; any child; or any human being without first suggesting the harmful side effects; or without first suggesting the remedy to said mental side effects.

C.) Due to the nature of this situation relative to the vast majority of the species is under the influence of the left hemisphere because they were not warned of the mental hindering aspects of the written education listed in (A); the rules, the ones that sense time, laws and suggestions contrary to this declaration are mere suggestions and may be considered or ignored at the discretion of the adherent to this declaration.

When a person gets the written education it veils their right brain intuition so they no longer have the ability to sense when they are doing harm mindfully. If I beat a dog you can see I am harming that dog, but if I mentally torment that dog you cannot see that so you assume it is not happening because your intuition is essentially gone. It is not about whether written education harms the mind of a small child it is the reality you cannot detect it because you were mentally harmed by the written education, so you right brain intuition is veiled. So children are being mentally harmed by written education but you are mentally blind to that reality because you were one of those children and thus are mentally blind because your right brain intuition is veiled.

2/8/2010 6:25 PM – Depression and people who are suicidal are not what you perceive they are. The depressed and suicidal are in the end stages as a being attempting to escape the neurosis, unveiling right brain traits.

So depression is the withdraw symptoms of a being attempting to unveil right brain after education veiled right brain, so any attempts to "fix" that person with antidepressants and encouragement for them to get well in fact harms that person. Society firstly put that person in that position with their wisdom education and then society tries to fix them when in reality society does not even know what it is dealing with. If society had an inkling of foresight it would at least be at the mental level of understanding to at least consider years of left brain education may in fact mentally hinder a person in one way or another but society is not even at that basic elementary level of awareness. Society has a stick of dynamite in their hand, written education, and it is lit and they are completely unaware there is any possibility it could be harmful. This is not an indication of societies intelligence on an absolute scale it is simply a symptom of how devastating this education is to a beings mind and since all of society gets the education, societies mind. The whole nature of neurosis is one is unaware they are in neurosis. One trait of a lunatic is they are paranoid or afraid of things that will help them. Let's look at this comment.

[I walk through the valley of the shadow of death and fear not evil.]
[I walk] denotes seeking. One has to walk through the door to escape the neurosis or hell. "I walk" shows intent and show's a choice has been made. It shows one is aware they are doing something and this is what a seeker is relative to seek and you will find. If one does not seek they will not find but since one is in neurosis and blind it is a blind seeking relative to the fact they are blind. This blind seeking is relative to the concept of let ones who are wise in the world become fools.

Then they have the next part of that remedy [through the valley]. A valley is a low point. Valley in this comment denotes depression but it is what one has to walk through not what one rests in, so it is not an end result it is something one has to do to get to another area.

X = neurosis or mental hell caused by written education
Y = depression and suicidal aspects
Z = leaving the neurosis

X + Y = Z

So try not to look at it like depression is a bad thing because in reality depression is just something one has to go through to break the neurosis. One is not going to deny their self if they are happy with their self. You cannot possibly know what right brain is like in the conscious state in your mind because it was veiled in from the conscious state before you were even ten and it does not even fully developed until later in your youth perhaps as long as eighteen or older so there is no possible way to know what right brain is like outside of what it is like in a subconscious state. So what this means is one cannot possibly be happy if one half of their mind has been reduced to a subconscious state so the assumption one is happy is a delusion of one in neurosis. A depressed person will seek out others to reaffirm their own understanding they are not happy. A psychologist perceives that person is seeking them out to get help but in reality that depressed person is not seeking help they are seeking death. The depressed person is telling the world they are seeking death it just so happens a psychologist is as good as any person to tell that to. The deeper reality of this is a child is born with right brain unveiled and in the conscious state so the mind is sound and once they get the written education the right brain is veiled to a subconscious state and so their mind is unsound and it is going to get back to being sound even if it kills the being unless the neurosis is so extreme the person is too far gone mentally. The complexity is one can do anything they set their mind to but one in neurosis has no mind or they have an unsound mind so it is not really a mind it is some hybrid mind but not a sound mind. A person on PCP is no different than a person in the neurosis because one cannot really assist that person in neurosis or on PCP, one can only attempt to suggest things with the understanding the person will most likely eventually jump out of a window. So the norm for ones in neurosis is literal death or being so far in neurosis they cannot ever escape so the deviation from that norm is once in a while a person escapes the neurosis. That is an indication of how devastating years and years of left brain favoring education is on the mind especially when its starts when the being is six or seven. This whole situation has never really been about attempting to wake up the ones in neurosis, ones who got the written education, it has really been about attempting to reach one in neurosis that is in a position of authority so they can perhaps adjust the education methods to avoid putting more people, children, in the neurosis. Since the neurosis caused by written education is essentially 99.9 % permanent the only real logical solution is to attempt to stop the ones in neurosis from putting more children into the neurosis. Jesus and Buddha and Socrates did not have 50,000 disciples for a reason. Moses freed an entire city of people in neurosis and he still did not have much luck on convincing them to apply the remedy.

[Exodus 32:19 And it came to pass, as soon as he came nigh unto the camp, that he saw the calf, and the dancing: and Moses' anger waxed hot, and he cast the tables out of his hands, and brake them beneath the mount.]

The spirit of this comment is saying Moses was not having any luck in convincing ones to apply the remedy and that is an indication that the neurosis caused by written education, the tree of knowledge, is essentially permanent. [and he cast the tables out of his hands] He threw every rule and moral and law on the ground and smashed them to pieces. He was saying, all bets are off. No rules and no morals and no class and no laws because this neurosis is so strong one cannot win or even make progress even with no morals and no rules and no class and no laws. All bets are off. Society puts children into the mental state of neurosis and then suggests the words, rules, laws and morals and that proves they are so far out of touch with reality I cannot explain it in infinite books. If I am mindful there is no solution then there is no solution, so all bets are off. Your freedom was taken from you starting at the age of six so why on earth are you speaking about freedom, you have no freedom, your mind was taken from you so why do you even suggest freedom? It was over for you before it even started it just has not hit you yet. You are trying very hard to achieve ideals you are no longer able to achieve. I will get back on track for no reason at all.

[I walk] means I seek.
[Through the valley] Valley denotes depression or self denial; a meek person is a depressed person; as in person that is attempting to unveil right brain and so they are mindfully in a valley, depressed, thus depression is a symptom one is trying to undo the damage education caused them.

[of the shadow of death] denotes seeking a place that you perceive you may literally die and at the same time not a place you perceive you will literally die. No shark frenzies but spooky dark places.

2/9/2010 12:42:04 PM - If I say you are pretty you feel good. If I say you are a loser, you feel bad. If I say you are ugly, you feel bad. That is only because your hypothalamus is not working properly. You are getting fight or flight signals from words and from sounds. If a person says to another person "You are an idiot" and that person punches that person, that is because they got a fight or flight signal from a word. This means their hypothalamus is making that person react to things they should not be fighting about. A parent will punish a child for saying a cuss word but that is only because that parents hypothalamus is telling that parent if that word is said that child will go to hell or die or something bad will happen to that child so that parent perceives they have morals or some righteous aspect but in reality it is just their hypothalamus is giving false positives because the written education has bent their mind so far to the left the hypothalamus is getting hits on things it should not be getting hits on. For any person to react violently or feel embarrassment or shame because a word is said shows clearly something is not working properly in that beings mind. Being afraid or ashamed or embarrassed because of sounds, words or music means a person is delusional because these things are in fact intangible. It is similar to being embarrassed because of a thought. A person that senses time will perceive they do not like certain words because they have a conscience but in reality it is just because of their ill functioning hypothalamus on a mental level and that aspect of the brain is relative to fear. So a television show will edit out any cuss word said which proves that television network fears words and also shows people who watch it and call in if cuss words are said, fear words because they all got written education and in turn have a hypothalamus that is afraid of a bad haircut and in this case even sounds. The adults perceive they are protecting children from spooky dangerous evil words and thus dangerous evil spooky sounds and that is a delusion. It is delusional to be afraid of a sound or word. Being afraid of a sound or a word is delusional. Their hypothalamus is telling them "death or evil will come if you hear that sound of that word." and that is a hallucination they are believing. They perceive they are righteous for being afraid of words or being mindful to scold anyone who says certain words because they are in a bubble and that bubble is neurosis caused by all of that left brain favoring education. Cuss words of 200 years ago are not necessarily cuss words of today so this fear of words is a sort of progression or mutation where the words change but the fears of certain words does not. All of society subscribes to this fear of words delusion and the only common denominator is all of society gets the written education. This is what Timothy was talking about.

[2 Timothy 1:7 For God hath not given us the spirit of fear; but of power, and of love, and of a sound mind.]

Spirit of fear. An adult will harm a child or a school will paddle a child for saying a word and that is insanity because that adult or authority truly believes the word is bad, evil, dangerous or life threatening but in reality it cannot be any of those things. Some being will have seminars about how evil certain music is but in reality their hypothalamus is totally out of whack on a mental level and they perceive true evil in music or in lyrics when that is not even in the realm of sanity. All of society fears words and all of society got the written education. It all comes back to the tree of knowledge and because the written education bends the mind itself so there is no way to determine how much damage is done because the damage is not uniform.

[B. B. (12) allegedly died from a self-inflicted gunshot wound] This twelve year old girl was an exceptional student which means she excelled in reading, writing and arithmetic and so her mind bent very fast to the left and as the mind bends to the left from the education the emotions start going through the roof and so does the fear caused by the hypothalamus and so minor incidents causes a person to snap. The students who are most suicidal and prone to depression caused by the mind bending to the left perhaps are the exceptional students or they show symptoms first. This depression suicidal aspect comes down to one simple reality. When right brain is at 50% in conscious state of mind the thought patterns are so swift and also random access mixed with sequential thoughts so a state of mind of depression and suicidal thoughts simply cannot be maintained at all. This goes along with all the other emotions from envy, shame, embarrassment, anger, hate, and lust. A person that can mindfully maintain any of these emotions for more than a moment relative to a clock in fact has to have right brain veiled to achieve that and the only way to have right brain veiled is for one to get some sort of conditioning that has rewards and punishments attached to it relative to how well one does at the left brain heavy aspect and that is written education. Even addiction is not possible with right brain unveiled because one forgets they are addicted because the thought patterns are random access and one has no sense of time and even if they do drugs there is no euphoric effect because euphoric effects are really right brain unveiling in ones that have right brain veiled for the duration the drugs lasts. This random access thought pattern means one is not able to covet a thought or the thoughts do not fester in the mind. The ambiguity and paradox of right brain will make one question if they are feeling euphoria on drugs and before a few moments have passed they will forget they should be feeling euphoria and on top of that, euphoria from drugs use is right brain being unveiled for the duration of the drug. One cannot unveil right brain when right brain is unveiled so one is always euphoric, so drug addiction is not possible and in some ways that will take some beings a while to get use to after they apply the remedy the full measure.

[Jeremiah 48:43 Fear, and the pit, and the snare, shall be upon thee, O inhabitant of Moab, saith the LORD.]

This comment sums it up perfectly. One has this huge spirit of fear because their hypothalamus is sending false positives about many things it should not be and that creates clutter in the mind and that in turn puts one's mind in a pit and so one's mind is in a snare. One's mind is trapped because right brain lightening processing is veiled so one thought can remain in that beings mind for years and years and that is what sloth is. After one applies the remedy and right brain unveils shortly after and one's mind is in such a processing frenzy for about nearly two months by the time they get past that initial stage any addictions or lusts are purged. This is not relative to how good one is, it is relative to the processing speed and random access thought patterns right brain has. One who is addicted to food will always have that food thought on their mind and one that is addicted to say sex or drugs will always have that thought on their mind but when right brain is in the conscious state or unveiled those thoughts have no more value than any other thought and they are processed through so fast they cannot even be maintained, so one is no longer controlled by these thoughts that seem to linger in the sense of time state of mind. One cannot even contrast to two states of mind, one with a sense of time and thus has right brain veiled to one with no sense of time that has right brain unveiled. One could say heaven and hell states of mind is the easiest way to contrast the two. An addict with a sense of time can have that addiction thought in their mind for their whole life and with right brain unveiled that addiction thought could never be maintained for more than a minute relative to a clock and so if one figures out the contrast in that alone they can see there is no comparison to those two states of mind. I mentioned in early volumes my mind was going so fast I thought I would overload but this is because I was accustomed to slothful sequential processing. Now I am greatly accustomed to it, but it took over a year to just get use to the powerhouse processing alone. The comment transformation or being reborn really means one can no longer even relate to how they use to be in the sense of time state of mind. Even people who show symptoms of right brain have not perhaps unveiled right brain all the way because if they got the written education they have to apply the remedy. It is mysterious because once right brain is unveiled it wants to figure out what veiled it. Right brain is a questioner and somehow that is its goal, to figure out what veiled it.

This comment is explaining Abraham pondered with right brain and figured out the spirit of fear was relative to this veiling of right brain [Genesis 15:1 After these things the word of the LORD came unto Abram in a vision, saying, Fear not, Abram: I am thy shield, and thy exceeding great reward.]

[the word of the LORD came unto Abram in a vision, saying, Fear not,] This comment could just as easily say right brain ministered to Abraham and did its lightening processing and Abraham came to the conclusion fear not was the remedy to this spirit of fear caused by the tree of knowledge, written education.. I am not wise I have right brain unveiled after accidentally applying this ancient fear not remedy after written education

112

veiled right brain. That will never ever change and so because everyone has a right brain when they unveil it fully using this method they will understand everything I understand because it is not me, it is right brain. I am not doing anything but relying on right brain lightening processing, pattern detection and intuition to write all of this and it is so fast I do not perceive it takes any effort at all. This is an indication that this righteous battle against the scribes in Sodom and Gomorrah for example was proper. These battles were not about ideology or politics or religion it was simply a battle about, it is better to have right brain unveiled than to have it veiled. It is better to have a sound mind than not have sound mind. It was better to have the mind you were born with than not have the mind you were born with. So it was a righteous battle. It was not about land and it was not about gold. It was not about resources and it was not about control. It was about allowing human beings to retain the mind they were born with. The entire point is, life is simple and easy with a sound mind and life is a wasted life with a mind bent to the left. Every problem we have as a species right now is because we mocked these wise beings when they said that tree of knowledge is dangerous and if you eat off of it you have to apply the remedy and since we ignored them we sit where we are at and wonder why all these problems are catching up to us now. Our species is built on the sand because we did not listen to these wise beings in the ancient texts. You may perceive we have some great thing going on in this world right now but you have no idea where we would be if we would have simply listened to this remedy these wise beings told us thousands of years ago. One will never ever top these variations of this fear not remedy relative to the remedy after getting all that left brain education so there is not even any point looking into it. The remedy un-bends the mind that was bent by the written education and all the drugs in the universe will never be able to accomplish that and the fear not remedy accomplishes that in one second and on a mental level so there is no money to be made in doing it and the ones that sense time are not pleased with that. It is not taxable. My hypothalamus said "Call for help or you will die from the pills" and I said "I don't care" and that was the remedy and it was done and nothing can take it back and so there is nothing that can complete with that. Fear not is an absolute remedy to the tree of knowledge. Knowing that does not mean one has applied the remedy but being mindful of that means one has applied the remedy, perhaps. Applying the remedy is the one thing a being with a sense of time does not want to do. The tragedy of the written education is the vast majority of people who get it have nothing to show for it but an unsound mind. They are brilliant cerebral giants sleeping and many will never awake. You take every single war mankind has fought in the last 5000 years and they do not compare to the suffering this written education taught improperly has caused the species. Society could not kill people mentally and literally more effectively than it does with written education. Abraham and Lot did not burn down those two cities and kill everyone in them for a few silver pieces, is another way to look at it. You will read this and discount it and doubt it and then you will go on with your life and never say anything about written education harming minds and you will understand why I suggest you no longer have a conscience or a soul.

[Leviticus 7:25 For whosoever eateth the fat of the beast, of which men offer an offering made by fire unto the LORD, even the soul that eateth it shall be cut off from his people.]

Anyone who eats off the golden calf, the beast, the tree, written education, has their right brain intuition veiled and so they have their soul cut out or veiled. = [even the soul that eateth it shall be cut off]: I don't write fiction.

[Deuteronomy 4:9 Only take heed to thyself, and keep thy soul diligently, lest thou forget the things which thine eyes have seen, and lest they depart from thy heart all the days of thy life: but teach them thy sons, and thy sons' sons;]

This comment is saying no matter what you do after you get the tree of knowledge you apply the remedy and in this case it's the "walk through the valley of the shadow of death and fear not evil" so you can keep your soul, right brain intuition, and make sure you explain it to your children and to their children. This is why it always goes bad because eventually people stop applying the remedy after they get the written education and stop telling their children in turn the remedy and then the whole society forgets the remedy all together.

[keep thy soul diligently] means apply the remedy no matter what but that's is not how it works out. The remedy is totally alien to ones who have the neurosis caused by the written education. Deny yourself means you are suicidal mindfully and society gives beings who are mindfully suicidal lots of pills to "fix them". The remedy is not needed if one does not force all that left brain favoring education on six year olds so it's not the remedy is harsh, it is harsh to veil a child's right hemisphere traits to begin with so a remedy is required to regain one's mind and thus soul, right brain intuition. If one sets a house on fire they should not complain it takes too much water to put that fire out because they should not have set that fire to begin with.

2/10/2010 7:48:14 AM – Relative to mental disorders.

Delusional Disorder : Non-bizarre delusions including feelings of being followed, poisoned, infected, deceived or conspired against, or loved at a distance. Non-bizarre referred to real life situations which could be true, but are not or are greatly exaggerated. Bizarre delusions, which would rule out this disorder, are those such as believing that your stomach is missing or that aliens are seeking you out to be their leader. Delusional disorder can be subtyped into the following categories: erotomanic, grandiose, jealous, persecutory, somatic, and mixed.

This is a complex disorder because a delusion is a persistent false belief held in the face of strong contradictory evidence. This comment is a form of evidence.

Evidence A -"What it comes down to is that modern society discriminates against the right hemisphere." - Roger Sperry (1973) - neuropsychologist, neurobiologist and Nobel laureate

This is a form of evidence.

Evidence B -"If you reflect back upon our own educational training, we have been traditionally taught to master the 3 R's: reading, writing and arithmetic -- the domain and strength of the left brain."

One delusion society has is years of reading, writing and arithmetic does not favor left brain enough to hinder the mind. One delusion I have is that I can convince society education does favor left brain and thus veils right brain aspects. It is a false belief that I perceive I can convince beings conditioned into extreme left brain by education that they have been conditioned into extreme left brain by education. If society believed in evidence A then they would have to ask "How does modern society discriminate against right hemisphere?" Then they would have to face the reality [reading, writing and arithmetic -- the domain and strength of the left brain.] is how modern society discriminates against right hemisphere. If modern society believed traditional education even had a one percent chance of hindering the mind by favoring one hemisphere over the other they would at least look into that belief and at most be concerned about that belief but modern society does neither so it is delusional because it believes something that stands in the face of strong contradictory evidence.

This is one aspect of a delusion [deceived or conspired against]. Deceived and conspired against suggests there is someone or a group that is pleased to veil everyone's right brain but I am mindful that is not what is happening.

Disharmony seeks disharmony and see's harmony as abnormal. Harmony seeks harmony and see's disharmony as abnormal. Because of these two realities one has to figure out what is disharmony and what is harmony to create a baseline standard. Rather than a conspiracy it is a simple equation of likes attract likes. A person gets the traditional education reading, writing and arithmetic and it bends their mind to the left and so they are a left brain influenced being. So this means if a being does not believe this : [reading, writing and arithmetic -- the domain and strength of the left brain.] would favor their left brain and leave them leaning towards being left brain influence that being is delusional. Because of that one cannot reason with a delusional person because they perceive they are not delusional, they believe false beliefs even in the face of strong contradictory evidence. So a left brain influenced being will base their understanding on the assumption no one would conspire against them or mentally bend their mind to the left so they are delusional in their belief that they were not mentally hindered as children. A left brain influenced being believes there is no possible way this: [reading, writing and arithmetic -- the domain and strength of the left brain.] bent their mind to the left, but this is not an indication of their lack of intelligence in an absolute way it is relative to their lack of foresight (awareness) in the left brain influenced state of mind. So a conspiracy is a secret plan that is illegal or subversive. So a conspiracy would mean the entire society is subversive against itself and this conspiracy would go back all the way to the start of written language and mathematics. That is very unlikely. One being suggested they, the ones that sense time, the scribes, know not what they do so that would negate the possibility it is a conspiracy. So that would mean written education appears very wise and like a good thing but in reality it has unwanted mental side effects but once a person gets the education they are not aware of the effects because the education has altered their perception and this perception altering left that being "blind" to the fact their perception has been altered by the education.

[Non-bizarre referred to real life situations which could be true, but are not or are greatly exaggerated.] This aspect of being delusional is relative to the observer. If veiling the right hemisphere of the mind as a result of the left brain favoring education is not a big deal then I am delusional. If making a sound minded being unsound minded is not a big deal then I am delusional. If altering a child perception permanently is not a big deal then I am delusional. If putting a person mentally in a state of disadvantage by veiling their right brain by way of education is not a big deal then rape, robbery and murder is not a big deal. If conditioning a child into a simple minded state of mind and robbing that child of their complex thought aspects is not a big deal them I am delusional. A person who has their right brain veiled is factually not able to relate to what complexity is because complexity is a right brain trait and their right brain has been turned down or veiled so they perceive simple minded aspects are complexity. Relative to a person that is simple minded, simple minded is complexity. Only a being that has negated being in the extreme left brain state can tell what the difference between simple minded and complexity is. A person that is left brain influenced will perceive complexity is bad or a symptom of mental illness because they cannot relate to complexity. This all relates to a left brain influenced being will always see right brain traits as bad because they are all contrary to left brain traits. I am mindful I am attempting to reason with the darkness so I digress.

9:52:55 AM – No matter how you have come into contact with these texts you are bound as a keeper of them. You are bound to maintain these texts and preserve these texts no matter what happens for the rest of your life and then you are to hand them down to the next generation. You are the keeper of the keys because you have the keys. Some keepers are better than others.

10:32:50 AM – Relative to this delusional disorder. There are a few subtypes of this disorder.
Erotomanic Type: Predominately erotomanic delusions. This is where a person perceives others love them but in reality that is not true. An example would be a person believing a popular personality is in love with them even though that popular person has never spoken with them or given them the time of day so to speak. One might suggest I do not have this delusion since I get spit on more than anything else when speaking about this tree of knowledge reality in most forums so that leaves talking about the lefts, the ones that sense time. The ones that sense time met the Africans and swiftly determined they were not intelligent because they did not have written education and so the ones that sense time turned them into slaves and so the ones that sense time love their self or love their ways when they really do not. The ones that sense time perceive the world of the ones with no sense of time loves them when in reality they are hated and despised and mocked and made fun of on so many levels and right in front of their face yet the ones that sense time do not perceive that is what is happening. All of recorded history has been spitting in the face of the ones that sense time but the ones that sense time have not figured that out yet. So the ones that sense time perceive they are loved but they are delusional in that belief. If I was pleased with the ones that sense time I would not be writing infinite books attempting to convince them to mindfully kill their self. If I was pleased with the ones that sense time I would be writing books praising how wonderful their ways are but contrary I am using every ounce of concentration I have to convince them to mindfully exterminate their self. So when the ones that sense time understand they are simply the mental abominations of the species as a result of the mental abuse they suffered as children as a result of the education being forced on them then they will no longer perceive the world of the ones with no sense of time loves them

and then they will not be so delusional. Your delusions about peace, love and happiness died about 5400 years ago, it simply has not caught up to you yet. All men are created equally but then society veils the right brain in everyone and some apply the ancient fear not remedy and they are known as Masters and the ones who do not are known as grasshoppers so all men are equal dies off at about the age of ten. By the age of ten the right brain veiling is well underway. So in that respect the last thing in this universe you and I are is equal because I applied the remedy and you have not. So get it out of your head we are equal, you wish you were equal to me in your big sense of time state of mind but that is as far as it goes.

[Rights are trusting--too trusting. They easily have patents and ideas stolen from them, usually to a left. Lefts know how to use an idea. They just can't come up with them on their own.] - Barbara Pytel

A true right is a conscious being. Some beings get the education and it does not take all the way or that being drops out of education before their right brain is veiled fully as in the case of Einstein, He dropped out of school at 16 but even then he was not necessarily conscious as in right and left brain are in the middle, the middle way, mentally sound. If he was fully conscious he would have written books about the tree of knowledge and the remedy to the tree of knowledge because when one is conscious nothing else matters but that. This is perhaps beyond the mental ability of ones that sense time to ever grasp fully. Jesus did not apply the remedy with assistance of John the Baptists baptism method of the fear not remedy and then go get a job as a carpenter. The disciples did not apply the remedy and then go back to their job as fishermen they became fishers of men, men being the ones that sense time and they nearly all got butchered for their efforts.

[Rights are trusting--too trusting.] A child is too trusting. A parent has to say to a child, "Don't trust strangers and don't get in the car with strangers." A deeper reality is that child trusted their parents to not allow them to have their right brain veiled and their parents failed them so that child was far too trusting.

The Africans saw the ones that sense time and trusted them and the ones that sense time saw they could take advantage of someone that trusts them so they turned the Africans into slaves because the ones that sense time saw a right brain influence as a savage and easy to take advantage of because right brain influenced being are too trusting as children are too trusting. This is a mirror image of what happened to the Incas and what happened to the Native Americans. The children of god, the ones with right brain unveiled are trusting and the sinister, the ones that sense time take advantage of that because that its nature is to kill the light because the darkness only see's the light as darkness.

[They easily have patents and ideas stolen from them] Abraham came up with the fear not remedy and Jesus came up with his "those who lose their life mindfully will preserve it" ideas and the ones that sense time have made untold billions off those ideas but they never even apply those ideas so they simply make lots of money off of the words of those wise beings because the ones that sense time are mindfully unable to come up with those words on their own.

[Lefts know how to use an idea. They just can't come up with them on their own.]

The ones that sense time do not have much cerebrally to offer so they are stuck with taking advantage of beings who applied the remedy and they have great cerebral wealth and thus lots of great ideas, creativity is a right brain trait. I suggested in earlier books you take every single idea I have freely so you do not perceive you are forced to steal from me, you are suffering enough as it is. So every person is born with right brain unveiled so every person should have great ideas and great cerebral wealth but society determines it is best to turn that aspect, right brain, off in them and they use written education to do it and once in a while a few escape that right brain veiling and they become "great minds" but that is only in contrast to mentally unsound lunatics not in contrast to sound minded beings. I am average relative to a person who is conscious and I am supernatural relative to a person who is unconscious. There is nothing special about my genes and the only thing special about my mind is I negated all the damage done to my mind by written education by accidentally applying the fear not remedy to the tree of knowledge. Writing fifteen 80k word books in

15 months is only special if one is mentally hindered and is normal if one is not, so in this case everything is relative to the observer. Relative to my perception, I am in the now or in the machine state so I do not mindfully perceive I have written any books or even started to write books because my mind does not sense any fatigue or stress. If I am writing this many books I should be fatigued but I am not fatigued so I am not writing books, is the mental perception going on. I do not perceive I am special I am pleased with the challenge of communicating with lunatics. It is quite a challenge to communicate in any meaningful way with lunatics, is perhaps the only wisdom I have achieved to this stage since the accident. Waking up to reality starts with one detecting delusions. My greatest fear is that ones that sense time will eventually understand what I say. Speaking of the great truth has more to do with fearlessness than morals.

When you apply this remedy the first thing you have to face is that the ones that sense time get all the children. The ones that sense time are going to veil the right brain in all the children using their wisdom education. You will implode as a being if you do not face that reality. The best you can ever do is focus on the log in your eye which means you look at that tragedy as a blessing to assist you to concentrate more. You have to look at the fact the ones that sense time are going to veil right brain, the god image in man in all the children as a blessing because if you do not you will implode because you will seek to stop it and you cannot stop it. You are not intelligent enough to convince a lunatic to stop harming innocent children but you are intelligent enough to look at that demon as an angel and use it as a method to concentrate more by focusing on yourself. You cannot defeat a demon you can only show a demon it cannot defeat you mindfully. Once you apply the remedy you will unveil right brain and so it will be a huge thing to you but since you will not longer sense time in a short period of time relative to a calendar you will forget how big of a deal it is and so you will be prone to deny yourself or deny that event. You will have a concept in your mind relative to how you use to be in contrast to how you are after the remedy but you will not be able to judge that very well and this will lead you to deny what happened. The ones that sense time will suggest it is not a very big deal written education veils right hemisphere even if it does veil right brain but they are unable to make such a judgment because they have right brain veiled so they are not possibly able to be an authority on right brain and so they will try to convince you that you are not either. They will attempt to convince you that you are like they are and then once they do that you will give up because you will doubt yourself and thus you will doubt right brain. It is simple to give up and it is impossible to go on. If you go on you will just keep getting your teeth kicked down your throat because you are attempting to communicate with lunatics so you have to disassociate yourself from them mindfully. The deepest reality is the vast majority of the ones that sense time are simply too far gone mentally to ever be revived. Because of that you cannot grow attached to them because they in fact are attempting to make you doubt yourself and relative to their perspective you are attempting to make them deny their self. There are two worlds and the ones that sense time will attempt to suggest you are of their world. Money does not encourage wisdom but it can mask lack of it.

[1 John 3:5 And ye know that he was manifested to take away our sins; and in him is no sin.]

This comment is suggesting the Masters, the ones who applied the fear not remedy and in this case Jesus applied the John the Baptist version of the fear not remedy. To take away our sins means ones who have a sense of time can exhibit these sins because their right brain is veiled. Lust for example is simply a thought or craving that rests in ones thoughts for long periods of time relative to a clock because right brain random access thoughts are absent from their thought processes. So ones with a sense of time can see a car they want but cannot afford and that lust for that car sits in their mind for long periods until they either let go of that thought or they do something to get that car. A man may see a women and that women does not want him but his lust for that women continues to fester because right brain is veiled and so that thought cannot be changed so that person is in a state of lust. Lust of course is simply seeking of control and control is a left brain trait. One might lust over land or money or any number of things and when that lust for control is in danger one may do some rather drastic things to defend their desire to control that object. So in the above comment [in him is no sin] simply means one is unable to maintain thoughts of these sins, lust ,greed, envy, jealousy because right brain random access keeps ones thoughts shifting so swiftly one is reduced to a neutral state of mind. So the sin of sloth is an indication one has left brain sequential linear thoughts in their conscious state of mind and sloth is why one can maintain these other sins in their thoughts. Sense of time is also one of these sins but not mentioned directly. Sin is simply traits one exhibits after the education has veiled their right brain so one is living in sin because they never applied the fear not remedy to the tree of knowledge. So living in sin is not an absolute and no being is born into sin they are pushed into sin as a result of the traditional education and then they can escape that state of mind by applying the fear not remedy. So sins are psychological aspects that are a result of having ones right brain traits veiled by the tree of knowledge, written education and math,

One major issue with having this sense of time caused by being in an unsound state of mind is one tends to covet time. Here is an example.

[P. R. (64) allegedly committed suicide on the 4th anniversary of his wife's suicide because he blamed himself for her death]

[B. P. (15) hung himself on the anniversary of his Mother's death]

Ones that sense time perceive time is real in relation to events in their life and so they act out on this perception of time. Both these beings killed their self on the anniversary of other beings death so they are coveting that time. They perceive every time that date arrives they relive that time of death of that loved one so they are being haunted by that anniversary and they also see some sort of value attached to that time of death. They perceive if they kill their self on that certain date their loved one died that will give them attachment to that loved one. On a certain date society celebrates certain events as if the event is happening again. Some pay homage to the deaths or births of certain beings in hopes that will bring them closer to that being. This is what sense of time does to people. It makes people covet time itself. If the above beings had no sense of time it would mean they had right brain unveiled so a state of mind of suicide would not be able to be achieved because right brain is simply switching up thoughts relative to its random access thought patterns so one could not fester on the thought of suicide. Secondly if they had no sense of time they would not have any attachment to the date their loved one died. Everyday is the same day if one has no sense of time so one day is not special from any other day is another way to look at it. [he blamed himself for her death] This comment suggests this being felt guilty or ashamed. Sometimes people have a terminal illness and they wish to end their suffering because they are mindful they will die from that illness anyway so that is not suicide. Some people in a war will jump on a grenade to save their buddies and that is not suicide. Suicide is killing one's self over depression but depression is not possible when right brain is unveiled. Depression is relative to shame, embarrassment and with no ego one cannot achieve those aspects. There are some cases of beings who have unveiled right brain that have killed their self but it was not because of depression. Einstein had a chance to get his heart repaired and he decided to not get his heart repaired and he died as a result of that but that is not suicide although one could argue if you are dying and do not seek to save yourself that is improper. Suicide is essentially the attempt of a human being in an unsound state of mind trying to escape their thoughts. The two beings above could not escape their thoughts of depression guilt or shame because their right brain was veiled as a result of written education. One can never escape their thoughts so it is wise one ensures their thoughts are of a sound mind. The act of crying itself is abnormal and because I am mindful that is true I ponder little children that cry. It puts a big hole in my understanding about written education because at first after the accident I did shed tears because the understandings caused by the heightened awareness were so strong even a thought would cause me to shed tears for just a moment but now I am pleased and I don't shed any tears at all. It is one thing to be in physical pain and shed tears but even then it is not so much about people crying when in physical pain as it is people crying over spilt milk from a leaking container. When someone dies sometimes people that knew them cry and that is an indication their emotions are way out of balance. The tear ducts are actually there to keep your eye balls moist and to assist in removing any object's that get in the eye like a grain of sand for example and that is it. If someone you know dies and you cry it is because your mind is unsound and what that means is your mind cannot understand everyone dies, so to cry over something you know is going to happen means you have very little foresight mindfully. It also means you have difficulty dealing with loss but of course left brain is controlling and does covet so loss means the absence of control. You cry over spilt milk from a leaking container because mentally you cannot grasp that container is leaking. Left brain cannot handle loss of control

124

because relative to death it has no control over that so it collapses in the face of something it cannot control but seeks to control. Sometimes people kill their self when a popular person dies because they cannot mindfully handle that loss and so since they cannot escape their thoughts they kill their self to escape their thoughts. When one cries it is a symptom even their own tear ducts no longer work properly in their unsound state of mind. Tear ducts are not something used to cry with. Tears are not supposed to be happening relative to tearing up when you see something or experience something. Once the mind is bent to the left everything goes haywire and that is why you cry over spilt milk. You do not cry over dead people because you care, you cry because you are an emotional wreck and thus mentally unsound. If you cared you would at least be able to sense written education veils the right brain of children so all of your tears are crocodile tears and they do not fool at least one being on this planet. About four years ago relative to a calendar my dog Sugar died and I cried and cried and was sad for over two weeks and recently, after the accident, one of my dogs died right in front of me and I did not shed a tear and I did not feel an ounce of depression. So you are thinking since the accident now I don't care because I don't emotionally implode in the face of death. The reality is my right brain is able to understand everything living has to die so it goes to that final conclusion and ponders it and is at peace with it and so I can skip all the crying and emotional crap because I am at peace with the reality everything has to die eventually. I am fully aware of reality so there is no need to become emotional in the face of reality because I cannot change reality. So I am at peace with impermanence because my mind can accept impermanence and so I have no reason to cry and you cry because you perceive your tears shows everyone how much you care when in reality it only shows everyone how emotionally unstable you are with your big sense of time state of mind. I have never witnessed a group of gazelle crying after the lion ate their buddy but I imagine you would assume because they do not cry they do not care. Your crying only means there is something seriously wrong with your tear ducts and that is relative to the fact there is something seriously wrong with your perception and thought processes. You trusted the adults not to mentally hinder you as a child and that was the biggest mistake of your life and you perhaps may never recover from that.

[Luke 9:60 Jesus said unto him, Let the dead bury their dead: but go thou and preach the kingdom of God.]

You create the mentally dead and I try to raise them. We have a working relationship. You create the mentally dead with your wisdom education and I try to raise them by showing them where the kingdom is. Now, who are you again? Do you want me to be ashamed and embarrassed like you are? The answer to all my questions is "perhaps". Patience is for those who have run out of ideas. Patience leads to sloth and thus stagnation. Learning is mimicking what others understood and understandings are what others wish to learn. The only thing worth learning in life is how to understand. Education has more to do with following rules than following your intuition. Thinking out loud is deadly in all tyrannies.

"When there is no enemy within, the enemies outside cannot hurt you." - African Proverb

If you are hurt by words then words own you. When you understand yourself you understand the enemy. If you only do things that are risk free you will never experience freedom. You are not born to follow rules you were taught to follow rules. Looking at a mistake as an understanding is the key to progress. One will never be surprised if they look at being caught off guard as a blessing. Impermanence doesn't hurt just the thought of it does. Concepts are easier to understand than apply. The water in a pond only moves up and down. The hardest part is usually the easiest part because you don't underestimate it.

2/11/2010 4:01:41 AM – It's not so much they sense time and have no conscience or intuition, the kicker is they believe they are allowed to speak. Now, back to the delusional disorder.

Grandiose Type: Predominately grandiose delusions. Let's first talk about my grandiose delusions I have been cured of. Shortly after the accident I perceived anyone could apply the remedy. Slowly as I continued to write and read the ancient texts I realized the fear not remedy is the only remedy. There are many forms of the fear not remedy but in principle the only remedy is to get the hypothalamus to give one the death signal and then one ignores it and the amygdala remembers that event and keeps the hypothalamus from sending so many false positives and that is what allows right brain to unveil. There are lots of details relative to that remedy but in principle that is the fear not remedy and the only way to fully unveil right brain after written education veils right brain. So my grandiose delusion was what I accomplished in the den by accident was easy to accomplish and now I am mindful it is not so easy to accomplish and that means the vast majority of beings who got this written education are stuck with their right brain veiled so my grandiose delusion has turned into .0024 %. That is the magic of right brain, it does not mind being mistaken because it see's all understandings are of value and understanding one was mistaken is of value. So I believed the remedy was easy to apply and now I am mindful it is not easy to apply relative to the fact ones that sense time are afraid of bad haircuts. This shouldn't be confused with the remedy itself. The remedy itself is painless and works every time it is applied properly and it takes one second to apply in the right situation but for a being with a sense of time getting to that right situation and mindset is the problem because it is a mind over matter situation. This is not an indication of anyone's intelligence as much as it is an indication that once one's mind is bent to the left they are hallucinating out of their mind and they are trapped by their own false perceptions. If a person is on PCP there is not much one can do to assist that person but to wait until the PCP wears off but in this situation the hallucinations never stop until that person applies the remedy and they won't apply the remedy because their hallucinations say they should not apply the remedy. When ones that sense time suggest to me they are fine just the way they are I am mindful they are a fatality to this written education induced neurosis and that is in line with the comment the meek shall inherit the earth which means the depressed and suicidal are the only ones who perceive they have no redeeming qualities so they are very aware as a being something is wrong. Tragically many believe literally they have no redeeming qualities so they kill their self but in reality it is just their right brain is attempting to unveil itself and they are experiencing side effects but that being perceives they have no way to escape the depression thoughts but to die literally. One has to go through hell to get to heaven and the exit from hell is the 9th circle, treason and so the comment seek first the kingdom means get it over with and don't hesitate. Seek the shadow of death with all your might and when it arrives fear not, and the word shadow is the operative word. These ancient texts are not about literal death they are suggesting these things with the reality once one get the written education, tree of knowledge one is mindfully dead, unsound, and so this remedy brings one back to mental life, restores their right brain to a conscious state. One has to come to terms with the fact written education is all left brain favoring and then they can come to terms it bent their mind to the left and one has to avoid assuming a conspiracy because the big players in society give the same education to their own children so it very obvious it's not a conspiracy it is just a very charming invention that has major side effects and once one gets the invention they are mentally unable to detect the major side effects until they apply the remedy. Beings would not put their own children in this place of suffering state of mind if they knew that's what they were doing so the only option is they know not what they do. Blaming someone in particular will not apply the remedy for you so blaming someone in particular is a method to talk yourself out of applying the remedy so avoid that line of thinking. Focusing on the log in your eye means you worry about applying the remedy firstly then once you do apply the remedy you focus on the log in your eye so you can come to grips with all the things you are going to become aware of and this way you will avoid this controlling aspect. You will want to fix everyone and that is not going to happen because the neurosis is simply too strong so you focus on yourself and speak things you are compelled to speak and perhaps some will be assisted by that but you don't worry about that either because it is far too deep and far too dark to be concerned about saving everyone. Focus on the reality you cannot make an impact on anyone but yourself. The kingdom and thus the battle is within your mind and so as long as you continue to get better in the inward battle you do well. Expectations are dangerous after you apply the remedy and attempting to retain pride and dignity is also dangerous because society is not going to stop pushing its brand of education on six year olds because you suggest they should look into its unwanted mental side effects. Society is never going to question its brand of education because its pride is infinite so one has to look at that as a blessing because that means one has infinite potential to focus on the log in their eye using that reality as a conditioning aspect. Once you apply the remedy your heightened awareness is going to be through the roof and there are no drugs on the planet that will help you escape that heightened awareness so you are either going to become a master of concentration or you are going to implode and there are no other options.

Now let's talk about the ones that sense time and their Grandiose Type: Predominately grandiose delusions. The ones that sense time have one basic grandiose delusion and all their other delusions are tied to it. They perceive there is no possible flaw in their brand of written education relative to unwanted mental side effects. Society perceives these two aspects are not possible:

[Evidence A -"What it comes down to is that modern society discriminates against the right hemisphere." - Roger Sperry (1973) - neuropsychologist, neurobiologist and Nobel laureate

Evidence B -"If you reflect back upon our own educational training, we have been traditionally taught to master the 3 R's: reading, writing and arithmetic -- the domain and strength of the left brain."]

Society has a grand delusion that its wisdom invention, written education, is perfect when in reality it could not be more devastating on the mind when taught improperly to beings starting at the age of six. Because society has that one grand delusion all of the other things they perceive after that are delusions. For example because they believe written education is perfect they perceive anyone who does not get enough of it is imperfect and even though Einstein dropped out of school at the age of sixteen they still do not detect that is a huge red flag. Society pays people money based on how much education that person gets because society has determined its manmade invention is the ultimate determiner of a beings mental worth and that is a delusion. Society is built on the grandiose delusion relative to written education and if that delusion is exposed society as we know it will collapse. It is just like a person who perceives a girl loves them but in reality that girl does not love them or even know them and then that person faces that girl and she says 'I do not and never have loved you." and that person collapses because their delusion is exposed to their self. The wise beings in these ancient texts knew exactly what they were talking about and the truth is the powers in society at that time also knew exactly what they were talking about. No matter what your government is, even if they knew 100 percent that written education veils the right brain they are not going to come on the news and say "Anyone who got the written education was mentally turned into a simple minded sequential based emotional wreck. Sorry about that." That is all they could say because there is no pill or shot that is going to undo that damage because it is on a mental level so this ancient fear not remedy is the only cure and it is not very simple to commit mental suicide when you are pleased with how you are in the neurosis state. Another way to look at it is, if your government came out and said written education veiled your right brain and you have to apply this fear not remedy you may assume they are insane and replace them. If the united nations came out and said the same thing you would assume they are insane and replace them because that would mean you got mentally hindered so drastically as a child you would deny truth as a mechanism to avoid self destructing as a being. It is easy for a being to relate to others being mentally abused but it is not so easy for a being to be mindful they were mentally abused to a devastating degree. You just keep telling yourself you sense time because everyone does so that proves you are mentally sound. The wise beings on this planet do not sense time and you do, so what does that tell you? You may emotionally collapse if you became fully mindful your sense of time is factual proof your right brain paradox was veiled to the degree it no longer factors into your perception of time.

5:09:00 PM –

Birds would not fly me away from all of this
Taken to the air; escaped from the abyss
The wind cannot carry me away from all of this
It tries to lift me but the ground does it resist
A butter fly has never tried; its colors are too faded
With its colors on my skin its light is rather jaded
A lion offered to carry me but now it stays well hide
It once was brave and fearless but doubt has closed its lid
The ocean would accept me but only to its depths
It cannot control its waves nor control their lips

A swan cannot fly too high but it would try its best
It stays close to the ground but must never leave its nest
A tree will not carry far but would blind my sight
I could use its steady trunk to reach a certain height
Some suggest it is best, some attempt to never rest
Some suggest to close your eyes will not remove the earth nor skies.

Chips - http://www.youtube.com/watch?v=avz7zGD-Joc

2/12/2010 7:09:41 AM – This is a partial list of what years of this left brain traditional education does to one from a physiological and neurological point of view. Some of these symptoms are over lapping.

Perception altering aspects:
Pain threshold very low; strong sense of pain or pronounced pain. Cause: absence of ambiguity and paradox from perception, right brain traits.
Fatigue threshold very low; strong sense of fatigue , tires easily mentally and physiologically: Cause: absence of ambiguity and paradox from perception, right brain traits. This is relative to why ones with no sense of time made good slaves, they worked their self to death and never complained, low fatigue because right brain was unveiled and did not allow them to sense great fatigue.

Hunger threshold very low ; strong sense of hunger; perceives the need to eat every four or six hours; loss of concentration and shows physical symptoms if even one meal is skipped. Cause: absence of ambiguity and paradox from perception, right brain traits.

Taste sensitivity very high; strong sense of taste relative to strong after taste: Cause: absence of ambiguity and paradox from perception, right brain traits.

Fear threshold very low; extreme fear of words, pictures, music: Cause: Hypothalamus sending many false positives due to the mind being mentally unsound, right brain veiled by education.

Emotional threshold very low; very emotional; emotionally up and downs stairs: Cause: right brain random access processing is veiled so emotions are pronounced and linger in thoughts.

Nervous threshold very low; very nervous; prone to nervous break downs over trivial aspects; becomes nervous and upset over words used for example: Cause: Hypothalamus is sending false positive and random access thoughts are veiled so one become nervous over even simple problems because the complexity aspect of right brain is absent so the being cannot mentally deal with simple problems that arise in life.

Because of these aspects many physiological aspects are also altered as well as mental aspects.
Thought processes are simple and sequential based, coping skills are greatly reduced. For example you cannot cope with the fact written education veiled your right brain or you would apply the remedy so you spit on the spirit of what I suggest because you cannot cope with reality.
Thought complexity is absent.
Creativity is greatly reduced.
Pattern detection is reduced.
Intuition is reduced.

So what all these aspects add up to is a being is in a state of suffering because of all these symptoms caused by written education veiling their right brain. It is exactly like a child is shot in the brain with novocain and then left to attempt to function for the rest of their life like that and you are that child. Avoid ever assuming I am talking to anyone but you. If you sense time you have a remedy to apply and your entire life and every detail in your life means zero until you apply that remedy. Avoid assuming anything you do in your sense of time state of mind is of value. One cannot alter absolute reality with belief and so one cannot alter absolute reality with disbelief. Your faith that your right brain was not veiled after years of written education means zero and your sense of time proves that. You believe making sure all the children get your brand of written education starting at the age of six or seven is of value so you are unable to mentally understand what value is and so in fact your sense of value is in reality backwards. Your right brain intuition is turned down to such a degree you devastate children and ruin them and kill them with your brand of written education and you feel nothing and in fact feel you did good by doing that so you have less than no soul and no conscience. You factually kill people's minds and kill their life in turn and you perceive that is good and righteous and proper so you are not even in touch with reality at all in your conditioned neurotic state of mind. Because of that nothing in your life is of value until you apply the remedy. One might suggest you would be wise at this point to throw down your nets and apply the remedy, because this is truth and fact and reality:

"If you reflect back upon our own educational training, we have been traditionally taught to master the 3 R's: reading, writing and arithmetic -- the domain and strength of the left brain."

Any human being on the planet or any group of human beings on the plant that teaches or encourages aforementioned written form of education must first inform the parents and the child getting the aforementioned written education of the potential mental effects that may occur; namely right brain aspects may be veiled or silenced as a result of the child being taught aforementioned education. Any human being on the planet or any group of human beings on the planet that does not give said warning to the parents or child is guilty of crimes against the mind and thus crimes against humanity. This law is to be known as the Sound Mind Protection Law. This Sound Mind Protection Law is valid and applies regardless of what any human being on the planet or group of human beings on the planet says contrary to aforementioned law. Said law is permanent and non negotiable. Punishments for breaking the Sound Mind Protection Law will be consistent with the punishments for breaking other grave crimes against humanity laws. Established : 2/12/2010 12:13:45 PM

[Psalms 98:9 Before the LORD; for he cometh to judge the earth(the ones that sense time): with righteousness(right brain, the god image in man) shall he judge the world, and the people with equity(impartiality).]

[Psalms 110:6 He shall judge among the heathen(the ones that sense time), he shall fill the places with the dead bodies(I won't be making any public speaking engagements); he shall wound the heads (Ruler scribes) over many countries.]

[Micah 4:3 And he shall judge among many people, and rebuke strong nations afar off(and the nations will cease to veil the children's right brain and teach the children oral education until the children's mind develops); and they shall beat their swords into plowshares, and their spears into pruning hooks(because they will no longer be mental abominations but return to being human beings; non violent and peaceful prone): nation shall not lift up a sword against nation(the species will no longer be divided), neither shall they learn war any more.]

My delusions are infinite.

[Rome Statute of the International Criminal Court Explanatory Memorandum, "are particularly odious offences in that they constitute a serious attack on human dignity or grave humiliation or a degradation of one or more human beings. They are not isolated or sporadic events, but are part either of a government policy (although the perpetrators need not identify themselves with this policy) or of a wide practice of atrocities tolerated or condoned by a government or a de facto authority. Murder; extermination; torture; rape and political, racial, or religious persecution and other inhumane acts reach the threshold of crimes against humanity only if they are part of a widespread or systematic practice. Isolated inhumane acts of this nature may constitute grave infringements of human rights, or depending on the circumstances, war crimes, but may fall short of falling into the category of crimes under discussion."]

[other inhumane acts reach the threshold of crimes against humanity only if they are part of a widespread or systematic practice.] = [widespread or systematic practice.] = Written education taught to children starting at the age of six or seven worldwide. = [widespread] = [systematic practice.] = school system.

Proof: [Evidence A -"What it comes down to is that modern society discriminates against the right hemisphere." - Roger Sperry (1973) - neuropsychologist, neurobiologist and Nobel laureate.

How does society discriminate against the right hemisphere?

Evidence B -"If you reflect back upon our own educational training, we have been traditionally taught to master the 3 R's: reading, writing and arithmetic -- the domain and strength of the left brain."]

= [crimes against humanity only if they are part of a widespread or systematic practice.]

Torture [any act by which severe pain or suffering, whether physical or mental is inflicted] = veiling right brain is torture because its rob's a being of the complex aspect of their mind and creativity, and in turn alters their perception so hunger and sense of pain and many other aspects are magnified and thus leaves a being in a mental state of suffering.

[(although the perpetrators need not identify themselves with this policy)] = They know not what they do, the scribes will deny their education does harm the mind of children in any way and that is not important at all because they are simply not (identifying themselves with this policy). The deny reality.

[Proverbs 12:20 Deceit is in the heart of them that imagine evil: but to the counsellors of peace is joy.] relative to [Genesis 2:17 But of the tree of the knowledge of good and evil, thou shalt not eat of it: for in the day that thou eatest thereof thou shalt surely die.]

[that imagine evil] = [tree of the knowledge of good and evil] The written education bends the mind to the left so one see's parts, so when they see parts they see words as evil [imagine evil], they see some music as evil [imagine evil], they see truth as evil [imagine evil], they see some foods as evil [imagine evil]. Simply put one is hallucinating and imagining evil where there is no evil because the written education has altered their perception, bent their mind dangerously to the left.

I have this intuition feeling that perhaps I will not be able to convince the beings in the west this is the proper explanation of their ancient texts but I may be able to convince the beings in the east this is the proper explanation of the west's ancient texts so perhaps they will perhaps begin to appreciate the ancient texts of the west. Perhaps that is as good as it will ever get.

2/13/2010 5:55:24 PM – I want you to know I am fully aware I will fail as all the other beings failed in their attempts to convince our majestic species of the dangers that written education, the tree of knowledge has on the mind but I am a trooper and I am pleased with the hottest coals and I will be pleased when the hot coals of awareness incinerate my being. My only toil is breathing.- 5:58:00 PM

7:02:39 PM – [Exodus 32:19 And it came to pass, as soon as he came nigh unto the camp, that he saw the calf, and the dancing: and Moses' anger waxed hot, and he cast the tables out of his hands, and brake them beneath the mount.]

There are a host of rules and laws before this line relative to how one should do things and how one should react to certain situations and then this line comes up [and he cast the tables out of his hands, and brake them beneath the mount.]. Keep in mind this concept of throwing all the rules down on the ricks and look at this comment. [Brake] is absent of sense of time. Sense of time would be [broke.]

"Right brains are honored in eastern cultures more than western. They are seen as less smart because of the manner in which they process information. Rights don't go from Point A to Point B. [Right brains don't like to listen to directions and don't like to read them.] They scan quickly and figure out what to do without reading details. Reading directions carefully is a detailed activity for the left-brain."- Barbara Pytel

[Right brains don't like to listen to directions and don't like to read them. They scan quickly and figure out what to do without reading details.]
Directions are rules. Think about a small child and they appear to just be carefree and oblivious to rules and regulations and then a parent will say "You follow my rules under my roof." Or even in school in

elementary education there is a section on the report card where they give out satisfactory and unsatisfactory grades relative to "Ability to follow directions."

It is looked at as a bad thing or an unwanted thing when a person does not like to follow directions so what that means is a person is frowned on when they want to think for their self. This is all a symptom of the neurosis caused by favoring left brain. Right brain does not like directions or rules and left brain likes directions or rules. Freedom is anarchy but that is what freedom is, determining your own direction. Schools frowns on ones who do not like to follow directions so school frowns on right brain because right brain does not like to follow directions. So a child does not follow directions because they still have some right brain aspects active and then a teacher will punish them and their parents will punish them and that child learns to hate their own right hemisphere. It's not the "big" rules it's all the anal retentive crap rules. One might suggest right brain does not take the lead of a mental abomination. One might suggest right brain does not need a mental abomination to give it direction.

[Right brains are honored in eastern cultures more than western.] In the west let me see, we nailed one wise being to a cross, we beheaded another wise being we stoned and tortured a host of other wise beings who unveiled right brain and fed many to the lions, made one drink hemlock, gave one poisoned lamb chops, burned a few at the stake, so one might suggest we do not honor right brain in the west. In the west we turned the tribes in various cultures that did not get the education into slaves and put them in concentration camps and took all their land and destroyed all the resources they spend thousands of years preserving. In the west we have a proud heritage of slaughtering any beings that unveil the god image in man, right brain or at least making them look like villains because they don't follow all the directions pushed on them by mental abominations. That's all you ever need to know about the history of the west, ever. Everything else you know about the west besides that are stupidity details. You sense time so you perceive you are so wise because you cling to all of your rules and details. You love details, a left brain trait.[They scan quickly and figure out what to do without reading details.] Here is what quickly means. I unveiled right brain about fourteen months ago and I am properly translating these ancient texts and it took me about perhaps six months to get to a stage I could do it efficiently after I unveiled right brain and you and every one of your friends and cult leaders still have not figured out what these ancient texts mean in thousands of years, that's what quickly means. One might suggest you are slightly leaning towards the sloth side of reality.

[figure out what to do without reading details.] This comment is relative to right brain intuition and getting the spirit of things. It is like speed reading so one looks at a sentence and gets the spirit of it and that sentence has a checksum and that is an ideal or a concept and so that concept is understood but the details are not retained. The complexity is every human being is born with that aspect but the education veils it or silences it. Now I just said every human being so because you are anal retentive and only focus on details so you are thinking, "Not every human being because some are born mentally hindered or without a right hemisphere." And then you will assume you are wise and clever but in reality you are just anal retentive and perceive your little simple minded ability to grasp details is some fantastic mental aspect. I did not lose my left hemisphere I can focus on details but in 50/50 mental harmony right brain traits rule. What that means is I was left brain dominate because I got written education and I did sense time and I did have all the aspects you have but then I accidentally applied the ancient fear not remedy and now I restored right brain to 50% and so right brain is my main perception engine now but if I want to I can use left brain traits. In your case all you have is left brain to rely on and your right brain is veiled to a subconscious state and the proof is you sense time so that's proves your right brain paradox aspect no longer factors into your perception. What that means is, you are not possibly able to compete with me on a mental level because you are factually mentally unsound and your sense of time proves it. It should upset you that I mock you on a world stage. That's unfortunate relatively speaking..

[Reading directions carefully is a detailed activity for the left-brain]
Following directions is a left brain trait. Being told what to do is a left brain trait. Left brain see's the more rules and the more directions the safer it is. So what that means is a being conditioned into this extreme left brain state caused by education is a shoe in for selling their freedom

for a little security. Freedom means few rules so that is right brain, left brain loves rules so that is the tyrant. The more rules the less freedom. So the education has conditioned you into a tyrannical state of mind. "You will follow my rules under my roof." That is a tyrant. The Governments of the world say "You will follow my rules in my country or you can get out." That's a tyrannical reality. The rules of the governments of the world are "Everyone will get our brand of education, written education." In American you will be sent to jail and deemed a threat to children if you do not give them written education, so you are legally not allowed to give children strictly oral education, until their mind develops, so that means it is factually illegal in America not to veil a child's right brain. The ancient texts suggest it is against the law to sin against God and the right brain is the god image in man so veiling it using the tree of knowledge, written education, is that sin against God. So you either adjust your education methods or you burn the ancient texts so I don't have to write in my book how schizophrenic you are, like I just did. You write on your money "In God we trust" and then you veil the God image in the children and you make it against the law not to do so. That is a symptom of how confused you are, Freud suggested you are neurotic I just call you a brain dead mole cricket, it makes better filler.

Think about this comment :

"Right brains don't explain what they feel well and are misunderstood. They think of one thing, say another because their brain has already moved on to another thought. " - Barbara Pytel

What this means is the processing power is so swift when right brain is at 50% power or when it is in the conscious state after one applies the remedy the full measure, ones thoughts have already moved on even before that person finishes what they were saying. In psychology this kind of a person would appear to be "babbling" but relative to the ancient texts the person is speaking in tongues and is quick. What this means is a person can appear to be under the influence of "spirit" because they are speaking in absolute verbatim or in real time or in the now. I can speak to someone and before I finish that thought I forget that thought and already speak another thought but the thoughts are random access so it appears I am babbling and my thoughts are all over the place and so a psychologist would say "here take these pills they will cure you." I do not remember what I write in these books after I write it and I also do not remember what I say to people in person after I say it and that is relative to this comment.

"Rights think and learn in visual, kinesthetic and audio images. They don't memorize well and need to visualize a picture so they can recall the facts. Abstract math is often not brain compatible. " - Barbara Pytel

[They don't memorize well and need to visualize a picture so they can recall the facts.] What this is saying is, right brain has a vast long term memory but it stores things as concepts or images. This is important, because a person who has right brain veiled stores things as absolutes. Their short term memory stores images, time stamps, and emotions, details, so when they recall them they get all that information back so they relive the event every time they y recall it and that is what PTSD is. When right brain is unveiled PTSD is not possible because all events are stored as concepts with no time stamps and no emotions so all images are equal and also short term memory is reduced so many things are simply forgotten so one never gets upset about petty details. For example sometimes a person with a sense of time will be insulted at work and they will brood about it over the next day and slowly that anger starts to consume them. With right brain unveiled one simply forgets and moves on.

So you see many of these "psychiatric orders" are really symptoms of right brain attempting to unveil itself or the result of right brain being veiled. One of the first tests they give a person who is baker acted is a memory test. They say a few words and then talk about something else and then ask that person what those words were. That test is in fact biased against the right brain because [They don't memorize well and need to visualize a picture so they can recall the facts.] It's easier to look at it once one unveils right brain they become an absent minded professor because at the level of concentration and awareness the mind has to turn down many things to be able to use the laser beam concentration and heighten and awareness. So the written education turns a mind that is a focused laser beam into a laser that has beams spread out over a vast area and thus is not very effective.

[Abstract math is often not brain compatible.] is relative to this [-"....
arithmetic -- the domain and strength of the left brain."]

So you are taught math in school and the better you get at it the more
your right brain becomes veiled. So written education costs you your right
hemisphere aspects and so you sell your "soul" your mind for the promise
of some money and some luxury and some vain acceptance by other people
who have also sold their mind for the same reason. Applying the remedy
is perhaps very harsh from your perspective and so you perhaps will just
determine it is best to not restore your right brain at all and so you were
robbed of your life, and what I find fascinating is you perhaps think that
is not absolute fact. Once you get this education your right brain is veiled
and certainly before you even finish many years of this education and so
you cease to be what you were as a child and you are some mental hybrid
and that means your perception is altered so it is impossible you are doing
things you would be doing before your perception was altered so you have
been thrust into an alternative reality of perception and you are acting not
like you would if that perception altering had not happened so you are
not even yourself, so you are someone else all together. This is why Jesus
said, you have to deny yourself because yourself is alternate reality self
and not your true self after you get all that education. So the proof you are
factually not you is the fact you sense time. Granted I fell off the tracks.

[Numbers 22:35 And the angel of the LORD said unto Balaam, Go with
the men: but only the word that I shall speak unto thee, that thou shalt
speak. So Balaam went with the princes of Balak.]

[Go with the men: but only the word that I shall speak unto thee, that thou
shalt speak.]

[the men] = the ones that sense time; the ones that got the written education
and didn't apply the remedy. Relative to [Genesis 11:5 And the LORD came
down to see the city and the tower, which the children of men builded.]

[children of men builded.] This comment means the adults that sense
time push the education on their offspring and then they deem most not
very intelligent because they didn't do well at it and they give them slave

jobs or remedial jobs. In general only the ones who do well at the written education get a luxurious life in this narrow and the rest become slaves.

[: but only the word that I shall speak unto thee, that thou shalt speak.]

This denotes a concept about strategic wording. If only these wise beings can form the perfect sentence the ones with a sense of time would grasp the written education does in fact hinder or veil right brain and then they would adjust their methods and use more oral education on the small children and perhaps right brain would not be veiled and thus our species would not be essentially mental abominations. This of course is not fantasy land. Strategic wording does not mean anything when dealing with beings conditioned into such a deep neurosis that they perceive all these abnormal symptoms of the neurosis are normal. All I can say is I had no idea I was in neurosis and I had no idea I was applying this ancient fear not remedy when I was applying it so it is impossible you would detect you are in neurosis until after you escape the neurosis. I am speaking to beings in full blown hallucination world and no strategic words are going to make up for that. People on PCP soon forget they took PCP and start believing what they see and perceive is real and the next thing you know someone says a word to them and they believe that word can harm them so they kill their self.

[R. N. (17) committed suicide after being "cyber-bullied"]
[M. M. (13) hung herself in her closet after becoming the victim of cyber-bullying]

This is why I don't speak to you because I don't pander to beings that kill children and then attempt to suggest they do not. You killed these children with your desire to swiftly make them as you are with no foresight into the possibility written education favors left brain just slightly too much as long as your definition of slightly is infinitely. You will find that God will not lift a finger to stop these innocent children you killed from exacting their revenge upon you in the afterlife so your only option is to pray with all of your might there is no afterlife. Attempt to forget I said that. I assure you I stopped trying a thousand lifetimes ago.

[Numbers 22:35 And the angel of the LORD said unto Balaam, Go with the men: but only the word that I shall speak unto thee, that thou shalt speak. So Balaam went with the princes of Balak.]

So this comment is similar to a situation where two people are doing something and one person says something and then the other person says "From now on let me do the talking." Maybe something like where a wife will say to a husband "From now on let me do the laundry." So before that comment Balaam killed this ass or donkey, one that senses time, three times and so that represents he was attempting to cram this message down a persons throat that senses time. So the spirit of this comment is kind of like patience. So it is saying "Go try again with the men, the ones that sense time, but no personal commentary let me do the talking." One could see that perhaps since he was going to only say what he was told to say everything would work out but in reality we still educate the young children with written education and are not even at a stage of thinking perhaps maybe perhaps all that left brain education may slightly veil perhaps the right brain perhaps. So you see these texts are relative to the time period. At this point in time when these texts were written there was still some hope that the species would come to understand the dangers these new inventions, written language and math, had on the mind. Now by the time period of the New Testimonies the attitude was more like this.
[Matthew 12:34 O generation of vipers, how can ye, being evil, speak good things? for out of the abundance of the heart the mouth speaketh.]

So it went from, "Be patient and speak calmly" to basically "You are all doomed." in about roughly eight hundred years.

All this comment is saying is [for out of the abundance of the heart the mouth speaketh.] your words are relative to your mind and if you mind is unsound your words are unsound and your methods are unsound and your life is unsound.

[how can ye, being evil, speak good things?] How can a being with their right hemisphere veiled to a subconscious state stand? How can a person with a mind divided to the point that right hemisphere is veiled amount

143

to anything? Without the right hemisphere in the conscious state of mind and at full power one is not really a human being relative to how they act so one is destroyed as a human being by this education but the catch is, without education in this narrow you get a slave job and are looked at as stupid and thus discriminated against. It is as simple as saying "Will you sell your child to the devil for some money and luxury?" and your parents and society said "yes" to that question for you and you do not want to believe that because truth may annihilate you in your current state of mind. I do not detect you are evil but at the level of neurosis you are in, it requires every ounce of your being to escape and if you are not willing to grasp that you might as well just give up on everything because you are doomed to a life of suffering. I don't care what neurotics that sense time say contrary to that. I am not talking about aliens, ghosts and lizard men I am talking about that "wisdom" education you got as a child. If written education and math are real then you are in a place of suffering you may never escape and if they are not real then I am in the afterlife and assuming I am not. Those are the only two possibilities.

If I type " There are people in the world." You will not detect any fault with that sentence.
If I type "Their are people in the world." You will assume I am stupid because I am using the wrong "there".
When right brain is unveiled it hardly notices the difference because it gets the spirit of the sentence or another way to look at it is , right brain gets the gist or concept of that sentence and does not focus on the details but you in the left brain conditioned state notice little details and miss the concepts. So while your abnormal mind is focused on the fact I typed "Their" instead of "There" you miss the concept of the sentence. What this means is that there are untold millions of things you do not notice or grasp because your mind is conditioned into a state it is only worried about meaningless details. You judge my entire mind and being on the fact I used "Their " instead of "There" which is simply illogical and quite delusional. To judge a child's mind and intelligence based on their ability to use a man made inventions syntax is insanity. It all comes down to the fact if you can spell well and use all the syntax in written language well you factually cannot think well because the language is all about left brain

144

orientated details. You can spell better than me and use commas better than me and use language syntax better than me but in a contest relative to concentration, pattern detection and intuition I annihilate you without even trying. It is all relative to what you want to test on. If you want a test on my ability to use abstract math and written language syntax you will win but when it comes down to concentration and solving problems using pattern detection and complexity you are not even within a billion light years of me. So you get to spell well but you leave the thinking and decisions to me, is the easiest way to look at it. That means avoid voting and go take a spelling comma test instead. What's very sad is I can use spelling and grammar syntax if I focus on it but then you might get the impression I pander to your stupidity language. I write novels at god speeds and all you can suggest is :[<Eps> ever heard of punctuation?] I give you secrets freely and all you can do is insult my grammar syntax.

[Genesis 18:28 Peradventure there shall lack five of the fifty righteous: wilt thou destroy all the city for lack of five? And he said, If I find there forty and five, I will not destroy it.]

This comment is great humor. It starts out with fifty. It is saying if there is fifty beings that sense time in this city that can be reached and convinced to apply the remedy, if so I will spare the city or I will see that there is a chance to communicate with the ones that sense time, that have the neurosis, and there will be hope. Then by the next few verses:
[Genesis 18:31 And he said, Behold now, I have taken upon me to speak unto the Lord: Peradventure there shall be twenty found there. And he said, I will not destroy it for twenty's sake.]

It is reduced to twenty. So Abraham and Lot are slowly starting to realize this neurosis caused by written education ruins the mind so greatly there may not even be twenty out of an entire city that can be reached. Then it is reduced down to ten :
[Genesis 18:32 And he said, Oh let not the Lord be angry, and I will speak yet but this once: Peradventure ten shall be found there. And he said, I will not destroy it for ten's sake.]

It is great humor, they started saying we will not burn this city to the ground if we can find fifty and then they are saying if we can find just ten beings that sense time we will spare this entire city. Then these two wise beings Abraham and Lot come to understand there is not even five in the entire city that sense time that can be convinced to apply the remedy and since they are going to just keep giving the children their "brand" of education it is best to just do away with the entire city:

[Genesis 19:13 For we will destroy this place, because the cry of them is waxen great before the face of the LORD; and the LORD hath sent us to destroy it.]

[cry of them] = [them] = ones that sense time = the neurosis in the ones that sense time is essentially permanent. If there were ten out of six billion that could be reached and salvaged I would try but I see no evidence of it. And even as I say that you are pondering if the tree of knowledge really is written education and math? Certainly it could not do any damage to the perfect mind of young children or our government officials would have told us by now, certainly they would have. Certainly our scientists would have told us by now if written education had any unwanted mental side effects by now. You speak of hope and optimism as if you know what they were. Your hope is really just a symptom of your ignorance and you optimism is just a symptom of your delusional state of mind. "Abandon all hope, all ye who enter here." That means once you get the education you are pretty much mentally doomed. The humor is, you are so mentally doomed you do not even perceive written education did any damage to your mind. It would be much easier for me if I could tell you ghosts and aliens and lizard men did this to you but it was your peers and your trusted friends that did this to you, the ones who wanted to "fix" you as a child. Once you realize you are not really any longer in touch with reality you will take yourself less seriously and come understand the ones on this planet that have applied the remedy to a degree do not take you very seriously either. It is a strange paradox that ones who have applied the remedy to a degree wish to assist you to come back to consciousness but the simple fact is you are essentially too far gone for any being to assist you so some will suggest you go meditate in a room for the next fifty years just to shut you up because you are not salvageable. Sitting in a room with your mouth

146

shut is a proper form of damage control but little else. Perhaps you should go mediate about that. Go focus on your breathing because when you are doing that you are at least not in the way. It is like when a person comes into a police station that is very high on drugs and delusional they put them in a padded cell until they sober up a bit and the good news is I am certain you will sober up eventually give or take 120 years.

2/14/2010 4:18:42 PM – Think about the remedy from strictly a neurological point of view. If one is in a room of people and someone says a cuss word some people get a shame or embarrassment signal and some people are indifferent and there is a wide range of reactions according to the person. What this means is the mental reaction to the cuss word itself is relative to each observer and so it is relative to how their amygdala has been conditioned. If a child says a cuss word and their parents wash their mouth out with soap that child's amygdala will remember that and so whenever that child's hears that cuss word their hypothalamus will get a signal sent to it by the amygdala relative to their memory of what happened when they said that cuss word when they were a child. So everyone does not react to fear the same way and relative to the remedy, fear of the dark or ghosts is paramount because that is the whole point of getting the hypothalamus to give that death signal in the perceived situation of the shadow of death which would be a ghost a perceived ghost. The remedy has nothing to do with ghosts or morbidity or cemeteries it just so happens these aspects tend to give that hypothalamus a good opportunity to give its false death signal to ones that senses time. It is not about the person being afraid of ghosts it is about the hypothalmus being afraid of shadows because the mind has been bent to the left by the education and so the hypothalamus is just giving false signals about things it should not be giving one false signals about. You perceive your fear of words is relative to your conscience but your conscience is relative to your intuition and you got the written education and so your right brain intuition is silenced perhaps totally so it's not your conscience it's your hypothalamus, its the spirit of fear that you perceive is your conscience.

[Genesis 2:9 And out of the ground made the LORD God to grow every tree that is pleasant to the sight, and good for food; the tree of life also in the midst of the garden, and the tree of knowledge of good and evil.]

[And out of the ground made the LORD God to grow every tree that is pleasant to the sight, and good for food;] This comment is a right brain holistic comment. [pleasant to the sight, and good for food;] Pleasant or pleasing to the sight is relative to after one applies the remedy everything they see or persons they see are pleasing so one loses their "judge a book by the cover" trait. Like you may see someone with a tattoo and assume "oh that person is displeasing" or you may see a person with certain clothes on and assume they are displeasing or see someone with a beard and assume they are displeasing. The antonym for pleasant among other things is beastly, embarrassing. Think about when you were young and you were getting ready to go somewhere and your mother said, "Comb your hair and put on some other clothes you look displeasing or beastly" so they were embarrassed by your appearance. If one shows up at a ballroom dance in a potato sack they should not be embarrassed nor should anyone who sees them be embarrassed or think that person is displeasing but because everyone got the education it happens often. The point is you are not embarrassed by how others dress for any other reason but because of all the written education you got as a child veiled your right brain aspects so what you see as displeasing or beastly is because your perception has been altered. When you were a child and you had dirt on your face from playing outside and your hands were all dirty you did not feel embarrassed by that even if the neighbors came over and saw you but now you are embarrassed by that. You would not go to work with dirt on your face because you would be embarrassed and you would be embarrassed because all your coworkers would be embarrassed by you but in reality it is because everyone got the education and so their perception has been altered. A sound mind should be indifferent to any picture it see's because a picture is just a visual. You know in society they will take a picture of starving children or some tragedy and then ask you to give them money so they are playing on your altered perception. You see good and evil in pictures. They will show a picture of a women in a nice dress and then everyone will be pleased by that and then they show another women

148

in another picture obese and then everyone will be displeased, this again is because their perception has been altered and so because perception is altered one can manipulate you because they play on that fact you are not indifferent to pictures. You have a favorite color so that means you have a color you are not pleased with but in reality you should be pleased or see every color as the same but since you perception has been altered you have favorites. It is not your taste at all, it is your perception has been altered by written education. Left brain see's part's. They suggest there is a certain color everyone is attracted to but that is only relative to people who have had their perception altered. Car dealerships have cars that are a certain color that sell better than cars of others colors but if the entire plant did not have their perception altered by education they would sell the same amount of cars of every color because right brain when unveiled is not a good judge and that is exactly what everything is, pleasing to the sight means: [pleasant to the sight].

If you think about the tribes that never got the written education and the women wear no top openly in public it is not because they are savages it is because everyone in that tribe is indifferent to that. It can be explained quite well with this comment: [Genesis 2:25 And they were both naked, the man and his wife, and were not ashamed.] This comment is pre-tree of knowledge, before they ate off the tree of knowledge.

That tribe is naked and they are not ashamed but then you look at society and people have heart attacks over nudity and assume it is because they have a conscience but in reality it is because they got the tree of knowledge and they are factually mentally unsound, it is not their conscience it is their unsound mind telling them things that are not true, it is their left brain seeing good and evil in pictures when in fact there is only pleasing images so they are hallucinating as a result of being conditioned into an unsound state of mind, extreme left brain state. This is how society is, and society all gets the written education, the tree of knowledge [Genesis 3:10 And he said, I heard thy voice in the garden, and I was afraid, because I was naked; and I hid myself.]

[afraid, because I was naked; and I hid myself.] = embarrassed as a result of having their perception altered by left brain favoring written education.

149

Evidence B -"If you reflect back upon our own educational training, we have been traditionally taught to master the 3 R's: reading, writing and arithmetic -- the domain and strength of the left brain."

[the tree of life also in the midst of the garden, and the tree of knowledge of good and evil.]

This comment is very simple. Right brain see's everything as good or as pleasing and left brain see's parts so it see's good and evil, and the tree of knowledge favors left brain so after one gets it they see good and evil when there is only good in reality. If you are walking around seeing parts such as good and evil you are not really living you are hallucinating, so seeing everything as one thing is living. Look at this way, we are on a planet in the middle of nowhere so exactly why would you be embarrassed about a picture or an image unless your mind is telling you things that are not true. Since you sense time you hear me say pictures are not bad and images are not bad but you assume bad things when you hear that. You are attempting to associate what I say with how you perceive things in your unsound state of mind. You are nothing like me so you have to attempt to never assume I think what you think. My perception is nothing like your perception. Our perceptions are completely different because I accidentally applied the fear not remedy and unveiled right brain and so I am of sound mind and you are not so you cannot relate to me but I was like you are now so I can relate to you. It takes one to know one. I know what you're thinking but you never felt right brain when it's at full power and in the conscious state so you factually cannot know exactly what I perceive I can just use words to explain things but you should perceive what I say is alien. This is relative to this transformation aspect. You are conditioned by education into one perception world and then you apply the remedy and are brought back to the perception you had as a child and so you are a child of God and God is pleased with what he sees, so to speak [Genesis 1:10 And God called the dry land Earth; and the gathering together of the waters called the Seas: and [God saw that it was good.]]

When I say a picture cannot be evil you may assume that cannot be true because you see many things you view as evil but that is just because you only have left brain to rely on and the education has ensured your right brain is in a subconscious state. So this comment : [the tree of life also in the midst of the garden, and the tree of knowledge of good and evil.] Is saying the tree of life is sound mind and that means when the mind is at 50/50 right brain traits rule so one sees everything is pleasing and the tree of knowledge induced state of mind, left brain dominate, see's good and evil and that is not the tree of life. An unsound mind is not the tree of life. I am pleased with everything I see but I am not pleased with everything I sense and that is relative to intuition a right brain trait. I am mindful there are ones who have applied the remedy to a degree who would never ever write a book and explain that written education veils the right brain and puts people to sleep but because I accidentally applied the remedy on my own I am totally alone and that means no one taught me anything so I just go with the flow and I am oblivious to any consequences that may occur from telling the world these things because I am back in the child state of mind, I have moments of my old self where I should not tell these things but mostly I just say what is on my mind and let the chips fall where they may because I don't have any reason at all to keep my mouth shut. That means I do not perceive potentially being harmed for explaining these things on a world stage is reason enough for me to keep my mouth shut so that means I see what I am saying or explaining is of more value than me. Perhaps I should run and hide in fear, but I doubt it.

[Genesis 18:28 Peradventure there shall lack five of the fifty righteous: wilt thou destroy all the city for lack of five? And he said, If I find there forty and five, I will not destroy it.]
[Genesis 19:13 For we will destroy this place, because the cry of them is waxen great before the face of the LORD; and the LORD hath sent us to destroy it.]

If you ponder these two comments you will see it is not possible out of an entire city they could not find fifty people who believed in God. From a supernatural point of view, one would be very hard pressed to pick out a city on the planet and determine no one in that city believed in God, supernatural, in some form or shape so they could not have determined to destroy this city because everyone did not believe in God but it is logical that everyone got the education and that is why they could not find even fifty that were "salvageable". This is an indication of how powerful this education affects the mind, it completely alters a person perception. One has to look at it just like a curse or just like a plague. You get the education and you got the plague and your chances to undo that plague is relative to your determination but first one has to understand they have the plague and it is nearly impossible to convince a person they have the plague when that person perceives the symptoms of the plague are normal because everyone around them has those symptoms essentially. I know what the plague is like because I had it, I use to sense time and then I accidentally applied this ancient remedy and now I do not sense time but that does not mean anything to you because all you have to do is go to the nearest person you know and ask them if they sense time and they will say "yes everyone does." and then you will conclude I am crazy and so you are in serious straights because it's my word against theirs and you do not know me from Adam, so to speak. That didn't come out right, but I doubt it. Relative to the west Abraham and Lot were the species' last chance to stop the spread of this neurosis or at least to slow it down. Think about mad cow disease and on a farm where they find it they have to kill all the cows but that farmer does not want to kill all the cows but it is best, so they do it but it's not because they are harmful and evil it is to get the disease under control and that is a lot like what Abraham and Lot had to do. They did not want to destroy those cities and kill all those people but they had this burden to do what was proper relative to their understandings and one should not be ashamed of that or embarrassed of that because it is our history as a species. We as a species invented a great invention that had devastating effects on our mind and that is nothing to be embarrassed about because we invent stuff all the time that ends up having bad side effects so one can just attempt to adjust to that reality but relative to this written education it is the most destructive thing ever invented ever into infinity relative to the effects on the mind even though it also has the best side effects relative to knowledge. All of the causes you perceive are of value and of worth in all of civilization mean zero in contrast to this cause because the vast majority of the causes are relative to this cause. Drug addiction, Obesity. Stress. Environmental destruction. War. Untold number of crimes and health issues. Child abuse. The general state of the entire species is relative to this written education neurosis. You perhaps may doubt that and I cannot

152

blame you for doubting that because it is far too far reaching for some to perhaps even grasp mindfully considering they have their complex aspects veiled. I am feeling infinitely defeated and I am pleased by that because that means I will perhaps start trying eventually, but I doubt it. If nothing else I am confusing lots of beings that sense time.

2/15/2010 7:13:50 AM
"I would rather be first in a little Iberian village than second in Rome."
Epicurus

Epicurus means ally or comrade and he lived 341 BCE – Athens, 270 BCE; 72 years) was an ancient Greek philosopher. A philosopher is reduced down to a person who applies the fear not remedy and unveils right brain and this is no different than what a true Jew, Muslim, Christian, Buddhist or Hindu is. It is one with no sense of time mindfully because that is a perception trait when right brain has been restored to 50% or returned to the conscious state of mind after written education veils right brain aspects. One of Epicurus' philosophical purposes was for a being to attain freedom from fear. As a boy he studied under a teacher that was schooled by Plato. So Plato was a student of Socrates and Socrates has a concept that no true philosopher fears death and that is identical to walk through the valley of the shadow of death and fear not. So in that respect Epicurus was a product of Socrates efforts but removed to the degree that his direct teacher was not Plato or Socrates but Pamphilus. So Pamphilus was a student of Plato and Socrates so all of these philosophers are descended from Socrates efforts or teachings. This is similar to the concept of disciples. This is not suggesting Socrates was better than any of these other beings because once right brain is unveiled its power is unnamable and everyone has a right hemisphere and so when a person unveils it they are essentially a spokesman for right brain or a right brain influenced being so they all know the same things so to speak. Socrates has a list of paradoxes. These were essentially some comments he made and the pattern here is paradox is a right brain trait so a being with right brain veiled has trouble grasping or thinking in paradox but only because right brain is the aspect of the mind that thinks in paradox and paradox is relative to the complex aspect of right brain. This paradox aspect is what leads one to understand there is no good or evil in many situations but often things just are. One paradoxal comment is suggested by Socrates was : No one errs or does wrongly willingly or knowingly. So relative to paradox this is also suggests, everyone errs or does wrongly willingly and knowingly. What this suggests is many things are relative to the observer and observation is relative to perception. So to look at the first aspect of this paradox:

No one errs or does wrongly willingly or knowingly. This is suggesting there are not people going around teaching written education to children with the intent of veiling children's right brain and leaving that child in a state of suffering knowingly and willingly because relative to their perception and so relative to the fact they had the same thing done to them they have right brain veiled so "they know not what they do." So this situation is relative to ignorance but not relative to intelligence. If a person has their right hemisphere turned way down or veiled as a child the deeds and actions they exhibit are relative to that so they in turn do not perceive the effects of what they are doing because an entire hemisphere of their mind is veiled. But the paradox is at the same time they know exactly what they are doing but that voice, right brain, is veiled so they are not in touch with it. I did not perceive I was applying the fear not remedy I perceived I was suicidal but now I understand I was not suicidal I understand being suicidal is a end symptom of right brain unveiling so in that respect I knew exactly what I was doing but I was not in touch with the fact that is exactly what I was doing because at the time right brain was veiled. So when I had right brain veiled I was asleep and I perceived I was harming myself but now I have right brain unveiled I understand I was not harming myself I was waking myself up. What one does consciously with right brain veiled is not what one would do consciously with right brain unveiled. The mind has two signals sent to the cerebral cortex the left and right hemisphere signals but these signals when one senses time are very left brain heavy and very right brain light so they are not harmony signals meaning equal input from both hemispheres so they become crossed signals. So one appears ignorant but the deeper reality is their mind is unsound so ignorance is a symptom of that. If one has their intuition, complexity, paradox, pattern detection turned down greatly or even silenced then a human being does not have all their mental aspects in their conscious mind to consider situations with. If I ask you how many fingers am I holding up but you

154

cannot see my fingers you are going to give me an ignorant answer or you are going to guess and that is what ignorance is. You were born with all of the left and right hemispheres aspects at your disposal to deal with any situation that may arise but the written education favored left hemisphere so much it neglected right hemisphere and slowly right hemisphere started to become silenced so now you are dealing with situations without all these hemisphere aspects at your disposal and so simple problems can appear to be quite difficult not because they are difficult but because you do not have all these aspects you should have mindfully relative to the hemispheres. So ones who push this written education on children have good intentions but they also have aspects of their mind no longer working so those good intentions are only relative to their perception.

"I had rather be first in a village than second at Rome."
Julius Caesar

This comment is identical to Epicurus' comment , what this comment is saying is identical to focus on the log in your eye because the eye of everyone else is relative to their perception. You can apply this remedy and then focus on your own understandings but you may never be able to convince anyone else to apply the fear not remedy so instead of looking at that reality as a bad thing you can look at it like you will become a master of your own house, your own mind. You may never be able to convince society written education veils the right hemisphere aspects when taught to young children before their mind is even getting warmed up but instead of allowing that reality to frustrate you, you can use it as a blessing that it is an infinite conditioning tool that will help you be aware of that and then concentrate even harder to explain it to yourself. It all leads back to one simple aspect. Even if you are dictator of the universe the beings who got this written education have their right brain veiled so you cannot force them to wake up, you cannot force them to apply the remedy because many do not even perceive they need to because their right brain was veiled when they were children so they do not even perceive their right brain is veiled at all. The absolute reality is this written education has created a complete nightmare relative to our species but it is so far along now one is left with attempting to be first in their village, first in their mind because the species is essentially all asleep. Focus on the log in your eye means focus on waking yourself up and then do as you are compelled to do and compelled to say with the understanding no matter what you say it is not going to solve this situation for the species. This battle our species is in is the ones who wake up are attempting to convince the vast majority who is still asleep to wake up. The ancient texts are testimonies of human being who woke up from the tree of knowledge neurosis and attempted to bear witness to its dangers. That is all one can do is bear witness because the ones who get the written education and have not applied the remedy are sleeping and so you are only bearing witness to yourself. I am writing explaining the exact same thing all the others explained when they woke up from the neurosis, "I was blind but now I see., "I was lost but now am found" That is all I can do because I am unable to deny what happened and so I bear witness and that's all I do now. This testimony is the key. These ancient texts are testimonies from many different people in many walks of life and from many professions spread out over hundreds of years so this eliminates the possibility it is an isolated incident. Socrates bared witness, the disciples of Socrates bared witness, Buddha bared witness, Jesus bared witness, John the Baptist bared witness, the disciples of Jesus bared witness, Mohammed bared witness, Abraham and Moses and Lot bared witness so this testimony is the key because the evidence is mounting. No single being is going to convince society but the combined efforts of these testimonies is the key. My testimony summed up is simply I got written education, it veiled my right brain and put me in neurosis and then I applied the ancient fear not remedy by accident and I unveil right brain and left the neurosis and returned to consciousness, but that is not good enough because the species is asleep so in turn I am very long winded, so to speak. Because I am under the influence of the right hemisphere when beings mock what I suggest they do not mock me they mock their self because they have been conditioned to see right hemisphere traits as improper traits by society.

X = how everyone is born left and right hemisphere in harmony.
Y = extreme left brain traits orientated after one gets the written education, right hemisphere traits veiled.

Y tends to see X as bad, alien, sick, insane, mentally undesired.

X does not see Y as bad, X see's Y as half of what it should be. Should be denotes everyone is born in the X state of mind so Y is a symptom something has happened to push one out of X state of mind and that something is years of left brain favoring written education. So the answer to the question: What is normal? X state of mind is normal and Y state of mind is abnormal. Sense of time is abnormal and relative to Y state of mind. No sense of time is normal and relative to X state of mind. Because these cornerstones of normal mindset are reality they alienate the vast majority of the species because the vast majority of the species was taught the written education and were never told about the fear not remedy that should go hand in hand with the written education. It is not important what my testimony may lead to relative to the safety of the entire species because that is totally irrelevant. One can argue that if as a species we were not supposed to put ourselves in this neurosis as a side effect of the written education we never would have but that is conflicting to Socrates paradox suggestion relative to "no one knowingly or willingly does wrong." We harmed ourselves as a species unknowingly with written education and so we may have to harm ourselves knowingly to get out. As a species we have to deny ourselves to get out of this situation.

[Mark 8:34 And when he had called the people unto him with his disciples also, he said unto them, Whosoever will come after me, let him deny himself, and take up his cross, and follow me.]

[let him deny himself] This applies on an individual level and a species level. Simply put, on a species level we have to mindfully kill ourselves and what that means is as a species we have to eat lots of crow. I am not concerned about anything else in this universe but assisting the species in eating lots of crow and whatever unwanted side effects that result from that are totally irrelevant.

[A. C. (19) allegedly died from a self-inflicted gunshot wound to the head]

This is what we as a species are going to do mindfully and you may not believe that and you may set your goals to resist that but on an absolute scale your efforts contrary to that goal are irrelevant. You will never be more important than the species because you are a subset of the species. You do not like the sound of that but that is irrelevant. I am not pleased to cram crow down the species throat but that is irrelevant. I am not pleased to inform you that you were mentally put to sleep as a child but that is irrelevant. I am not pleased to create a division among our species but that is irrelevant. There are only two subsets of our species on this planet. Left brain influenced beings who seek knowingly or unknowingly to create more left brain influenced beings using the written education and beings who have negated the written education left brain influence mindset. Until that conflict is resolved our species is dead in the water. Until that division is resolved our species is stagnate. Neither side is going to give in and that is why there is war among our species. Since we are a species at war we are only capable of symptoms that indicate we are at war. The war must be resolved so we can go back to being a united species because a species divided against itself cannot stand. If the resolution of the war destroys our species that is the same thing that will happen if the war is not resolved because a species divided cannot stand. The beings who are left brain influenced will suggest peace but that only means they get to keep turning all the children that are born in X state of mind, sound minded into left brain influenced beings of unsound mind, Y state of mind. So the left brain influenced suggest peace in order to remain in a position to continue to turn others into left brain influenced. Disharmony seeks disharmony.

X = how everyone is born left and right hemispheres in harmony.
Y = extreme left brain traits orientated after one gets the written education, right hemisphere traits veiled.

A (Y) will always see an X(harmony) as bad and seek to turn it into a (Y). A parent (Y) seeks to turn their child (X) into a (Y). A nation (Y) seeks to turn all its people into a (Y) and that is what the traditional education system is and does. If one does not believe that, it is totally irrelevant because only a (Y) would not believe that. Only a (Y) would not want that to stop and (X) would be totally aware of that and seek to stop it because an (X) is harmony and only seeks harmony. On an individual level, right brain seeks to return to mental harmony and a side effect of that is depression and suicidal thoughts in that being so right hemispheres desire to return to harmony may kill that being as a side effect. What this means is harmony will destroy things to achieve harmony and disharmony will destroy things to achieve disharmony. Because one in the Y state of mind is in disharmony, has right brain veiled, the only way for them to achieve harmony is to deny their self which is destroy their self mindfully. A suicidal person's only goal is to destroy their self so they are a human being in disharmony mindfully attempting to seek harmony, unveil right brain so they are attempting to deny their self but because this is not fantasy land many end up literally destroying their self. As a being they are seeking harmony and the side effect of that is they may destroy their self literally instead of just mindfully denying their self. Because of this reality there cannot possibly be any rules or morals and standards in this war our species is in. Our species is divided and the only solution for either side is destruction. The left brain influence destroys the children and the right brain influenced attempts to stop that and both require destruction to achieve those goals mindfully or literally. This is all relevant to the fact as a species this written education has divided us against ourselves. If you sense time you are in mental disharmony so you are destructive and if you apply the remedy you deny yourself so you are destructive so it is impossible this situation means one side is destructive and the other side is not because the core of our species is destructive because we are divided against ourselves as a result of this perception altering invention called written education and mathematics. If you perceive your well being is greater than the species well being then you assume you are not of the species. The species is divided so peace is not possible. Any illusions of peace are symptoms of denial of the division. The left brain influenced containers caused by the written education can never win because no matter what someone will always negate the neurosis and wake up and become sound minded X state of mind. The X state of mind can win because if they convince everyone to apply the remedy and convince the world education should be taught properly then the Y state of mind will become extinct. This suggests harmony will always win because mindful harmony is the only possible solution to viability on a species level. So the remedy is deny one's self or commit mental suicide but a left brain container will suggest that is bad or improper because a left brain container only seeks disharmony because left brain dominate beings are in mental disharmony. Harmony suggestions appear as improper to disharmony because disharmony see's harmony as illogical because disharmony is against itself.

Everyone is doing the best they can based on their perception.

"When in Rome, live as the Romans do; when elsewhere, live as they live elsewhere. " - Saint Ambrose

This is a great truth but it is also a great paradox. Rome is the ones that sense time. If I was doing as they do I would never write a single word so in that respect I am not doing as they do. On the other hand I am mindful I stand no chance because their numbers are far too great. What that means is there is this "political" party, the ones that sense time, and when a child is born they give that child the education and never suggest the fear not remedy and thus create another member of their political party, the left brain influenced containers. So in a system of majority rules there is no possible way to stop all the children being conditioned into left brain influenced container's. So In America for example if a parent applies the remedy and decides not to allow their child to get written education but instead oral education until that child is older that parent will be arrested and deemed a threat to that child. So this sense of time, left brain influenced political party is dictating what will be for everyone relative to that beings mindset but that negates the constitution, life liberty and the pursuit of happiness. One's life is dictated by their perception and education alters a being perception so in turn they are robbed of their choice of which life they wish to have by law and that law is voted on by the majority, left brain influenced beings. The left influenced beings want everyone to be left brain influenced and the proof is they were all determined to be conditioned into left brain influence by the beings before them or when they were children. A majority of mentally unsound beings, left brain influenced will dictate all mentally sound beings should be conditioned into a mentally unsound state. That is really all that is happening. So majority rules is a good thing on some levels and a death sentence on other levels. This is exactly why there is no mention of education in the founding documents of America. That means each person gets to determine what kind of education they get, oral or written but at this point there is only one choice, written education and if a parent even suggests they do not want that education pushed on their young mentally developing child they are arrested and deemed a threat to that child when in reality they are protecting their child. A dictatorship is achieved in a democracy when the voters have all been indoctrinated into one doctrine party. One is born and then when they are six another group of humans determines what that child's perception is going to be and that is left brain perception and they achieve that by forcing written education on that child and if anyone attempts to protect that child from that they are deemed a threat and a criminal. That is what a dictatorship is. One is no longer able to determine their own free will, it is dictated for them using subtle fear tactics and punishments. "You get written education or you will not make any money and be discriminated against in this society and end up with a slave job and a hard life." So no one can stand against that kind of scare tactic. "You do as we say or we will make your life miserable." That is what written education laws are saying. The left brain influence is controlling so it is going to make sure every single child is turned into what it is and although there are people involved in that influence they are all acting the same way. Go tell the school board you do not want your child to get written education until they are much older and they will make sure your child is taken from you not because they desire to harm your child but because they want all children to become like they are, left brain influenced. They perceive they are doing good because left brain always sees itself as good and see's right brain as bad because right brain aspects are contrary. Before you stick any pills in your hyperactive child you better make sure it's not just they are hyper because they still have right brain unveiled to a degree and are not as slothful as you are, so you don't give me the impression you just kill what is different than you. Are you sure your courts of law and your understanding's about psychology are not simply right brain biased tyrannies? It is understood the education system is biased against right brain and everything in society is relative to the education system of that society.

You suggest you are open minded to the existence of afterlife and supernatural and perhaps aliens but are you open minded to the reality written education hinders the mind? Are you open minded enough to understand this comment-

[Evidence B -"If you reflect back upon our own educational training, we have been traditionally taught to master the 3 R's: reading, writing and arithmetic -- the domain and strength of the left brain."] is saying right brain is hindered because written education favors left brain.

I am not suggesting ghosts, aliens or lizard men. I am suggesting something that is right in front of your nose. The tree is not as important as where it is planted. Ignorance is relative to joy as wisdom is relative to grief. Some see suffering as an excuse and some see grief as a gift. Attachments start with control and end with suffering. Some are human beings and some are human becomings. All ideas are either popular or risky.

2/16/2010 7:08:29 AM – There are these things called facts. A fact is something that can be shown to be true. It is difficult to show a blind man a fact. A fact is relative to the ignorance of one shown the truth. The ones that sense time are very physical based because their complex cerebral aspect right brain is veiled so their intuition and pattern detection is veiled so they are only able to essentially deal in very obvious evidence. That is a nice way of saying the ones that sense time have one physical world based perception of facts and so the entire other world of cerebral or mental facts are blind to them because their mind is only at a small fraction of its capacity. These statements do not mean anything to the ones that sense time because they have nearly no intuition and nearly no pattern detection in their thoughts at all.

Proof: [Evidence A -"What it comes down to is that modern society discriminates against the right hemisphere." - Roger Sperry (1973) - neuropsychologist, neurobiologist and Nobel laureate.

How does society discriminate against the right hemisphere?

Evidence B -"If you reflect back upon our own educational training, we have been traditionally taught to master the 3 R's: reading, writing and arithmetic -- the domain and strength of the left brain."]

One might suggest the ones that sense time are special needs type beings. They have special needs because they are cerebrally in need. When the special needs beings hear this [-"What it comes down to is that modern society discriminates against the right hemisphere." - Roger Sperry (1973)] They say prove it to me and show me it is a fact", when in reality they should see this comment and their intuition, pattern detection and vast memory of right brain should kick in and explain to them instantly what it means they would understand it is fact and what its implications are but instead they are left with no valued conclusions because their right hemisphere is sleeping. Being very tactful I will just say the fact they sense time proves they are mentally damaged goods beyond the understanding of even their self because of all that left brain favoring education. A perfectly healthy physiological brain has nothing to do with the fact their mind has been bent to the left. Modern medicine is looking at the brain itself and attempting to figure out symptoms but this mental bending caused by education is on a cerebral level so it cannot be detected with a machine and this is why the ones that sense time only have a small spectrum of things they can understand are facts. One has to look at my purpose more in the range of mocking the ones that sense time than an actual attempts to prove to them facts relative to this situation. I like to mock them as opposed to teach them. That is an indication that no matter what I prove to them at the end of the day they have to apply the remedy and they are perhaps no longer at the mental level of fortitude as a being to be able to do that so this fact proving aspect is relative to whom I am attempting to prove facts to, not my actual ability to find and show facts. I cannot prove to a blind man blindness is abnormal. My proof is only relative to whom I am telling it to. I can go tell a rock the sky is blue but I do not expect it to agree with me. Perhaps the ones that sense time do not want to see truth because they would have to understand they are a lie.

The frontal lobe in mammals covers an area on each hemisphere. So humans has a frontal lobe on the left and right hemispheres.

Giedd, Jay N. (october 1999). "Brain Development during childhood and adolescence: a longitudinal MRI study". Nature neuroscience 2 (10): 861-863. http://www.millersville.edu/~bduncan/465/articles/giedd.pdf.

I am adding this whole "who gets credit for saying this" because the comment they make is so profound because it gives an indication of the damage the written education does on the mind. This is the comment : "In humans, the frontal lobe reaches full maturity around only after the 20s, marking the cognitive maturity associated with adulthood" - Giedd, Jay N.

[the frontal lobe reaches full maturity around only after the 20s] A child starts this education at the age of six or seven: [reading, writing and arithmetic -- the domain and strength of the left brain.] What is profound is in all of civilization there is not one single human being that got this education and has not applied the remedy that has the mental capacity any longer to detect this maturity of the front lobe at the age of 20 combined with the fact the traditional education is all left brain favoring, and thus left mind favoring could possibly have even .000001% negative mental effect on the child. I am certain it mentally destroys that child but civilization on all levels from leaders, to scientists to psychologists cannot even understand at all there may be a problem with pushing strictly left brain favoring education on the mind of a seven year old child whose mind is not even going to fully develop until they are at least 20.

So a child is essentially a fetus and that fetus is becoming mentally mature until the age of 20 but the education starts messing with that fetus' mental aspect at the age of seven.

Fetus relative to a child, so seven years is like a trimester in contrast to an embryo. So the first trimester for an embryo is three months and so that means at the first trimester, age seven, is when the education is pushed on the child. So this means the child is not even near developing mentally and the education is pushed on them and by the time that child is at the second trimester, at age 14 they are mentally ruined and that is the age children start killing their self. So if you inject drugs into a mother that is three months pregnant you will perhaps destroy that embryo or affect it in one way or another and it's the same with a child, that child is seven so they are 1/3rd on their way to mental development and you push education that is all left brain favoring on them and so you factually ruin them mentally. That is all that your education does. I have faith eventually your pinprick sequential laughable mind will grasp something I say. You rape children mentally and then brag about it and perceive you are doing good so that proves you were mentally destroyed as a child also. You know not what you do. Are you starting to understand what Abraham and Lot were thinking when they decided this : [Genesis 19:13 For we will destroy this place, because the cry of them is waxen great before the face of the LORD; and the LORD hath sent us to destroy it.]

When people who were mentally hindered on a devastating level continue to mentally hinder the offspring to that same degree because they are not mentally able to even understand that is what they are doing, what else can you do to stop it?

[because the cry of them is waxen great before the face of the LORD] This is suggesting they are so mentally ruined they are destroying the offspring and have zero conscience to even be aware that is factually what they are doing. A lunatic is a person who has no foresight so they know not what they do. A lunatic will destroy another being and not even be aware they did that at all. They can only be locked in cages to protect the children but we don't have six billion cages so we need to work on our cage building infrastructure perhaps because there is going to be very soon a lot of beings that are going to be caged to protect the children. Because of your neurosis I will attempt to rephrase that concept again.

A child is born and it takes 20 years for that child's mind to get up to speed or get warmed up and you push this left brain favoring education on them starting at the age of six or seven [reading, writing and arithmetic -- the domain and strength of the left brain."] and you do not even believe that may affect their overall mental development. Because you do not believe that, you are factually out of touch with reality and in turn factually mentally unsound as a being. Any country on this planet that does this : [reading, writing and arithmetic -- the domain and strength of the left brain."] to seven year old children is factually a threat to the species and committing crimes against humanity. Now I have to start the infinite books over from right here. I will go play my video game before I implode. Implode: to collapse inwardly. Black hole: Black holes are believed to form when stars collapse in on themselves.

2:53:39 PM - So because of this: "In humans, the frontal lobe reaches full maturity around only after the 20s, marking the cognitive maturity associated with adulthood" ,education is nothing but a form of mental

165

abortion. Even if the education was right brain favoring it would still be mental abortion because the point of abortion is to stop the fetus from developing. So traditional education favors left brain and thus interrupts the development of the mind of that child and so it aborts that development and because the mind is relative to the physical aspects of that child it aborts that child all together from developing. You do not believe that because you have slight right brain intuition and thus no conscience but it is fact none the less. Oft, nothing is more profound than something. One cannot reach consciousness unless they first uncover all their delusions. I am speechless paradoxically speaking. When you find everything is perfect on all levels you have passed away.

There was a mathematician Georg Ferdinand Ludwig Phillip Cantor and he played around with infinity. On a scale of numbers in infinity there are infinite fractions between each number and for example infinite fractions between 1 and 2 and this continues on with every number into infinity so there is infinity within infinity. Infinity only works with parts, other words the opposite of infinity is everything is one thing. So if everything is one thing there is no infinity or infinity itself is one thing. Cantor started to notice this paradox aspect to infinity but because he was a mathematician he had right brain veiled. He was attempting to grasp paradox and complexity using his left brain and he went insane. Math itself is a paradox. To be good at math one has to see parts a left brain trait so the better one is at math the more right brain is veiled , right brain see's holistically, so one gets better at math and loses their ability to think with complexity and paradox, a right brain trait. What may have happened to him is he started to unveil right brain and so he went to the 9th circle of hell, he had severe bouts of mania and depression and paranoia and that is the 9th circle of hell. So he was trying to grasp paradox while studying infinity and attempting to grasp complex aspects of infinity and started to favor right brain and as right brain starts to unveil one gets closer to the 9th circle of hell, treason. E= Mc2 suggests everything is one thing, energy and mass equals one thing a total, menergy, but if one looks at parts they can find infinity within this one thing aspect of everything. Cantor set music aside as a child and went into math. Music is creativity a right brain trait and math is a left brain trait. Math is such a strange invention because it requires complexity and paradox to use at high levels but it veils right brain to get to those levels so it is self defeating. It is very deep but mankind lived without math for tens of thousands of years and in the five thousand years or so with math mankind has perhaps not really accomplish anything. For example math by itself without creativity, a right brain trait, does nothing at all. The tree of knowledge has not assisted our species in progression it has only created more details and thus pushed us further into favoring left hemisphere.

2/17/2010 7:08:48 AM - S = K log W : This is the equation relative to entropy and probability. It was invented by Ludwig Eduard Boltzmann. It suggested that in a system there are not really absolutes but simply probabilities or no absolutes. This went against the thinking of the time relative to mechanical physics. The concept was that everything could be proven in an absolute form and then Ludwig came along and said many systems in life and inanimate systems like a fire for example were really easier to predict using non absolutes or probability and probability suggests paradox because absolutes do not tend to allow paradox. So Ludwig was really bringing the philosophical reality into physics and it did not go over well. Ludwig was saying there are no absolutes and that means even the system of life itself is not absolute and the "minds that be" did not take kindly to that. Ludwig was so good at math, he favored his left brain so much, he eventually became depressed and hung himself, the more you favor left brain the stronger your emotions become, it is an interesting trade off. Darwin suggested in spirit that life itself is not really this perfect God planned reality it is more along the lines of anything can happen at any time and so nothing is carved in stone, so to speak. Everyone knows what Moses did to those absolute rules carved in stone. Ones that sense time think like left brain, they perceive God would never make a contradiction, paradox, and God is simple minded so what they see, relative to God the only way they can see, using their left brain aspects, sequential, absolute and linear aspects. Ludwig and Darwin on their own were more suggesting an experiment mentality to life which means a solar flare could happen right now and wipe out the entire planet and that is just the way it goes, that would be just another event in the experiment and the system as a whole relative to the universe would continue. That goes against this absolute linear concept of reality because it suggests God is not pulling the strings God just created the strings. For example I see this religious show and there are thousands of people listening to this preacher and he walks up to a boy and puts his hand on the boy and prays and then asks the boy "Did you feel God when I touched you." And the boy hesitates and is aware thousands of people are watching him and he responds into the microphone "Yes" as if he could say anything else in that situation.

This comment suggests God see's everything as good [Genesis 1:10 And God called the dry land Earth; and the gathering together of the waters called he Seas: and God saw that it was good.]

This comment is interesting from a grammar point of view because if you look at two different translations:

[^{NAS} Genesis 1:10 And God called the dry land earth, and the gathering of the waters He called seas; and God saw that it was good.]

[^{KJV} Genesis 1:10 And God called the dry land Earth; and the gathering together of the waters called he Seas: and God saw that it was good.]

You can see they corrected the grammar.

[and the gathering together of the waters called he Seas:]

[and the gathering of the waters He called seas]

[called he Seas:] is out of sequential order , it is in random access order so some being with a sense of time determined it is best to correct the author of this texts grammar [He called seas].

In Hebrew this reverse or random access aspect does not exist.

New American translation:

"God called the dry land earth, and the gathering of the waters He called seas; and God saw that it was good."

King James:

168

"And God called the dry land Earth; and the gathering together of the waters [called he Seas]: and God saw that it was good."

American King James:

"And God called the dry land Earth; and the gathering together of the waters [called he Seas]: and God saw that it was good."

American Standard:

"And God called the dry land Earth; and the gathering together of the waters [called he Seas]: and God saw that it was good."

English Revised:

"And God called the dry land Earth; and the gathering together of the waters [called he Seas]: and God saw that it was good."

Literal Hebrew Translation:

"And God called the dry land Earth and the gathering together of the waters called the Seas and God saw that it was good."

So the random access "speaking in tongues" aspect does not show up as obviously in some languages at least in this verse.

"And God called(passed tense) the dry land Earth and the [gathering together] of the waters called(time tense) the Seas and God saw(time tense) that [it was](time tense) good."

This Hebrew translation is full of time denotations. So to translate this comment using no time tense at all it would be.

God create dry land earth and water sea and God see it good.

So [Genesis 1:1 In the beginning God created the heaven and the earth.] would be without time denotations. God create heaven and earth. [In the beginning] denotes time.[created] denotes time. These texts if written with no time denotations would not make any sense to ones that sense time. So if a being that has applied the remedy finds these texts they are battle plans, strategic and tactical aspects on how to battle the ones that sense time, and if one that has not applied the remedy finds these texts they are traps and are inviting because they make the ones that sense time believe they are like the ones who wrote these texts because of all the time denotations.

You are good I am bad. You good I bad. In school they grade a student on their ability to use past, present and future tense words. The further one goes into left brain the better they become at using time tense words so the ones who are not taking the left brain education well do poorly at past, present, and future tense word usage. So the children in school that gets poor grades have right brain unveiled the most or are not as "willing" to having their right brain veiled. So students who get poor grades are simply human beings who are resisting having their right brain veiled and so they are punished with bad grades, and thus poor job opportunities in society and thus they are discriminated against.

"What it comes down to is that modern society discriminates against the right hemisphere." - Roger Sperry (1973) - neuropsychologist, neurobiologist and Nobel laureate

The entire spirit of society and thus civilization is simply, you veil your right brain with our wisdom education and if you do not, we will make sure you pay for it, this of course is done unknowingly by the beings who have their right brain veiled. There is nothing else happening in civilization and thus society but that, everything after that reality are simply details relative to that reality. The definition of society and thus civilization is : A group that discriminates using various methods against right hemisphere. Society is a tyranny against right hemisphere. All society does is discriminates against any human being that exhibits right hemisphere traits and thus discourages right hemisphere traits and that is why society is, simply left hemisphere containers. Only left hemisphere would see right hemisphere traits as bad because they are all contrary to left hemisphere traits. Someone of sound mind would not see left hemisphere traits or right hemisphere traits as bad and what that means is when a person misspells a word I do not insult them because I am fully aware of what the word is they were typing anyway. A school teacher punishes a child that misspells a word by giving them grades that suggest that child is not intelligent so grades are nothing but a form of fear tactics and threats. "If you get another bad grade you will go home with a bad report card and your parents will berate you and punish you and insult you."

"What it comes down to is that modern society discriminates against the right hemisphere." = Society is a monster that dislikes an entire hemisphere of the mind and thus is divided against itself. Since society looks at one entire hemisphere of its mind as unwanted traits then the species is doomed. If a species looks at a child that is hyperactive and that is simply a right brain trait, being quick and energetic and then gives that child drugs to silence those aspects then the species hates itself. It is logical if you do not understand that is what is happening because you sense time and thus are a left brain influenced container and it is logical you would never find fault with yourself. If a left brain influenced container found fault with their self they may deny their self. The deeper reality is if society even questioned if traditional education favored left brain even slightly too much they would have to admit perhaps traditional education does hinder the mind even slightly and all of society as we know it would collapse. It would not be the males that would revolt it would be the women. The very first conclusion a female would come to if society questioned if traditional education mentally hindered children is they would tell their husband or mate "Society is harming the children.", and the males would do what they do best, defend the children at the women's request.

12:02:21 PM – Do not take the word of a blind man ask questions. - Buddha

[word] denotes written language ; word as in the written word

[blind man] denotes mentally hindered; one who learns written language is mentally hindered so they are mentally blind

[ask questions] denotes before you are taught the word, written language make sure you ask about it because the one who teaches it to you is mentally hindered or a blind man. Right brain is the curious aspect and it asks lots of questions like small children do.

Do not get written education without asking questions about its potential mental effects because the one who teaches it is mentally hindered because a mentally hindered being taught it to them. Do not take the teachings relative to written education (word) from a mentally blind man because they will make you mentally blind like they are. A mentally hindered being is unable to detect any potential unwanted mental side effects from written education because they would first have to face the reality they were mentally hindered by it.

[Acts 10:42 And he commanded us to preach unto the people, and to testify that it is he which was ordained of God to be the Judge of quick and dead.]

[Judge of quick and dead.] Only the quick, the ones that negate the mental effects of the written education, the ones with no sense of time, can judge who is quick and who is still in the neurosis, mentally dead. The ones that sense time, the dead, cannot judge properly because they are mentally unsound, dead. The ones that sense time only see the ones who have applied the remedy and returned to sound mind as everything in the universe except of sound mind based on their ability to use language. For example: This is an actual comment from a being who finds fault with the fact I cannot use the written language very well.

"You do realize schizophrenics write in this manner?"

What he is really saying is, "If you cannot use the language well it proves you are mentally unsound." In reality right brain when at 50% in the conscious state is not a good judge and because the language is based on judgment, like when to use a commas and when to use paragraph breaks etc, one is simply not very good at using it anymore, also written language is all sequential based. The being who made that remark is quite the defender of the "golden calf" and literally hates right brain traits and is attempting to make it seem like I have mental problems because he is not aware if I am not mentally unsound then he factually is mentally unsound. The deeper reality is he is totally unaware he is against right brain traits because he is "asleep" mentally, his right brain intuition is gone so he is a "blind man".

172

[and to testify that it is he which was ordained of God] This comment causes quite a bit of trouble for some. Firstly testify means once one applies the remedy right brain aspects minister to them and they become a witness to the fact written education veiled their right brain traits. What this means is after one applies the remedy they become a teacher unto their self and they no longer need assistance because they can think for their self. Other words these beings in the ancient texts were equals because they all applied the remedy, they all unveiled right brain, they were prophets, so in that respect no one was leader of this group they were all equals. They all were saying the same thing and it was not because one told them to say these things, they said them because they were compelled to say them. For example John the Baptist was not greater than Jesus and Jesus was not greater than Mathew, Mark, Luke or John because when everything was said and done they were all under the influence of right brain and so they were right brain influenced beings speaking on behalf of right brain, the god image in man. Ones that sense time tend to covet and idolize and so they idolize these beings but that is not the plan in these texts. The plan in these texts is for one to apply the fear not remedy and unveil right brain and then one becomes a witness to the power of right hemisphere and then they testify that to the world and everyone who does apply the remedy has their own story to tell. For example the disciples went out and gave their own testimony after Jesus was killed and that is the same thing Jesus did after John the Baptist was killed so there is no leader that is required because a being with right brain unveiled has the power to think for their self, right brain intuition. The only beings that would suggest that is not truth are beings who do not even know what the tree of knowledge is and that would mean they also have not even applied the, those who lose their life mindfully will preserve it. Jesus said quite clearly in the Gospel of Thomas:

[13 - Jesus said, "I am not your teacher. Because you have drunk, you have become intoxicated from the bubbling spring that I have tended."]

This means once you apply the remedy you become the teacher because you have the bubbling spring, right brain in your conscious state and you are of sound mind and you have the power to teach and to explain the remedy and you no longer need a teacher relative to a teacher that explains to you how to apply the remedy. I am mindful if a being senses time then they have not applied the fear not remedy to the full measure so they cannot possibly know what these texts are really saying and so I will just leave it at that because I am mindful that some of the beings that do sense time are only trying to make living off these texts and the reality is, the beings in these texts did not make a living off of testifying, they all essentially got killed for explaining the remedy to written education, the tree of knowledge. If you are making a living off of your testimony you clearly are not saying what you are compelled to say, you are just watering it down for your protection so perhaps you should apply the remedy the full measure so you are not so afraid. The rule of thumb is if you need someone to tell that you are a teacher or you are capable of testifying you have not applied the remedy the full measure because you still have self esteem issues because ones who have applied the remedy the full measure are compelled to speak or testify about the tree of knowledge because they can think for their self. These texts had nothing to do with me applying the remedy. I woke up on my own, the hard way, so these texts are not my salvation these texts are pleasing to talk about because they explain the actual history of mankind relative to last few thousand years and that is a curious history because it is not the history the ones that sense time are preaching and perhaps for good reason. I am not idolizing the beings in these texts I am explaining what they attempted to explain and that is as far as it will ever go. I have left the world of hesitation, sloth and low self esteem, one might suggest. Once one applies the remedy they return to being a sound minded human and so it is not possible there is any other human that is wiser than they are, and that perhaps is beyond the grasp of ones that sense time to understand because they perhaps are all about coveting and idolizing and thinking others are so much wiser than they are because their grades were not perfect in their schooling. If you are not one of the wisest human beings on the planet after you apply the remedy you clearly have not applied the remedy the full measure, so keep trying. I understand one very important thing about life and that is if you go around basing your actions on what you perceive others will say or think about you in any respect you have major self esteem issues because there is no one else on this planet that knows better than you do after you apply the remedy because you are a sound minded human being then. That is the whole point of the remedy, once you return to being a sounded minded human being as you were born you cease being a sheep that has to be herded. Once you have right brain on your side this life poses no problems you cannot handle on your own; no stress, no nervousness, no panic, no fear because you have mental clarity and thus you can think. Perhaps you cannot relate to that at all.

[Acts 2:15 For these are not drunken, as ye suppose, seeing it is but the third hour of the day.]

[For these (the ones with no sense of time, the ones who applied the remedy) are not drunken, as ye(the ones with a sense of time, the mentally unsound, the dead) suppose(judge),

The only thing I can say to the being that suggest this: "You do realize schizophrenics write in this manner?" is "I am not drunken as ye suppose."

So Acts 2:15 is a being with no sense of time telling the ones with a sense of time , "No, they are just mentally sound beings because they applied the remedy but because you sense time and thus are mentally hindered you see sanity as drunkenness"

So society see's Einstein as "special" or "gifted" and studies his brain attempting to find an alien implant because society cannot grasp Einstein was just very close to being conscious because he did not get to much of that written education. He left school at the age of sixteen and even when he was in school he did very poorly at it, especially math. Since Einstein is just very close to normal, conscious, sound minded, then that means all of society is a poor judge because it perceives he was "special". Simply put Einstein was just a conscious human being and so that means society itself is so mentally hindered they see conscious beings as mental giants because society could never face the reality, all their written education has done to them is mentally hinder them into a mental state called hell and they may not be able to escape that.

[Hebrews 4:12 For the word of God is quick, and powerful, and sharper than any twoedged sword, piercing even to the dividing asunder of soul and spirit, and of the joints and marrow, and is a discerner of the thoughts and intents of the heart.]

[For the word of God is quick, and powerful, and sharper than any twoedged sword] One with right brain unveiled is very swift in contrast to one who has right brain veiled only because right brain has lightening random access processing. So their words appear to be wise as in they can come up with lots of nice "wisdom sayings" but that is just right brain attributes.

[sharper] denotes they have mental clarity and can explain concepts and solutions to problems not because they are special but because they are of sound mind because they got the written education and kept the covenant which is "apply the fear not remedy after you eat off the tree of knowledge so your right hemisphere does not remain veiled."

[a discerner of the thoughts and intents of the heart.] This is an attempt to explain the right brain intuition aspects of right hemisphere when it is at full power. I can tell what you are thinking and when you speak, I can tell whether you have applied the remedy or not instantly. I am not supernatural it is simply a right brain traits called intuition, pattern detection and lightening random access processing power. I have to ponder why would society veil such a powerhouse aspect in the mind and the only logical conclusion is society is mentally unsound and knows not what it does. I am saying to your face if you sense time you are factually mentally a lunatic and factually mentally unsound and you should have a problem with that. If your right brain intuition is working at all it should be telling you that you have serious problems now. It is proper to defend children from all threats in order to keep them from having their right hemisphere veiled. Having said that you are not going to do anything because you are going to focus on the log in your eye and if the entire universe starts mentally raping innocent children you are not going to do anything but use that understanding to concentrate harder and if you cannot concentrate you will literally emotionally implode and end up destroying yourself and that is just as well. You are going to allow the ones that sense time mentally harm every single last child and you are not going to do anything about it but observe it. You are going to condition your mind to see this as beauty:

[A. M. (19) committed suicide by jumping off the Sunshine Skyway Bridge.]

If you are unable to see the horrific reality caused by written educations mental side effects on the mind of children as beauty you will emotionally implode and eventually kill yourself and I will see that as beauty. I oft only speak in paradox. The ones that sense time essentially cannot be recovered because they are fatalities so you let them go or they will drag you down with them. I will now discuss something of importance.

1:11:32 PM - The story about Jonah and the whale is a concept story on one hand. One can plug the concept from this story into many aspects of the ancient texts. For example Jesus was a big fish and he spoke to the disciples and they followed what he said and they became big fish or spokesman for the cause so to speak. Abraham was a big fish and Isaac listened to Abraham and applied the remedy Abraham suggested and so Isaac became a big fish. So the concept of being swallowed by a big fish is along the lines of listening to what a big fish suggests and if one does that they will become a big fish. So for example Jesus said if you want to follow me deny yourself. If one seeks the shadow of death and when they find it they fear not, they deny their self, they deny their instincts that suggest they run from the shadow of death. Psychologists suggest everyone has a chemical imbalance except them.

[Jonah 1:1 Now the word of the LORD(right brain) came unto Jonah the son of Amittai, saying,]

This comment means Jonah applied the remedy partially and he was compelled to speak out against the dangers of the tree of knowledge, written education, and he saw the vast armies of Goliath and he was scared so he did not apply the remedy to full measure at this stage.

[Jonah 1:2 Arise, go to Nineveh, that great city, and cry against it; for their wickedness is come up before me.]

This means Jonah was fully aware of what was happening the children as a result of the written education and was fully aware of what the authorities that sense time(the wicked) were doing to children.

[their wickedness is come up before me.] This means after you apply the remedy your heightened awareness and intuition is going to be off the scale and you are going to be fully aware of what is going on in this narrow.

[Jonah 1:3 But Jonah rose up to flee unto Tarshish from the presence of the LORD, and went down to Joppa; and he found a ship going to Tarshish: so he paid the fare thereof, and went down into it, to go with them unto Tarshish from the presence of the LORD.]

This means after you apply the remedy you are going to come up with every single excuse in the universe to not speak out against written education so you can save your worthless life from the ones that sense time because they butcher anyone who speaks out against their whore demotic, the golden calf, written education.

[Jonah 1:4 But the LORD sent out a great wind into the sea, and there was a mighty tempest in the sea, so that the ship was like to be broken.]

This means after you apply the remedy and you become fully aware of the dangers of written education and if you do not speak out against it you deny your own understandings so you curse yourself.

[Jonah 1:5 Then the mariners were afraid, and cried every man unto his god, and cast forth the wares that were in the ship into the sea, to lighten it of them. But Jonah was gone down into the sides of the ship; and he lay, and was fast asleep.] This comment proves Jonah had already applied the remedy.

[Then the mariners were afraid] = the ones that sense time had the spirit of fear; 2 Timothy 1:7

[But Jonah was gone down into the sides of the ship; and he lay, and was fast asleep.] = ones that do not sense time , they are not afraid because fear itself is a symptom of the neurosis relative to [2 Timothy 1:7 For God hath not given us the spirit of fear; but of power, and of love, and of a sound mind.]

[For God hath not given us the spirit of fear;] = [But Jonah was gone down into the sides of the ship; and he lay, and was fast asleep.] = Jonah was not afraid of the storm because he applied the remedy to a degree and was without the spirit of fear, he could stand any storm, problem, because he had a sound mind. This is similar to how Job could stand all the "storms" he encountered and also how Jesus could stand the "storm" in the boat on the sea when all of the beings with him were: [Then the mariners were afraid]. This is an indication of the spirit of these texts repeating itself over and over, on a scale of hundreds of years.

[Jonah 1:6 So the shipmaster came to him, and said unto him, What meanest thou, O sleeper? arise, call upon thy God, if so be that God will think upon us, that we perish not.]

This is saying the ones that sense time notice Jonah, one that didn't sense time, was not afraid and since the darkness only see's the light as darkness they assumed Jonah was evil. For example : "You do realize schizophrenics write in this manner?" This is the same concept of when the ones that sense time saw the Native Americans and the Africans, they judged them to be evil or savages so they took advantage of them because the darkness only see's the light as darkness and must kill the light because the light reveals to the darkness what the darkness is and the darkness cannot stand itself so if it does not kill the light it will destroy itself.

[Jonah 1:7 And they said every one to his fellow, Come, and let us cast lots, that we may know for whose cause this evil is upon us. So they cast lots, and the lot fell upon Jonah.]

[cast lots] is a symbol for gambling and thus money, so gambling is a symptom of the ones that sense time. So the fact they settled this situation with lots is a hint they were ones that sense time.

[that we may know for whose cause this evil is upon us.] So the ones that sense time are using their pin prick sequential logic to determine who is evil.

[So they cast lots, and the lot fell upon Jonah.] The lot always falls on the odd man out so to speak, the outcast relative to outcasts. Jonah was exhibiting odd behavior in contrast to the ones that sense time so they automatically assumed it was Jonah who was evil because it certainly could not be all of them that were messed up. This is a common reality because I have no sense of time and I write books faster than any human being with a sense of time can so with their pin prick sequential logic, they will assume I am on drugs or supernatural or above average because they cannot imagine I am just mentally sound because I accidentally applied the ancient fear not remedy to the tree of knowledge. I am only quick relative to the dead. I am only special if you contrast me with a mental abomination.

2:08:34 PM - I searched the internet for the phrase "you can't even spell". The ones that sense time in their pin prick sequential logic world of delusions have concluded a misspelling is a symptom of one's lack of intelligence because when they were children in school and they misspelled a word the teacher gave them a bad grade and that suggested they were not intelligent for misspelling a word so now they simply have become a product of what they were conditioned into so they have lost their ability to think for their self. So here are some comments on the internet relative to ones that sense time assuming misspelling is proof one is not intelligent. For the record I do not assume you are not intelligent because you misspell words I simply understand you are mentally unsound because you sense time.

[Good grief. You can't even spell ammunition correctly, yet you own a Beretta. The world has gone mad.]
[You can't even spell "business".]
[You can't even spell Gretzky FFS.]
[Why make a group or page, when you can't even spell the title correctly?!]
[Hannity so capitalist, they can't even spell "comrades"]
[Yeesh. You can't even spell 'doubt' right?]
[The fact that you can't even spell "booger" is]
[You can't even spell "playa".]
[Besides, you can't even spell 'Moveable'"]

[Let's start with the most ironic piece of this farce tale. "Compliance" is actually misspelled in the title. I could stop there... But you know I won't.]

[You can't even spell "probably"]

[Are you sure you can play the saxophone? I mean, you can't even spell it.]

[dude, you can't even spell his name right]

[After reading that rambling rhetoric, it is sad to discover you can't even spell can you?]

[You can't even spell Amendment? ...geez!]

[You can't even spell....go to school!!]

["I bet you can't even spell poker"]

[If you can't even spell your own name correctly how do you expected to take you seriously?]

[Take some more Xanax, Jeff! Ha! (you can't even spell) lol (nt)]

[If you can't even spell or abbreviate your job title correctly, you're out. Do not pass go, do not collect a paycheck. I'm serious. Ask anyone]

This comment is what I am suggesting, if you can't do well at the education you get a slave job but if you are good at written education and math you are mentally hindered because right brain is veiled so you in fact sell your "soul" for the prospects of money. Simply put your parents sold your soul "right brain" when they decided to "educate" you and now you wonder why you cannot think well, it is because you are only playing with half of a mind and that is no mind at all.

[Hell, you can't even spell you illiterate fuck. Not to mention, that what you wrote makes no sense at all...sentence structure, if you had passed grade 3]

This is another being that has determined "school" is the complete and absolute measure of intelligence and that is only true if ones definition of intelligence is mentally hindered and thus mentally retarded.

[Considering you can't even spell "word", it's a bit rich telling people they can't spell.]

[you can't even spell or write full sentence.]

[correctly] comes up in these comments. This indicates these beings are subconsciously aware the education has harmed them. What I mean is a teacher tells a student, "You didn't spell that word correctly." Now that teacher does not say "So that means you are stupid" but it is implied. "You did not do it correctly." implies you are stupid but in reality correctly is often relative. If you do something and it does not kill you, you did it correctly and even that is a paradox. All of these beings that made these comments have been conditioned into detail noticing left brain influenced mental abnormalities. Left brain notices details and that is not improper but when one notices details in words when they know what the word is and then they go to the trouble to make a speaking point relative to the speakers intelligence based on that petty detail they are neurotic. An English teacher can get a paper from a student that has a very important concept in the spirit of that text but the teacher only has one goal, to look at all the details in the text and judge the student on them so that teacher is not even judging the content of that paper they are just judging the details in that paper because they were conditioned into extreme left brain and they perceive all the little petty details are more important than life itself. A teacher will tell an innocent child that he or she is stupid to protect the sanctity of the spelling of an inanimate word, because that teacher was told they are stupid when they did not respect the spelling sanctity of an inanimate word when they were a child.

[Not to mention, that what you wrote makes no sense at all...sentence structure, if you had passed grade 3] This comment is a being who is assuming school is the end all be all, relative to wisdom. This kind of pin prick logic is exactly why the "white man" made the Africans slaves and why they took advantage of the Native Americans and locked them all in concentration camps where they remain to this day, of course the ruler scribe also lock their own kind in concentration camps called cities. The reason people are not all spread out is because they can be controlled easier if they are all concentrated. This concentration aspect is what caused the plague and many diseases and many other conditions. The ones that sense time met the Native Americans and the Native Americans got many diseases from them but that is because the ones that sense time are cursed with so many curses and one of them is disease which is a symptom of their fruits and one of their fruits is concentration camps which are cities. The Native Americans were not stupid because they did not have all the diseases the ones that sense time had, they were in fact infected by the cursed ones. If you hang around someone who is cursed long enough you may get the curse or experience symptoms of the curse. This is why there are tribes in the wilderness that are very hostile to ones from civilization because they are aware of the curse in one way or another. They are not anti-social they just are wise enough to avoid associating with abominations , one might suggest. Let's get back to Jonah and his experience with the mental abominations that sense time and have no conscience.

[Jonah 1:8 Then said they unto him, Tell us, we pray thee, for whose cause this evil is upon us; What is thine occupation? and whence comest thou? what is thy country? and of what people art thou?]

Notice all the questions. The ones that sense time have many questions because their right brain intuition is silenced. If these beings had their right brain intuition they would know the answers to these question, they would be aware Jonah had applied the remedy. They would know [what people art thou?] what kind of person Jonah was.

[Jonah 1:9 And he said unto them, I am an Hebrew; and I fear the LORD, the God of heaven, which hath made the sea and the dry land.]

So now Jonah has to start explaining who he is. Hebrew is the same as Jew and a Jew is one who gets the written education and applies the fear not remedy relative to this time period so is one with no sense of time, one with a sound mind. So Jonah was one that did not sense time but in explaining who he is, the ones that sense time cannot grasp who he is because they are mentally unsound, so Jonah is attempting to explain who he is but he is using words that go way above the ones that sense time heads. [I fear the LORD] is simply saying he had faith written education veiled the god image in man, right brain, which is why he applied the remedy but the ones that sense time cannot grasp that so he is getting himself into trouble attempting to reason with the darkness.

[Jonah 1:10 Then were the men exceedingly afraid, and said unto him, Why hast thou done this? For the men knew that he fled from the presence of the LORD, because he had told them.]

This is interesting as you can see [I fear the LORD] Jonah said he feared but then in this line it says [Then were the men exceedingly afraid] so it is saying the men were afraid of something other than the Lord. Also [Then were the men exceedingly afraid] this comment is out of sequence it should be [Then the men were exceedingly afraid] so this is a signpost of authenticity. In this comment even the Hebrew translation keeps the out of sequence aspect.

Then were the men

'enowsh (en-oshe')

[For the men knew that he fled] This is using men as an insult. Men are ones that sense time.

[Jonah 1:11 Then said they unto him, What shall we do unto thee, that the sea may be calm unto us? for the sea wrought, and was tempestuous.]

This is similar to the story where Jesus was in a boat and a storm came and everyone in the boat was "afraid" but Jesus.[What shall we do unto thee, that the sea may be calm unto us?] This comment is explaining what the ones that sense time do when they are afraid. [What shall we do unto thee] denotes the "men" where willing to do anything so the fear would go away. Kind of like how the "men" will give away their freedom for a little security because they are afraid of a bad haircut. This is why the ones that sense time are so easily controlled using fear tactics, they will sell their soul if they fear they won't have money or fear they won't have friends or fear they will become afraid. This spirit of fear is of course a side effect of all that left brain written education and mathematics, it is an abnormal aspect not a naturally occurring aspect in humans. Humans are fearless then they get the traditional education and become scared like dogs because their hypothalamus starts sending many false positives.

[Jonah 1:12 And he said unto them, Take me up, and cast me forth into the sea; so shall the sea be calm unto you: for I know that for my sake this great tempest is upon you.]

The point of this comment is Jonah fled from his duty to confront the "wicked" ones in the city after he applied the remedy to a degree and give his testimony about the tree of knowledge and because he fled from that duty now he is in an even worse situation. Another way to look at it is Jonah is finding out he is damned if he does and dammed if he doesn't, so to speak. If he would have confronted the wicked and gave his testimony he would never have been on this boat so he wouldn't have to throw himself into the sea. This comment is relative to the comment " it is better to throw yourself into the sea than harm one of the little ones." For example once one applies the remedy if they sit on their hands and do not speak up and give their testimony about the tree of knowledge they are as bad as the ones who harm the children with the tree of knowledge but if one does speak out against the tree of knowledge the ones that sense time most certainly will perhaps slaughter you but that is better than hiding like a scared dog and denying truth but always keep in mind "when in rome". This is an indication that this written education threw our species mentally into some alternate perception reality and we are divided against ourselves and have been simply reduced to war against ourselves. Eat, drink and be merry for tomorrow we shall die pretty much sums it up.

[Jonah 1:15 So they took up Jonah, and cast him forth into the sea: and the sea ceased from her raging.

16 Then the men feared the LORD exceedingly, and offered a sacrifice unto the LORD, and made vows.

17 Now the LORD had prepared a great fish to swallow up Jonah. And Jonah was in the belly of the fish three days and three nights.]

The spirit of these comments is important. Notice the word sacrifice. So what this story is suggesting is Jonah only applied the remedy to a degree and then he had to apply it again to go the full measure. Other words, Jonah applied the remedy and became aware of the "wicked" ones but he was still afraid of them so he did not purge the "spirit of fear" fully so he had to apply the remedy the full measure.

[And he said unto them, Take me up, and cast me forth into the sea] He is sacrificing himself and the remedy is sacrificing one's self. Look at it this way, if you are in a spooky dark place and your hypothalamus tells you "run like the wind or you will die." and you ignore that, you sacrifice yourself mindfully. Abraham sacrificed Isaac but on a mental level. This remedy has nothing to do with literal sacrifice but the one applying the remedy has to fully believe it is a literal sacrifice or it will not work because the left brain aspect knows everything the being it "possesses" does.

[Jonah 2:2 And said, I cried by reason of mine affliction unto the LORD, and he heard me; out of the belly of hell cried I, and thou heardest my voice.]

[the belly of hell cried I,] This is out of sequence, it should be [the belly of hell I cried]. The belly of hell is the 9th circle of hell, treason.

[Jonah 1:12 ...., Take me up, and cast me forth into the sea] this is treason against ones self, mindful self sacrifice which is the remedy.

2/18/2010 8:48:09 AM – Hortus deliciarum is a medieval manuscript and in Latin it means Garden of Delights. In this manuscript there is a painting or picture called hell. I will explain to you what that picture means so perhaps you want to look it up as I explain it.

On the right side margin of the painting are bodies and there are nine bodies and they represent the nine circles of hell. The actual body of the painting only depicts four circles of hell but the bodies in the right margin suggest nine circles, nine bodies, so the painter has compressed the nine circles of hell into four circles perhaps to save space.

The upper level represents the first circle of hell and that is limbo. You can see there is some suffering going on but the characters on the left that are standing are not being tormented greatly. You can see the women has a snake wrapped around her and even some of the males have indications of a snake wrapped around them so the beings in this first circle are in full

186

grips of the left brain influence, known in the ancient texts as the serpent. This is not an indication about literal females it is a type of person that got the written education and for one reason or another they became popular or wealthy in the ways of the world and so they are oblivious to what the tree of knowledge has done to them mentally. Avoid assuming these people in limbo were born like this, the proper way to look at it is the education veiled their right brain so drastically they are what is known as the absolute chaff which means the education was fatal to them mentally. The beings in limbo cups are full which means they perceive their popularity or wealth proves they have figured out life so they cannot be reached which is a nice way to say their right brain ambiguity is so silenced they have closed minds completely. Relatively speaking the important thing to note in the upper circle is the people are not being tormented in contrast to the lower three circles. This is the trap of limbo, everything looks fine so everything must be fine. The beings in the first circle limbo are trapped by that perception. Something along the lines of "I have lots of money and comfort so I must be doing something right." And that is basing their understandings on a false indicator of value, vision or sight. Their mind is in a place where money equals happiness so that wealth proves they are wise and that proves there is nothing wrong with them. This level , limbo , is relative to , it is easier for a camel to do the impossible than for a rich man to find the kingdom, which is apply the remedy that is required to unveil right brain. Pontius Pilate and Herod were certainly not going to allow a being they had their guards pick up in the wilderness and wearing commoners clothes tell them about wisdom because they both had already assumed the material wealth they were surrounded by proved they were wise.

On the second level in this painting you will notice the beings are starting to be tortured, one being is lying on the ground and a demon is stabbing him. If you notice the first circle no one is being stabbed so this second circle shows that the suffering is starting to increase. The reality is one has to go through hell to get to heaven because a side effect of right brain unveiling is depression and suicidal thoughts and those are symptoms of grave suffering but depression is not depression it is a mental state where right brain is starting to unveil or starting to show signs it is coming back to the middle or coming back to the conscious state of mind. Simply put all the suicides in the world are essentially beings that did not make it through the depression stage of right brain unveiling after education veiled right brain. Another way to look at it is, right brain is going to unveil itself even if it kills the being because it should be in the conscious state of mind and a symptom it is close to unveiling is depression or suicidal thoughts. Simply put society makes no people wise with its education but it kills millions attempting to make them wise..

[C. S.(17) committed suicide, method unknown] This is what happens to the majority of beings when right brain starts to unveil. So this being was sensitive and so the education did not completely destroy their mind, so they were leaning to right brain unveiling and a symptom of that is suicidal thoughts but this being was not suicidal they just believed they were, in reality they were attempting to restore their mind but they perceived it was hell and treason against their self was the only solution, so they committed literal treason against their self. The last thing in this universe the ones that sense time understand is psychology because they are all mentally factually unsound. If you trust your children in the hands of a lunatic you are a lunatic.

In the third circle or level you will notice the large fire under the caldrons' the people are being cooked in. The large fires represent even more suffering. There is more suffering in this third circle than in the previous two circles above it. So these are people who are not suicidal but they are certainly depressed so that means right brain is starting to unveil but often they either go back up to the circle above it closer to limbo or they stay at this circle for the rest of their life but some go down to the 9th circle, treason.

The fourth level in this painting represents the ninth circle of hell and it is very obvious the suffering is greatest there. If you look at the picture of the devil in this ninth circle you will see there are heads underneath him, literal suicides, and also you will see mouths attached to him eating people. This represents the reality that once a person gets to the ninth circle they may very well end up literally killing their self. This is the price that has to be paid when traditional education which is all left brain favoring is pushed on the mind of a child starting at the age of seven when their mind does not even develop until they are twenty. That is what this comment means [Genesis 2:17 But of the tree of the knowledge of good and evil, thou shalt not eat of it: for in the day that thou eatest thereof thou shalt surely die.] If you are attached to the world in your sense of time state of mind you perhaps will not even attempt to apply the remedy and that means you will never restore your mind because you are not meek. Only the meek can apply the remedy and even then many of them do not make it. This is not an indication of the remedy it is an indication of how damaging all that left brain education forced on a child starting when they are seven is. One has to pay the piper and that is the one thing in this universe a being with a sense of time does not want to do. Your mind is your worst enemy in your sense of time state of mind and so you are your worst enemy. There is no one on this planet that cares if you apply the remedy or not, and no one is going to stop you from applying the remedy but you, and "you" is that left brain influenced aspect because it knows if you apply the remedy is loses all its power because right brain rules the mind in a 50/50 sound minded state of mind and that left brain cannot stand that reality so it is going to say everything in the universe to you except "Apply the remedy." I am not your enemy, you are.

On the left side of the painting in the lowest level, the ninth circle, there is a "saint" or what is known as the good shepherd. The good shepherd is not in the other circles but only in the ninth circle, not in the circle kind of on the side, so he is in that area, because the good shepherd knows only the meek , the depressed, the suicidal have a chance to "wake up". Jesus said if you want to follow me deny yourself and that is never going to go over well with a person that has even an ounce of arrogance. Do not save your life mindfully to preserve it. The only beings that sense time that are capable of grasping that reality are the depressed and suicidal so this good shepherd in there in the ninth circle of hell calmly suggesting to the depressed and suicidal "Before you literally kill yourself at least consider seeking the shadow of death and then letting go or fearing not or submitting." That is all the good shepherd can do because once a person is in the ninth circle they perhaps are going to literally kill their self. The ones that sense time literally kill people by pushing this written education on children and I write that in my book clearly. Any human being on this planet that supports, teaches or encourages written education being taught to small children without suggesting the potential mental side effects is a murderer. If you pay taxes to support it you are a murderer. If you teach it you are a murderer. If you are a leader and support it you are a murderer. If you are a parent that does this to your child you murder your own child. If you do not speak out against it you are a murderer. I would not tell you that if it was not fact. Now I will discuss something of value.

[C. S.(17) committed suicide, method unknown.] This child's parents murdered him, his government murdered him, his fellow citizens who support the education being forced on young children murdered him, his teachers murdered him, but he did not murder himself, he was in the ninth circle of hell attempting to undo the damage civilization did to him mentally and he did not make it through the meat grinder that is treason, the ninth circle of hell. It has never been about written education being bad on an absolute scale but like any tool if you do not use it properly you can run into problems. You teach that left brain favoring education on a child of seven whose mind is just starting to develop, you kill that child and there is no need to prove it to you because the above being C.S. has proved it to you. Perhaps you are not longer able to understand proof when you are looking at it. The main point about right brain relative to psychology is when right brain is at 50% in the conscious state it has random access thoughts so one thought such as depression or lust or greed cannot be maintain for more than a moment ever. So a state of depression cannot be maintained ever and since that is the case one cannot even reach a state of suicidal thoughts so suicides are a symptom right brain traits have been veiled as a result of all that left brain favoring education everyone gets as children. Even if you understand that, it does not mean you have applied the remedy so avoid talking yourself out of the one thing in this universe you do not want to do. Avoid allowing your infinitely low self esteem from thinking anything I say is a symptom I am special, I simply applied the ancient fear not remedy by accident so I am not special at all, you just have not applied the remedy so do not idolize me, idolize your right brain and you do that by applying the remedy.

11:26:40 AM – An email to someone about something.

[Clearly you have developed some strong views, ideas and theories.]

190

I am pleased you are mindful my theories and ideas are strong. It is important you question everything I suggest in my books because if I get warmed up to a stage I can make a convincing argument that traditional education taught to children at such a young age does in fact mentally hinder them there is going to perhaps be problems.

Giedd, Jay N. (october 1999). "Brain Development during childhood and adolescence: a longitudinal MRI study". Nature neuroscience 2 (10): 861-863.

"In humans, the frontal lobe reaches full maturity around only after the 20s, marking the cognitive maturity associated with adulthood"

[the frontal lobe reaches full maturity around only after the 20s] Since this is truth then pushing this [we have been traditionally taught to master the 3 R's: reading, writing and arithmetic -- the domain and strength of the left brain.] on children when they are seven is the same as pushing drugs on a pregnant mother when her fetus is in the first trimester.

fetus 9 months to mature
Child 20 years to mentally mature ["In humans, the frontal lobe reaches full maturity around only after the 20s]

So first trimester in a fetus is 1-3 months
So first trimester in a child is 1 to 7 years roughly

I can only humbly suggest I had a non physiological traumatic near death experience and this shocked me out of the neurosis the education caused and now I am showing lots of right brain traits.

"Neurosis is the inability to tolerate ambiguity." - Freud

Ambiguity is a right brain trait relative to [-"What it comes down to is that modern society discriminates against the right hemisphere]Roger Sperry (1973) - neuropsychologist, neurobiologist and Nobel laureate

Neurosis is society, because they all get the left brain favoring education which veils right brain.

.Neurosis(society) is the inability to tolerate ambiguity(right brain) = [What it comes down to is that modern society(neurosis) discriminates against the right hemisphere(ambiguity and other right brain traits)]

I only operate in real time, I am in a machine state now and as I typed this message I just figured out what Freud was saying or maybe I just figured out what Roger Sperry was saying about Freud.

I mean no harm but my purpose has already been determined I am nearly finished with the 15th book. I have published 14 in the fourteen months since the accident. They average book is about 80 to 100k words each. You do not know any human being in history that has published 14 - 80K word books 14 months in a row.

I will give you a demonstration of how powerful the right brain is. It uses its intuition and pattern detection to swiftly translate any information that is put in front of it. Here are some patterns.

"The tree of knowledge is not the tree of life! And yet can we cast out of our spirits all the good or evil poured into them by so many learned generations? Ignorance cannot be learned."
Gerard De Nerval

[tree of knowledge] = [[we have been traditionally taught to master the 3 R's: reading, writing and arithmetic -- the domain and strength of the left brain.]

[is not the tree of life] = tree of life is being mentally sound , both hemispheres in 50/50% in the east this state of mind is known as consciousness or nirvana, the middle way, Plato suggested this state of mind is the ideal plane, and in the ancient texts this state of mind is heaven

[And yet can we cast out of our spirits all the good or evil poured into them by so many learned generations?]

[good or evil poured into them] is relative to this ancient texts comment [Genesis 2:17 But of the tree of the knowledge of good and evil, thou shalt not eat of it: for in the day that thou eatest thereof thou shalt surely die.]

[good and evil] is seeing things as parts, a left brain traits , right brain is seeing holistically and when the mind is at 50/50 mental harmony right brain traits rule. This means any human being on the planet that is left brain dominate is mentally unsound because a being that is mentally sound shows right brain traits. The one deciding factor is sense of time. If one sense time mentally it means their right brain paradox aspect is absent from their perception. This no sense of time si also known as the fountain of youth, if the mind cannot sense time the body does not show symptoms of fatigue as readily.

[poured into them by so many learned generations?] This denotes the ones that get the written education became left brain influenced containers and left brain see's right brain traits as contrary and thus evil or bad. So an adult get the education and they are left brain influenced and when they see their child they determine they need to "fix" that child because left brain wants to make everything left brain (misery loves company)

[Ignorance cannot be learned.] Simply means children are conditioned into ignorance by this left brain favouring education, tree of knowledge. This line means children are not taught to be ignorant they are made ignorant by traditional education because it veils their right hemisphere.

So this comment :
"The tree of knowledge is not the tree of life! And yet can we cast out of our spirits all the good or evil poured into them by so many learned generations? Ignorance cannot be learned."
Gerard De Nerval

Written education is taught to children by the adults that got the education and it is only making the children see parts, good and evil, a left brain trait and that means it veils their right brain, it see's holistically.

Interestingly this being could not convince society of this and he eventually killed himself because some who wake up cannot stand the heat in this narrow so to speak. It is difficult to convince the neurotics, the ones that sense time, they literally mentally kill children with their wisdom education. That is unfortunate.

Here is another pattern:

"Sorrow is knowledge, those that know the most must mourn the deepest, the tree of knowledge is not the tree of life."
Lord Byron

[Sorrow is knowledge] This means once one gets the tree of knowledge, written education, their right brain is veiled and so they are mentally suffering, or put in the place of suffering, hell, because they have the powerhouse right brain veiled to a subconscious state so life becomes very hard for them which is logical because any creature needs both hemispheres to survive.

[those that know the most must mourn the deepest] This is relative to a comment in the ancient texts.

[Ecclesiastes 1:18   For in much wisdom is much grief: and he that increaseth knowledge increaseth sorrow.}

[[Sorrow is knowledge]] = [knowledge increaseth sorrow] Byron repeating the same premise in the ancient texts.

Simply put.. one gets the tree of knowledge and they have right brain veiled so they are in a mental state of sorrow, and ones who apply the remedy to the tree of knowledge, return to sound mind and become fully aware of what the tree of knowledge has done to the species and they have much grief because they cannot stop the lunatics from doing what they'd o to the children with the tree of knowledge.

194

[For in much wisdom is much grief:] The wise are ones who apply the fear not remedy and unveil right brain

[the tree of knowledge is not the tree of life.] This comment is a repeat of what the other being said [The tree of knowledge is not the tree of life!]

There is this pattern of repeating the same thing over and over because the ones that sense time are in such deep neurosis from the education they are what one might suggest is Slothful, or slow to understand and quick to judge.

The good news is understand the remedy and how anyone can apply it and the bad news is one that sense time is left brain influenced and the left brain does not want right brain to come back to 50% because then left brain traits are second fiddle to right brain, so that means any being that sense time is their own worst enemy and perhaps will not apply the remedy.

DONE

3:20:38 PM - Insanity: extreme foolishness, or an act that demonstrates such foolishness.

Foolishness: showing, or resulting from, a lack of good sense or judgment

[a lack of good sense or judgment] Right brain traits are fast processing speed relative to random access thoughts, intuition and pattern detection. The traditional education favors the left brain so in turn veils the right brain traits and intuition and pattern detection are certainly required so one can avoid [a lack of good sense or judgment]. Good sense is intuition. If you had good sense you would just sense improper cerebral deeds and improper actions but since your right brain is veiled you not only cannot sense written education with all its left brain favoring aspect may hinder the undeveloped mind of a seven year old, even when a person explains that to you in great detail you still cannot grasps that because you do not have good sense because you do not have anything but slight intuition because if you had good sense you would drop your nets and apply the remedy but since you have bad sense you just sit there on your hands because in your state of mind you cannot grasp the complexity, a right brain trait, that society itself robbed you of the only thing that matters in all of life and this is your sound mind you had as a child. I assure you the only beings on this planet that assume what I say is my opinion are beings with a sense of time and thus beings with right brain veiled and thus beings in full neurosis and thus beings that are factually insane. I am blessed that no one can understand anything I say ever into infinity.

2/19/2010 6:29:13 AM – A letter to someone about something.

[Mind always appreciates hearing people's opinions.]

I pondered your message and I am mindful you do sense time. If you were not in deep neurosis you would never say the spirit of what I suggest in my books is opinion.

I will tell you a fact and then when you read it and perceive it is an opinion you will understand you are in neurosis and out of touch with reality.

I walk through the valley of the shadow of death and i fear no evil.

This comment is a concept that is a fact.

If any human being on the planet that senses time gets into a situation they can get their hypothalamus to give them a death signal, and then they close their eyes and instead of running like a scared dog they just ignore that signal in about 30 days their right brain will unveil. That is a fact. This method takes one second to apply in the proper situation and works every single time it is applied and it is a one time thing. It is the remedy to the tree of knowledge. That is a fact.

The problem is one that sense time is in neurosis so this remedy appears dangerous to them because they are under the influence of left brain so they will attempt to explain how this remedy cannot work or is just opinion or how it is not important to apply this remedy because they are in neurosis and no longer have the mental ability to grasp reality and grasp an important concept when they hear it.

The main reason ones that sense time will not even attempt to apply the remedy is because going to a "spooky" place alone at night to get the hypothalamus to give that death signal scares them because their hypothalamus is giving them many false positives. The ones that sense time are scared little dogs, is the best way to look at it. Neurologically speaking it is a one second self control mental exercise.

The many years of left brain education has turned the mind into an abnormality.

[2 Timothy 1:7 For God hath not given us the spirit of fear; but of power, and of love, and of a sound mind.}

 [For God hath not given us the spirit of fear} This comment is saying Normally human beings should not be scared of dark spooky places. Now you are in the neurosis so there are perhaps many locations you would not want to go alone at night, perhaps a spooky house in the woods that has been abandoned. Human beings of sound mind are not afraid of spooky places at night but mentally unsound human beings are afraid of things they should not be afraid of. Perhaps the catacombs in Paris , going down to the 5th level and then turning out your flashlight and throwing it away should get that hypothalamus to give you the death signal and then you can ignore that signal and return to the world of the mentally sound, the ones that don't sense time. This comment is saying:

[For God hath not given us the spirit of fear; but of a sound mind.}
So if one reverse it:
The spirit of fear is a symptom of an unsound mind.

The problem with the ones that sense time is they do not know the difference between a fact and an opinion.
The ones that sense time perceive written education the tree of knowledge factually makes one wise but in reality it veils the right brain so written education pushed on a child starting at the age of seven factually makes one mentally hindered which means it makes one mentally retarded.
[Genesis 3:6 And when the woman saw that the tree ....to be desired to make one wise,]

You factually would not teach children an invention you factually understood make them mentally hinder and thus mentally retarded so you are out of touch with reality because you do support and encourage teaching children an invention that factually does make them mentally hindered, veils right brain aspect, and thus mentally retarded.

You believe factually written education, reading, writing and math does this : [make one wise,] but it does not because when pushed on a child of seven who mind is not even developed until the age of 20 it ruins their mind, factually. So you are out of touch with reality and thus in neurosis or simply put you know not what you do.

Friedrich Nietzsche "A casual stroll through the lunatic asylum shows that faith does not prove anything."

[lunatic asylum] = the ones that sense time, the ones who got the written education and did not apply the fear not remedy. Nezchez hit it right on the head because as I type this to you I am fully aware you are unable to grasp the concepts I am saying because at the end of the day you will mock this fear not remedy and you will do that by not even attempting to apply it because you are trapped by your own perception and you are trapped by your pride and so you have a full cup and have already determined there is no way this remedy could be true because if it is true, your entire world will collapse, so it is best that you just mocked this fear not remedy because if you discover it is truth and fact and works then you have to start your entire life over and throw away everything you have learned up to this point in your life and few are ever able to face that fact. If I had any faith in the ones that sense time I would write one book and leave it be, but instead I write infinite books. If I had any faith the ones that sense time would stop harming the children by pushing the written education on seven year old innocent beings who's mind is not even close to being developed I would write one book and get on with my life but instead I am trapped here in infinity writing books for the rest of my life because I am fully aware I cannot convince a blind man blindness is abnormal.

END

Talk about toying with the mice.

Because left brain is sequential based it is also simple minded in contrast to right brain, it lacks the ability to think on a complex level. So one's that sense time lack the ability to think on a complex level because they only have sequential based thought processes. What this means is whatever the ones that sense time cannot control they destroy and whatever they cannot destroy they control. Control is a left brain aspect. Since the ones that sense time only have sequential based thoughts they cannot make a very convincing argument and so they are not really able to control ones that are of sound mind, ones with no sense of time, so they tend to resort to the next best thing which is physical violence or physical control. A good example is the ones that sense time could not get Jesus to stop saying what he was saying.

[Luke 4:32 And they were astonished at his doctrine: for his word was with power.]

It is one thing to have a doctrine. It is another thing to be able to explain that doctrine flawlessly. The ones that sense time have many little doctrines but they just never reach the stage they can explain it flawlessly so they falter in their ability to explain things because the complex machine, right brain is veiled in them. Jesus along with the disciples had the doctrine explanation down perfectly and many listened to them and started to "see the light" relative to the dangers this written education has on the mind. But they were not suggesting some original idea they were simply agreeing with what the ones in the Torah were suggesting.

[Mark 12:37 David therefore himself calleth him Lord; and whence is he then his son? And the common people heard him gladly.]

[Mark 12:38 And he said unto them in his doctrine, Beware of the scribes, which love to go in long clothing, and love salutations in the marketplaces,]

So Mark 12:37 is saying the people heard David suggesting "Beware of the scribes", the ones that sense time, the ones that got the education and did not apply the remedy and they heard him gladly.

[Beware of the scribes, which love to go in long clothing, and love salutations in the marketplaces,]

This comment is saying the ones who eat off the tree of knowledge and do not apply the fear not remedy show symptoms of being physical focused relative to what they see as value because their right hemisphere is veiled so they lost their cerebral power. So this being is saying you did not spit on David when he said what I am saying but now you spit on me. What this indicates is, after some time passes people start forgetting to apply the fear not remedy and they eventually all become "cursed" again. They all fall back under the curse caused by the tree of knowledge. But the complexity is written education looks flawless, it looks like there could not possibly be anything wrong with it ever. Go ask anyone that senses time anywhere if there are any possible mental side effects from learning all that left brain favoring education starting as a child of seven and they will say "There is no indication it could ever harm the mind." That is reality to them because no government on the planet has ever suggested there could be some mental side effects caused as a result of traditional education. No government on the planet. So either this is the greatest lie in the history of mankind, civilization [Beware of the scribes] or civilization is a greatest liar or at least the most ignorant fool in the history of mankind. The deepest reality is the ancient texts give a version of history that suggests written education, the tree of knowledge, does in fact hinder the mind and thus the spirit and civilization gives an exact opposite suggestion that written education not only does not hinder the mind but it actually makes one wise. But the proof is when one applies the remedy and they wake up to the fact civilizations argument is anti-truth and anti-fact and the ancient texts are the truth and the fact and the light. It is one thing to call civilization a liar and anti-truth and out of touch with reality but it is another thing to explain why it is flawlessly. That's what the beings in the ancient texts could do and civilization was unable to stop them or control them or shut them up so they had to eventually just come up with an excuse to kill them because they would have exposed civilization for what it is, a mental harmer of children, and the common people would have had civilizations head on a stake sooner or later. One big problem in this situation is women are very protective of their children or women are the protectors of the offspring and these beings were explaining that this written education was harming their children and it may appear that the men would be most upset but in reality the men became upset because the women became upset. For example if someone harms a child the mother of that child will explain that to her husband or male mate and then that male mate will take action so it is more the women are the ones who find this mental harm of children more devastating than the men. The pecking order is males are defenders of the women and the women are defenders of the children but these ancient texts appear to be mostly male dominated but that is only because the males did the fighting, but the females were behind that fighting but did not do the actual fighting. The story about Helen of Troy launching a thousand sinking ships full of men is a good example of this. In many species the males do not have the same attachment or feelings about children or the offspring like the females do. So the females are the protectors of the offspring and the males assist the females to facilitate that reality. The story about a woman's honor being insulted and the male defending that woman's honor is another way to look at it and even in nature one can usually see the female protecting the young from the males. There is a saying behind every great man is a female is another way to look at it. Even from ant colonies in nature the males have been systematically purged completely so the ant colony is all females but it would never work the other way around so clearly the females are the dominate, they just are so clever so to speak they allow the males to believe they are not dominate. Because of this one can see why explaining written education hinders the mind of children would upset the females and the females would suggest the males should therefore defend the children.

[Deuteronomy 2:34 And we took all his cities at that time, and utterly destroyed the men, and the women, and the little ones, of every city, we left none to remain:]

And we took all of his cities, of the ones that sense time, and destroyed the men that sense time, the women that sense time and the little ones that sense time and left none to remain. The logic of this tactic is once the women get the curse the offspring are doomed. Once the women get the education their offspring will also get the curse because the women are the big influence in a child's life. When a soldier is dying on a battle field they yell for their mother not for their father.

There are patterns in these texts were they suggest women and little ones, children, as being connected .

[Joshua 8:35 There was not a word of all that Moses commanded, which Joshua read not before all the congregation of Israel, with the women, and the little ones, and the strangers that were conversant among them.]

[with the women, and the little ones]

[Deuteronomy 20:14 But the women, and the little ones, and the cattle, and all that is in the city, even all the spoil thereof, shalt thou take unto thyself; and thou shalt eat the spoil of thine enemies, which the LORD thy God hath given thee.]

[women, and the little ones]

This comment is actually suggesting the women are discussing the exploits of the men as if they are calling the shots.

[1 Samuel 18:7 And the women answered one another as they played, and said, Saul hath slain his thousands, and David his ten thousands.]

[women answered one another] = having a meeting or conference among their self.

[, and said, Saul hath slain his thousands, and David his ten thousands] = the exploits of the men and what exactly are the exploits of the men?

[[Mark 12:37 David therefore himself calleth him Lord; and whence is he then his son? And the common people heard him gladly.]

What was David's doctrine or what was David's drive? [Beware of the scribes]

Who was the Goliath David faced fearlessly? Civilization, the ones that sense time, the ones that push the tree of knowledge on the children and in turn veils the children right brain, the god image in man.

[[Mark 12:38 And he said unto them in his doctrine,[Beware of the scribes], which love to go in long clothing, and love salutations in the marketplaces,]

Why would David's doctrine be , beware of the scribes? Because the scribes harmed the children and the women are not pleased when their offspring are harmed.

[1 Samuel 18:7 And the women answered one another as they played, and said, Saul hath slain his thousands, and David his ten thousands.]

The women are having a meeting and saying David and Saul are defending the offspring as we suggested they do.

[Saul hath slain his thousands, and David his ten thousands.] Who are they slaying? The scribes, the ones that sense time, the ones that push the education on the children and mentally hinder the children and thus harm the children.

[Beware of the scribes] David and Soul are defending the offspring of the species at the request of the women. Simply put the males are not the protectors of the offspring the females are and the females use the males to accomplish this defending of the offspring aspect.

[Exodus 35:25 And all the women that were wise hearted did spin with their hands, and brought that which they had spun, both of blue, and of purple, and of scarlet, and of fine linen.]

[And all the women that were wise hearted] = The women who did not get the written education or got the written education and then applied the fear not remedy were [wise hearted], had right brain unveiled. The females are calling the shots it is just the males are the warriors and that appeals to males so it appears the males are the dominate topic in these texts but in reality they are doing the bidding of the females because the females are the protectors of the children. There is a story about a child that was sexually abused by a male and the father of that child took a gun down to the police station and shot the one who abused his child so it appears the father avenged his child being sexually abused but in reality it was the mother who the father was acting for. It was the mother of that child the father of that child was avenging. The male was protecting the offspring for the mother. In contrast to the females the males do not really care about the children and this is obvious in nature in many ways especially in mammals. There will perhaps not be any females that would argue with that but perhaps there are many males that will argue with that. Even in a pride of lions the female is protecting the cubs from the males. In a pride of lions without the females there the males would perhaps kill the cubs. Males are not supposed to be good with children, males are supposed to defend any threats to the females because the females are good with children so to speak. Perhaps it does not take any great amount of wisdom to understand this reality. We are mammals and perhaps with all the other mammals the females defend the offspring so it is logical this tree of knowledge appeared, written language, and it harmed the little ones, and so the males were called on to defend the little ones at the request of the females thus : [1 Samuel 18:7 And the women answered one another as they played, and said, Saul hath slain his thousands(scribes, ones that sense time), and David his ten thousands(scribes).]

This neurosis caused by the education has made our species forget what reality is. Our species has their perception altered by the education so our perception of reality is altered so we are in some altered reality that is opposite to actual reality as a species because the written education has altered our perception. So there are not many books in the ancient texts written by women because they did not get the "script" education because they were keepers of the offspring. Simply put, it is not women were dumb because they did not get the written education it is because they were [And all the women that were wise hearted]. One is not dumb if they cannot use written language well it is factual proof they are wise, do not have right brain veiled, but civilization only see's the opposite of reality because their perception is altered so they say "if you cannot spell words you are dumb" but the fact is, a being that cannot use written language at all is a being that is of sound mind and there may only be 50,000 or less of them left on the planet and they live in the wilderness and all the gold and money in the universe would not convince them to come live in civilization. Other words if a person lives in civilization, around ones that sense time, even if they cannot use written language they still are influenced by the curse the ones that sense time have, so the only true sound minded beings left are the ones that live in the wilderness and civilization calls them "savages" and that is perfectly logical because civilization has it perception altered and see's everything as the reverse of what it really is. This of course is complex because the beings in the ancient texts explained this fear not remedy and that means one can negate the mental neurosis caused by the written education and return to sound mind but they are still going to be surrounded by the ones that sense time. So one can negate the curse but they can never get back to how they were before the curse so this means the curse does take a toll on one's mind. A human being that is seven cannot have their mind bent to the left when their mind is not even developed before they are twenty and expect to undo that and everything is fine but one can greatly improve the situation they are in mentally by applying the remedy. Another way to look at it is, it takes one a while to adjust back to sanity after the education puts one in neurosis. This is relative to this transformation aspect , one completely has to learn everything all over again after they apply the remedy but not relative to someone teaching them but relative to [Mark 1:13 And he was there in the wilderness forty days, tempted of Satan; and was with the wild beasts; and the angels ministered unto him.]

[and the angels ministered unto him.] Right brain once it is unveiled will minister to you. It is a machine so it will take everything you know and have in your mind and everything you have ever learned and sort it all out and then you will teach yourself in real time from then on out and no one can really teach you anything anymore they can just say things to you and that puts more data into the machine and the machine will come to further understandings. It perhaps sounds very arrogant but that is only because you have been conditioned to hate right brain aspects. This is the proper way to look at it [Matthew 20:28 Even as the Son of man came not to be ministered unto, but to minister, and to give his life a ransom for many.]

[the Son of man] = a being who got the written education . Man being the ones that sense time in this comment relative to [Genesis 11:5 And the LORD came down to see the city and the tower, which the children of men builded.]

[children of men] = [son of man]

The logic being, if one never gets taught the written education they have no need to apply the remedy but also if one hangs around the ones with a sense of time they also may start to exhibit their traits which is relative to the concept of contact. Like in the television shows where they say "This native tribe has never had contact with civilization." So that means that native tribe does not have the curse of civilization, of course that perhaps is beyond your ability to grasp.

Another way to look at this situation relative to Jesus is , if Jesus did not get the written education he would not have been able to read the ancient texts in the temple as a child. So since he did read , he also could write and that means he did get the tree of knowledge and so he had to apply the remedy, which was in his case John the Baptists version of the fear not remedy, baptism, dunking you under water and when the hypothalamus says "you will die if you do not rush to the surface" you then "fear not", which is a rather dangerous version of the fear not remedy and that is perhaps why Jesus adopted his own version "those who lose their life (mindfully) preserve it." Buddha starved for 39 or 43 days and at one stage in that progression it occurred to him that he may die and lose his life but he did not fear that so he feared not, and that is how he woke up, but he did not go around telling people to starve to death nearly to wake up, he said go sit in a dark cemetery at night alone and mediate. I am not suggesting you take a handful of pills and then when your mind says "you are going to die" you fear not, because it does not have to be that dangerous. So Jesus went through the baptism and realized it does not have to be that dangerous, and that is why he say "deny yourself;" which is what "those who lose their life(mindfully) preserve it" means. Jesus realized it was a mental exercise not a physical exercise. The kingdom is within, right brain is within, your mind is within, so there is no reason to put yourself in literal danger to apply this remedy only a situation where your hypothalamus that is giving lots of false signals to begin with, will perceive the shadow of death and then you fear not. Another way to look at it is you may not be afraid of death but if you sense time your hypothalamus is afraid of a bad haircut and words and you are at the mercy of your ill functioning hypothalamus and until you shock it back into reality it will keep your right brain veiled and you will be stuck with simple minded sequential thoughts and have to live out your life with your emotions turned up to dangerous levels and stuck with the inability to think clearly. This is a very interesting comment relative to when Jesus was a child but it is more relative to children or speaking about children.

[Luke 2:46 And it came to pass, that after three days they found him in the temple, sitting in the midst of the doctors, both hearing them, and asking them questions.

Luke 2:47 And all that heard him were astonished at his understanding and answers.]

[sitting in the midst of the doctors, both hearing them, and asking them questions.] Think about someone that has a doctorate degree. That means they have lots of traditional education. So this child is speaking to beings who have lots of education and [And all that heard him were astonished at his understanding and answers.] These beings with lots of education were astonished by his understandings. These beings with lots of education were listening to child with no education and they were astonished and wondering what all their education did for them at all, if this child with no education was wiser than they were. Simply put , I only have a high school education but since I accidentally applied the ancient fear not remedy I understand things you will never ever learn in school so what did all your schooling do for you outside of make you mentally hindered and thus simple minded and thus unwise? What did your big doctorate degree do for you if a stupid high school educated being is infinitely wiser than you will perhaps ever be. Perhaps your degree is nothing but a piece of paper you can boast about and be proud of and allow you to make money but has nothing to do with your mental clarity outside of the fact you perhaps have none at all if you have not applied the remedy after getting all that traditional education. You are astonished by my understanding but my purpose is to convince you that you have a right hemisphere that was veiled by traditional education and all you have to do is apply the fear not remedy and then you can astonish the ones that sense time with your understandings. I cannot veil my right brain, my mind is developed, all I can do is explain right brain is very powerful and explain how you can unveil it but no matter what happens I cannot go back to the neurosis I was in. I cannot go back to blindness I can only attempt to convince you to come to the world of sight. If you do not believe you are blind you cannot come to the world of sight because you believe you are already in the world of sight so your cup is full, you are arrogant. If you see the darkness world you are in as light then you will see the light as darkness and you will avoid it. You have to have faith that even in the dark spooky place you go to apply the remedy even if your mind tells you something in that dark spooky place will kill you, you must understand dark spooky places have never killed anyone so you just ignore what you mind says when it says "Run like a scared little dog a spooky dark thing is going to kill you." If you desire you can take your diploma and rub it on your forehead and see if you that will make you lose your sense of time and unveil your right brain just so you can come to the understanding that piece of paper you spent all that effort acquiring is totally worthless in this narrow.

10:01:16 AM –

"Is it not a species of blasphemy to call the New Testament revealed religion, when we see in it such contradictions and absurdities."

Thomas Paine

One may read these comments and assume Thomas Payne was not fond of the ancient texts but in reality he was denying himself. Thomas Payne certainly had not applied the remedy so he was saying things he perceived were wise but in reality if one flips them they will see they were exactly opposite of wise. Here is an example : [when we see in it such contradictions and absurdities.] A paradox is two contradictions that equate to a truth. One who has right brain veiled, one that senses time, will assume contradictions are absurd. So this comment by Thomas Payne : [when we see in it such contradictions and absurdities.] is proving the ancient texts are authentic because they were written by beings who had unveiled right brain and so it is logical they would have lots of paradox, paradox denotes complexity a right brain trait, in their words and ones that sense time see paradox as a contradiction and thus as absurdity. So Thomas Payne was insulting the ancient texts but that only made people that sense time think poorly of him and so he was denying himself, he was bringing insults upon himself and that is a form of denying one's self. Prostration is a from of denying one's self and also submission is a form of denying one's self and that is what is required for one to unveil right brain. If one walks through the valley of the shadow of death and then fears not they deny their self because their self, the left brain influence, wants them to run and fear the shadow of death. The deeper reality is everyone has a right hemisphere relatively speaking and once one gets the education it becomes veiled and so they are often saying things that are accurate but they do not aware they are accurate because they see the reverse.

Thomas Payne is making this [when we see in it such contradictions and absurdities.] sound like it is a bad thing but in reality it is proof the ancient texts are authentic. Simply put he knows not what he is saying. He said this comment with the understanding he is making an insult to the ancient texts but now it is revealed he is showing they are authentic. This is what the reverse thing is. In psychology it is understood just because a person says something it does not mean that is what they mean. For example a female may leave a male and that male may assume that female dislikes them but sometimes that means that female likes them so much she is leaving him because she likes him too much. But even then that does not mean that female is consciously aware that is why she is leaving him. This is the reality of what this written education does to the mind. It makes a person unconscious mentally. Not literally asleep but simply not in touch with the thoughts signals that are in their mind. Another way to look at it is every single person has moments of clarity but the reality is when the remedy is applied ones only has clarity and that is consciousness. One should not have an epiphany they should be an epiphany at all times in their thoughts. Every thought they have should lead them to new understandings always no matter what but if one has right brain veiled then they may only experience that reality a few times in their entire life. Right brain does not detect a beginning or an end so the epiphany never stops. I detect wisdom in everything everyone says but they may not detect it but that reality is because they have right brain inputs coming into their thoughts that are veiled or silenced so they often get translated backwards. Religion is simply a method to undo the mental damage written education does to the mind and the beings who wrote these texts had the foresight to understand everyone was going to get this written education because it is a very attractive Trojan horse so there cannot be any being of sound mind who would suggest the religious texts are bad because then they are suggesting a sound mind is bad and only a being of unsound mind would ever suggest a sound mind is bad. If a being does not understand that is what the ancient texts are talking about, the perils of this tree of knowledge, written education, then they cannot possibly be a proper judge of the texts. The texts are not based on opinions they are factual testimonies of human beings who applied the fear not remedy after getting the written education. If one takes a gun and shoot their self in the leg and then writes a book and says "I shot myself in the leg and the bullet harmed me." that is not an opinion that is a factual testimony.

This is not an opinion:
"In humans, the frontal lobe reaches full maturity around only after the 20s, marking the cognitive maturity associated with adulthood"
This is not an opinion:

[we have been traditionally taught to master the 3 R's: reading, writing and arithmetic -- the domain and strength of the left brain.]

This is not an opinion:

"What it comes down to is that modern society discriminates against the right hemisphere." - Roger Sperry (1973) - neuropsychologist, neurobiologist and Nobel laureate

This is not an opinion:

[Genesis 2:17 But of the tree of the knowledge of good and evil, thou shalt not eat of it: for in the day that thou eatest thereof thou shalt surely die.]

This is not an opinion:

[Luke 17:33 ....; and whosoever shall lose his life (mindfully) shall preserve it.]

If one cannot determine what an opinion is and what a fact is then they are in a serious pit of mental trouble. If one cannot detect wisdom when they see it then they will end up following fools and thus become fools.

This is not supernatural:

[we have been traditionally taught to master the 3 R's: reading, writing and arithmetic -- the domain and strength of the left brain.]

This is not supernatural :

"In humans, the frontal lobe reaches full maturity around only after the 20s, marking the cognitive maturity associated with adulthood"

This is not supernatural :

"What it comes down to is that modern society discriminates against the right hemisphere." - Roger Sperry (1973) - neuropsychologist, neurobiologist and Nobel laureate

What it comes down to is YOU discriminate against the right hemisphere, because you are a left brain container and the proof is that you sense time, of your own child or you would not push all that left brain written education on them when they are seven so it is best you give your child over to beings that are intelligent enough and dedicated enough to ensure your child's mind is not ruined by the education. Do not do it for yourself, do it because you do not want to do it, deny yourself. You sense time, so you are not supposed to do things that please you, you are suppose to do things that deny you. You are suppose to destroy your temple in that sense of time state of mind you are in not build upon it because it is built upon sand and thus cannot stand. I have infinity to rip you to shreds mentally and I am pleased with that prospect. I will now discuss something relevant. I do not sense time and you do so one of us is factually hallucinating and I am wise enough to understand that.

One complexity of this creativity leading to God as the Pope suggested, right brain the God image in man is creativity is a subtle path. The fear not remedy and the like is the beeline and then there are many subtle paths and the problem with the subtle paths is one slowly goes into the 9th circle of hell, treason. This is exactly why some very creative people from artists to musicians and singers sometimes end up committing suicide or dying from drug overdose and the like. This is not a recent reality, this spans all the way back in history and this is also not relative to just creative aspects relative to the arts, it also applies to creative aspects relative to science and math because they are require creativity.

Alexander, Henry (ca. 1860-1894) - American painter - Drank carbolic acid.

Arbus, Diane (1923-1971)American photographer - Took a lethal dose of barbiturates and slashed her wrists.

Gertrude Margaret Lowthian (1868-1926)- English architectural historian - Overdosed on sleeping pills in Baghdad.

Bonvin, Léon (1834-1866) French watercolorist - Hanged himself from a tree in the forest of Meudon, after a Parisian dealer rejected his paintings.

Borromini, Francesco (1599-1667) Italian architect - Threw himself on a ceremonial sword, then lingered for another 24 hours.

Bugatti, Rembrandt (1884-1916) - Italian sculptor and draftsman - Put on one of his finest suits and gassed himself.

Bupalos and Athenis (active ca. 540-ca. 537 BC) Greek sculptors - Rumored to have been driven to suicide by the nasty, albeit poetic, written attacks of Hipponax (who apparently didn't like their sculpture of him).

Carrington, Dora (1893-1932) - English painter and decorative artist - Shot herself a few weeks after the death of her companion, Lytton Strachey.

Czigány, Dezsö (1883-1937) - Hungarian painter - Committed suicide in a psychotic fit, but not before killing his family.

Fagan, Robert (1761-1816) - English painter, archaeologist and dealer - Jumped out of a window in Rome.

There are some common facts relative to all of these people. One fact is they all got written education which is, they were taught the script and perhaps many were also taught the mathematics as children. [we have been traditionally taught to master the 3 R's: reading, writing and arithmetic -- the domain and strength of the left brain.] So they had their right brain veiled and as one embraces creativity more and more a right brain trait they get closer to the circle of hell called treason and once a person is in the 9th circle one will either literally kill their self, wake up, or go back to the higher circles of hell and in these beings cases they did not wake up they literally killed their self. So as one favors creativity or starts favoring right brain aspects at all, such as saying perhaps often, the side effect of that is depression and suicidal thoughts because one has to go through that treason level of hell to get to heaven. So the Pope suggested creativity is one path to God but in reality it is suggesting creativity is one path to the 9th circle of hell treason and if one survives that they find heaven, they unveil right brain. Now because you sense time you are thinking this is all dangerous but the reality is, it is dangerous to push left brain education on the delicate mind of a seven year old child, so do not complain about the remedy because you started the fire to begin with. The ones that sense time start the fire and then complain about the water needed to put the fire out.

There are infinite books of wisdom in these two comments:

[Exodus 2:11 And it came to pass in those days, when Moses was grown, that he went out unto his brethren, and looked on their burdens: and he spied an Egyptian smiting an Hebrew, one of his brethren.

Exodus 2:12 And he looked this way and that way, and when he saw that there was no man, he slew the Egyptian, and hid him in the sand.]

[when Moses was grown] This means Moses applied the remedy in one way or another and one understands he had to because he was found by royalty relative to civilization and it is understood they certainly "educated" Moses. Royalty in civilization would certainly give a child the best education civilization could offer, so to speak. So Moses applied the remedy and then his intuition, a right brain trait, kicked in and he became aware, or his eyes were opened and what he saw was: [and looked on their burdens:]. The burdens of the common people relative to what this education was doing to them then [he spied an Egyptian smiting an Hebrew, one of his brethren.] So Moses saw one with a sense of time taking advantage of one that did not sense time and he killed him. But the comment is much more complex than that. Moses freed the people from the tyrants, the ones that sense time and also killed the army the tyrants sent to try and get back their slaves so he killed them there also. The reality of this line is Moses applied the remedy and went on a war path against the ones that sense time, civilization. You may be under the impression you are going to apply this remedy and reach inner peace and spend the rest of your life with a smile on your face. Here is how you will feel after you apply the remedy. You will feel like you just realized you got raped into hell and there is nothing you can do to stop others from being raped into hell and that is all you are going to understand for the rest of your life and so the initial sensation you will get after the several months of right brain unveiling is you are going to be the most angry being on the face of the planet and righteously so. You are going to wake up after you apply the remedy and fully be aware someone abused you mentally beyond the scale that any law could compensate you for so you only have one emotion shortly after you wake up and that is infinite rage on a cerebral level. If you doubt that even slightly it is only because you sense time and you are still asleep. What is interesting is the no sense of time is actually the biggest shock to your mind at first and then the rage and then the heightened awareness just keeps getting strong and stronger and you become aware of so much suffering around you and you cannot do anything about it and so to even suggest the beings in the these ancient were anything but full of this cerebral rage or this cerebral grief means you do not understand the texts at all. Go ask a rape victim how they feel about being raped and then multiply that by a billion and then factor in your mind was stolen from you and you have to mindfully kill yourself to get it back and then factor in you get no compensation for that and then factor in when you tell people your testimony they laugh in your face and spit on you and say you are crazy. I do not detect you are going to be feeling much peace, love, and happiness after you wake up although your delusional fantasy land ideals perhaps suggest you will. Love is a being that wakes up, one with no sense of time, and is willing to shepherd the ones that sense time down to the 9th circle of hell with the understanding that once in that circle some will literally kill their self and not wake up. Is that what your teacher told you love is because if they didn't they are a liar. You have no idea what this narrow is. I am feeling writey.

[Exodus 2:12 And he looked this way and that way, and when he saw that there was no man, he slew the Egyptian, and hid him in the sand.]

[And he looked this way and that way, and when he saw that there was no man] This suggests first degree murder or intentional intent to kill someone.

[and hid him in the sand.] This is tampering with the evidence or concealing the evidence. What this shows is he knew exactly what he was doing. He knew exactly what he was doing so he had no doubt about who the adversary was. The good news is this rage you will feel after you apply the remedy will soon be reduced by the extreme cerebral aspects. It works like this. After you wake up the rage will be intense and you have to block that rage and as you do, you will concentrate better and better and that is what the warming up process is all about. You will either be destroyed by your grief and rage after you apply the remedy or you will purge them and become a master at concentration. This does not mean you will not have moments of rage but instead of going out and harming someone you will use your "ministered unto him" purpose to vent that rage. Of course some beings are given the go to actual war purpose. I got the write infinite books purpose, some get paint pictures purpose, some get make movies purpose and some get, go speak in public purpose. I cannot assist you at all after you apply the remedy because then you are a sound minded being and can think for yourself. You defeat your fear of death so then you get a purpose or a mission and then you carry out that mission and no being with no sense of time will ever get in the way of your purpose but there are many that do sense time that will attempt to. All of this could be avoided if the ones that sense time simply had a little patience with the children and taught the education with slightly more foresight but that is fantasy land thinking because they are all asleep and have no idea what that even means. To suggest to the ones that sense time they should perhaps not be pushing all the left brain education on the mind of a seven year old child whose mind does not even develop until they are twenty seems like evil or hateful or the devil to them. It is simply obvious common sense but the ones that sense time have absolutely no common sense because that is intuition, a right brain trait. My purpose is that I am not allowed to raise a finger to harm anyone but when it comes to my books I let all my rage out with all of my might into infinity and that is righteous. So you see your fear tactics do not work on me in any meaningful way because death itself ran from me so death is the one thing in the universe that is no longer real to me, so anything less than death is laughable and so is death. Self defense applies on both fronts. I am pleased if they determine it is best to burn my books because then the common people will have to hang them from the tree of liberty.

[That whenever any Form of Government becomes destructive of these ends (freedom of speech, freedom of press), it is the Right of the People to alter or to abolish (exterminate) it, and to institute new Government,]

You are going to need a bigger boat. I keep forgetting you do not even know what the tree of knowledge is in literal terms. I am avoiding finishing the Jonah story. I go to great efforts to avoid efforts.

"America is a mistake, a giant mistake."

Sigmund Freud

It's a mistake as long as your definition of a mistake is an anarchy, anarchy is what freedom is. Has that occurred to any of you in America yet? We are an anarchy.

Anarchy: the absence of any formal system of government in a society.

"Government is not reason; it is not eloquent; it is force. Like fire, it is a dangerous servant and a fearful master. " - George Washington

[the absence of any formal system of government] = [Government is not reason] = there should be no government at all because it is insane, antonym of reason is insane. Only a tyrant would argue with that fact.

You would not know an anarchy if you lived in a country founded by anarchists. We sure have a lot of laws considering we are an anarchy. I will approach it from another angle.

[[That whenever any Form of Government becomes destructive of these ends (freedom of speech, freedom of press), it is the Right of the People to alter or to abolish (exterminate) it,] We are allowed and it is our right to abolish the government at any moment and so we are an anarchy. Independence is anarchy. It means you get to determine for yourself your life liberty and pursuit of happiness. That is what an anarchy is. You get to make your own decisions in an anarchy and you do not get to make your own decisions in a tyranny. There are no other forms of government on the planet but tyrannies. In a tyranny people are not equal, there is a ruler and then the ones lower than that ruler are his servants and in an anarchy everyone is equal so there is no ruler. In America as long as you do not infringe on another person's right to life, liberty and pursuit of happiness it is proper and that is anarchy.

Anarchy: the absence of any formal system of government(a ruler) in a society.

Only a tyrant or control freak would argue with that fact. Think about a school of bait fish and there are thousands of them and they are all swimming around and no one is telling them what to do but somehow they remain in a school but still there is no ruler bait fish telling them what to do, that is anarchy, other words, people are allowed to do as they please with the understanding eventually they may school together and accomplish something or not. Of course when you were seven some ruler control freak decided you are going to get their brand of education and so your delusions of freedom and free will died then. I find it hard to believe Freud's job title wasn't "World's greatest comedian" because he has such a long list of inside jokes my ribs hurt when I even think of his name.

Neurosis is the inability to understand what the tree of knowledge literally is. Neurosis is the ability to sense time and the inability to understand that ability is abnormal.

2/20/2010 7:21:02 AM – [Jonah 2:5 The waters compassed me about, even to the soul: the depth closed me round about, the weeds were wrapped about my head.]

This is a cerebral comment relative to what one experiences after they apply the remedy to full measure. So Jonah applied the remedy to a degree but then when he was compelled to speak his testimony he feared so he had no applied the remedy all the way so then he sacrifices himself and in this case into the water, the sea. This is perhaps where John the Baptist got his baptism idea, using water as a method to get the hypothalamus to give one the death signal.

[the depth closed me round about, the weeds were wrapped about my head.] This is relative to cerebral aspects. This is saying Jonah was confused after he applied the remedy. After the right brain unveils about a month after the remedy is applied one is very confused because one is not accustomed to such cerebral power and this is relative to the transformation cerebrally speaking. It is like going from tricycle cerebral thought's to space shuttle rocket booster thoughts and it takes time to get accustomed to. One will literally assume something is very wrong because they have never felt such cerebral power but one adapts and this stage passes within several months.

[weeds were wrapped about my head.] This denotes confusion.

[Jonah 2:6 I went down to the bottoms of the mountains; the earth with her bars was about me for ever: yet hast thou brought up my life from corruption, O LORD my God.]

[I went down to the bottoms of the mountains] What is the bottom of a mountain? A valley, relative to I walked through the valley of the shadow of death and fear not evil. So by throwing himself into the sea he was seeking the shadow of death, so to speak. A valley is a depression, and is relative to the state of mind one has to be in to apply the remedy, depressed , relative to the meek shall inherit the earth. The meek are the depressed.

[thou brought up my life from corruption] This is just saying this time the remedy worked the full measure. Jonah was brought from the neurosis,

218

mental corruption(right brain veiled), into the light, he unveiled right brain fully, returned to sound mind, both hemispheres working equally.

[Jonah 2:7 When my soul fainted within me I remembered the LORD: and my prayer came in unto thee, into thine holy temple.]

This is suggesting he died to himself. He let go of his old self. "Soul fainted within me". The holy temple is the right brain, the god image in man, the holy spirit. This is also similar to the comment about the angels were ministering to him. Right brain was starting to sort things out in his head. So at first when right brain unveils one is confused [weeds were wrapped about my head.] and then one starts to slowly come up to speed this is relative to the mental transformation or being reborn.

[Jonah 2:8 They that observe lying vanities forsake their own mercy.] This is a conclusion he is coming to during the adjustment period. He is starting to become aware. He is speaking about the ones that sense time. The ones that sense time deny the tree of knowledge has any effect on their mind so they forsake their mind because they never apply the remedy. This comment is another way of saying the ones that sense time are their own worst enemy. Of course on an absolute level left brain does not want right brain to become unveiled because when left and right hemispheres are in equal power right brain traits dominate and left brain is reduced to second fiddle and it cannot stand that reality, it is jealous of right brain and in turn hates right brain. Simply put, Cain cannot stand Abel because well Abel, right brain, is just so powerful Cain cannot compete and is always reduced to second fiddle in contrast to right brain in an equal contest. No beings defeated the ones that have applied the remedy they only defeated their self by talking their self out of applying the remedy.

[They that observe lying vanities forsake their own mercy.] You can mock what I suggest about this remedy and spit on me but in the end it's your sound mind you are mocking and robbing yourself of by not applying the remedy. Have mercy on yourself and apply the remedy to return to sound mind because by not applying the remedy you leave yourself in a mental state of suffering, the place of suffering, hell.

[Jonah 2:9 But I will sacrifice unto thee with the voice of thanksgiving; I will pay that that I have vowed. Salvation is of the LORD.]

The key word in this comment is sacrifice. So now Jonah has sacrificed himself into the sea to apply the remedy the full measure, he is now ready to sacrifice himself by speaking to the ones that sense time. He is no longer afraid of Goliath and his vast armies, is one way to look at it. Once the right brain unveils this aspect called ego goes away and ego is relative to the spirit of fear so when the ego goes so does the fear. If one has fear they will be hesitant to give their testimony after they apply the remedy about the dangers of written education on the mind so this comment is saying: Jonah applied the remedy the full measure this time and he is ready to testify. All one can do after they unveil right brain is to keep testifying and getting better and better at explaining the situation with the understanding they are speaking to beings who have been mentally pushed into such a deep neurosis they may never actually convince the ones that sense time of anything at all. It is not the people that will dislike you, it is the people are under the influence of left brain and left brain only see's right brain traits as bad because they are totally contrary to left brain. If you try to appease the ones that sense time all you will really do is deny your own testimony. By telling the truth you make enemies and that is as good as it gets in this narrow.

[Jonah 2:10 And the LORD spake unto the fish, and it vomited out Jonah upon the dry land.] So this is similar to this comment, [Mark 1:13 And he was there in the wilderness forty days, tempted of Satan; and was with the wild beasts; and the angels ministered unto him.]

So Jonah was ministered to for three days and nights, in that fish, but that is just a contrast statement, similar to how Jesus said I will tear down the temple and rebuild it in three days. [And he was there in the wilderness forty days] and this comment is similar to Jonah who was in the belly of the fish for three days, the ocean is the wilderness.

[tempted of Satan; and was with the wild beasts;] this is similar to saying I was in the belly of a big fish, a beast. I prefer not to reason with you but logically if this is not a concept statement this being in the belly of fish, then it means he defied the laws of nature because there is no oxygen in the belly of a fish, so one has to be mindful these comments are not literal they are concepts. Right brain deals with concepts. It uses parables to explain cerebral concepts. For example and not that I ever get off topic:

[John 2:19 Jesus answered and said unto them, Destroy this temple, and in three days I will raise it up.]

This is a concept statement relative to the transformation one under goes mentally after they apply the remedy but the ones that sense time are left brain influenced and they assume it is literal and they said this.

[John 2:20 Then said the Jews(ones that sense time that say they are Jews(Lord Lords) not True jews), Forty and six years was this temple in building, and wilt thou rear it up in three days?]

They assume Jesus was speaking literally but he was not so Jesus was coming across as being violent by saying "tear down this building" but the building he was speaking about is within and is relative to the transformation of the mind after one applies the remedy but because he was speaking to ones that sense time, the ones in neurosis they could not understand what he was saying and so they assumed he was a dangerous man. One has to be careful what they say to the lunatics, the ones that sense time. I am no such fish because I do not pander to what I own. The ones that sense time will attempt to put you on the defensive because they perceive they do not mentally harm children with written education so it is important you understand who is who. They are at fault, they harm children, they are in neurosis, they are mentally unsound so they cannot even grasp that so pay no heed to their attempts to get you to deny your testimony because they are in deep neurosis and are doing the best they can to make you flounder. They are factually mentally unsound mentally ill beings and so take everything they say with that in mind or they will start to make you doubt yourself. Look at them as illusions and then they just become voices that are not even relevant. Do not reason with them because they do not have the ability to reason because they are insane. It's harder than it seems because your eyes will only see perfection in them but their words are only lies so it is quite a battle even after you apply the remedy or perhaps the real battle starts after you apply the remedy is another way to look at it.

[Jonah 3:1 And the word of the LORD came unto Jonah the second time, saying,]

So now that Jonah applied the remedy to the full measure he was again compelled to testify against the tree of knowledge, written education.

[Jonah 3:2 Arise, go unto Nineveh, that great city, and preach unto it the preaching that I bid thee.]

What is he preaching? He is telling the ones that sense time all that left brain favoring education is veiling their right brain, the god image in man, and they must apply the fear not, sacrifice remedy to restore their mind or preserve their mind. [preach unto it] denotes the ones that sense time are no longer human beings they are a beasts, "it". Where are these beasts at? [go unto Nineveh, that great city] in the cities. So this city is just like Sodom and Gomorrah. Cities are a symptom of the left brain education but also cities are just cities so they are not good or bad just like all these aspects relative to the ones that sense time are not good or bad they just are. The whole point of these texts is, written education is a tool and if taught improperly, to children at a young age, one has to apply the fear not remedy to restore their mind and that is all. These physical details are not a problem as long as one keeps the covenant, applies the remedy, and in turn restores their sound mind after eating off the tree of knowledge. The ones that sense time are in the cities and like today the ones that do not sense time, the ones that never got the education are in the wilderness, for example the ones that live deep in the Amazon. So in part this story is talking about how Jonah was in a battle because he was at first afraid to testify to the ones in the city and then he applied the remedy the full measure and now he is fearless. I can make vague comments, the tree of knowledge and fear not, relative to written education and relative to the remedy until the end of time and perhaps never accomplish anything but I am mindful to just come right out and say specifically written education and math and specifically the fear not remedy and explain it in detail, and the ones that sense time perhaps do not understand either of those

222

explanations so there is no point to beat around the bush. The ones that sense time do not understand either method. The ones that sense time only see the truth and the facts as lies anyway so no need to create vague explanations.

[Jonah 3:3 So Jonah arose, and went unto Nineveh, according to the word of the LORD. Now Nineveh was an exceeding great city of three days' journey.]

This comment is saying Jonah was finally ready to begin is testimony so he went to the cities to begin speaking his testimony.

[Jonah 3:4 And Jonah began to enter into the city a day's journey, and he cried, and said, Yet forty days, and Nineveh shall be overthrown.]

This comment is saying this particular city listened to Jonah or would listen to Jonah and they would apply the remedy. Overthrow means this city would apply the remedy and go from left brain influenced containers back to sound mind, right brain influenced containers. So Jonah knew he applied the remedy so well he could explain the problem and convince this city before he even entered the city, his intuition was at full power.

[Jonah 3:5 So the people of Nineveh believed God, and proclaimed a fast, and put on sackcloth, from the greatest of them even to the least of them.]\

[So the people of Nineveh believed God] This is saying Jonah gave his testimony and the people of this city believed his testimony and believed in right brain so to speak and they began to deny their self, which is what the remedy is. They fasted, that is a form of denying one's self but also a symbol their sense of hunger was reduced, because when right brain paradox is activated after the remedy is applied one has no sense of hunger.

[and put on sackcloth] is a form of denying one's self relative to this comment [Mark 12:38 And he said unto them in his doctrine, Beware of the scribes, which love to go in long clothing, and love salutations in the marketplaces,]

[Beware of the scribes, which love to go in long clothing] The scribes, the ones that sense time are very material focused because they have no cerebral aspects because their right brain is veiled so the opposite of [love to go in long clothing] , which is nice pretty clothes, is [and put on sackcloth]. This is not suggesting anything but a contrast. The proper way to look at it is once one applies the remedy all these material things lose their value or one is no longer focused on material thing as much because their cerebral wealth is so great the material things all take a back seat. This has nothing to do with morals it is just one restores the genius mind they were born with and the material desires tend to fade away.

[Jonah 3:6 For word came unto the king of Nineveh, and he arose from his throne, and he laid his robe from him, and covered him with sackcloth, and sat in ashes.]

Jonah pulled a cu de gra , which is what this comment is saying [Yet forty days, and Nineveh shall be overthrown.] All this means is Jonah convinced the King the ruler that written education does veil the right brain the god image in man and this King saw the "light" and so the city became mindful of that and so they were mindful to apply the remedy after getting the written education. Moses spoke to the King, the Pharaoh and attempted to do the same thing but was not successful. There is a story in the New Testament where the disciples spoke to a governor of a country and they were unsuccessful but in this story Jonah was successful in reaching the King and making a valid argument. The complexity is, once a King or Government is convinced, they must inform the common people of the mental side effects written education has , and that is a huge can or worms due to liability and payment to the people who got the written education or at least methods to assist them to apply the remedy and restore their minds. This of course also means the governments are not going to be trusted by the common people perhaps ever again after that. But this story of Jonah is suggesting at least one city and one king was reached and Jonah convinced that king of the need for the remedy and the king understood him and adopted the remedy so this story is certainly an optimistic story up to this point. The logic is the left brain influenced common people will listen to their King or ruler and so if one can convince the ruler or King the remedy is needed then that King will tell the common people and they will follow that direction because left brain likes to follow directions or like to be told what to do and this is contrary to right brain intuition so right brain can think and figure out what to do on its own. So in that respect this story is a tactic. It is saying skip over all the common people and attempt to convince the rulers of the ones that sense time and if one can accomplish that then the common people that sense time will also be convinced because they will listen to their "ruler". It is certainly a bold tactic. Moses attempted this tactic on the Pharaoh for example.

[he laid his robe from him, and covered him with sackcloth, and sat in ashes.] This is just suggesting the King applied the remedy and all the sudden all his great material wealth was not very important to him because he found the kingdom, so to speak. This is very similar to the Queen in modern times who was on her death bed and found the kingdom after being mindful of death from being bed ridden so long and said something along the lines of "My entire kingdom for a moment more" just before she died. One might suggest unveiling right brain makes all material wealth look like a folly for fools, Right brain is simply so powerful one cannot even explain it in infinite books but one is so pleased to return to sound mind they are compelled to explain it to others.

[Jonah 3:7 And he caused it to be proclaimed and published through Nineveh by the decree of the king and his nobles, saying, Let neither man nor beast, herd nor flock, taste any thing: let them not feed, nor drink water:

Jonah 3:8 But let man and beast be covered with sackcloth, and cry mightily unto God: yea, let them turn every one from his evil way, and from the violence that is in their hands.]

So these two comments are what is known as denying one's self. This King is making everyone apply the remedy.

[taste any thing: let them not feed, nor drink water:] this is relative to denying one's self, and fasting. [be covered with sackcloth] this is also relative to denying one's self and detachment.

[let them turn every one from his evil way, and from the violence that is in their hands.] And this comment is what is hoped to be accomplished as a result of the above denying of one's self. Turn from their wicked ways, which simply means they unveil right and return to sound mind. So wicked is simply a being that senses time and that ability to sense time is evidence right brain paradox no longer figures into their perception of time so they do sense time mindfully, and after the remedy is applied they lose sense of time and that is because right brain aspects are restored so they are not longer wicked or a beast, mentally unsound and so they act less violent and behave more docile and peaceful and in harmony like mammals should.

[Jonah 3:9 Who can tell if God will turn and repent, and turn away from his fierce anger, that we perish not?

Jonah 3:10 And God saw their works, that they turned from their evil way; and God repented of the evil, that he had said that he would do unto them; and he did it not.]

The spirit of this comment is simply saying, the people applied the remedy and returned to sound mind and the people in this city were better off for it. They started to notice a reduction in the problems that were caused by being in an unsound state of mind such as greed, lust, envy, anger. This of course is logical. If one returns to sound mind life itself becomes easy again and so there is not all this stress and nervousness on an individual level and thus the stress of this entire city was reduced so life returned to how it should be, a pleasing stress free experience instead of this stressed out fear filled existence one experiences when one has their right brain veiled, being able to think clearly is also a nice perk. The city achieved this "good will among men" state because the King was reached by Jonah and he understood what Jonah said and so the king forced the city to apply the fear not remedy or deny one's self remedy. Do not become complacent by this story. The reality is written education is taught and there is no mention firstly of its mental side effects in society and secondly there is no mention of the fear not remedy. When all is said and done one must seek the shadow of death in the valley, depression, and then fear not, deny their self, or submit when the hypothalamus detects that shadow of death coming. Do not attempt to assume because you read my words you are me. I applied the remedy accidentally you have not so we are adversaries in every definition of the word adversary. I do not sense time and you do so you are not me. Avoid trying to talk yourself out of applying the remedy. You are reading concepts and ideas that can only be achieved when right brain is unveiled. You sense time so your right brain is veiled so you have to apply the remedy. If you understand what I say but do not apply the remedy you do not understand what I say.

[and he did it not.] This is a form of random access because it should be [he did not do it]

[Jonah 4:1 But it displeased Jonah exceedingly, and he was very angry.] So Jonah reached the King of this city and convinced the King to force the city to apply the remedy but Jonah was angry or displeased. Jonah applied the full measure remedy. He sacrificed himself in the sea but he did not tell the King that is the full measure remedy. Jonah settled for explaining a lukewarm version of the remedy, simple fasting and denying material wealth. So again Jonah was in a battle because he did not do what he was compelled to do instead he settled or he reasoned with the ones that sense time. He did not say "seek the shadow of death and fear not" because if he did the King would have laughed at him and mocked him and called him crazy so he settled and just said fast and avoid material things and mediate but that is not the full measure remedy it is just a lukewarm version of the remedy.

[Jonah 4:2 And he prayed unto the LORD, and said, I pray thee, O LORD, was not this my saying, when I was yet in my country? Therefore I fled before unto Tarshish: for I knew that thou art a gracious God, and merciful, slow to anger, and of great kindness, and repentest thee of the evil.]

Jonah is simply saying "Why have you forsaken me Lord." The reality is the mental damage this written education does to the mind is so devastating it is not ever about these beings not having a proper explanation or reasons one should apply the remedy, it is simply a child is seven and gets the education and their mind is not even developed until they are twenty so their mind is bent into some state that in all reality they may never achieve the mind set to even understand they need to apply the remedy. It is essentially fatal to the mind and once in a while a seeker will be able to apply the remedy but essentially the damage is permanent in most people. Jonah is starting to understand the scope of the devastation relative to how damaging the education is on the mind and he is unable to stop it or hardly even convince anyone to apply the remedy. He is throwing the rules down on the rocks as Moses did, so to speak. Jonah is coming to understand there is no way to reverse the "curse" on our species relative to [Genesis 3:14 And the LORD God said unto the serpent, Because thou hast done this, thou art cursed above all cattle, and above every beast of the field; upon thy belly shalt thou go, and dust shalt thou eat all the days of thy life:]

[thou art cursed... all the days of thy life] This means once this education is taught to a small child the mind is essentially ruined for the rest of the beings life and it is a miracle above all miracles if one is able to apply the remedy the full measure and return to sound mind. No wonder I no longer speak to you.

[Jonah 4:3 Therefore now, O LORD, take, I beseech thee, my life from me; for it is better for me to die than to live.]

Jonah is struggling with the awareness that he cannot stop the curse. Jonah is experiencing the exact same thing Moses experienced and what all beings who applied the remedy the full measure experienced.

[Exodus 32:19 And it came to pass, as soon as he came nigh unto the camp, that he saw the calf, and the dancing: and Moses' [anger waxed hot], and he cast the tables out of his hands, and brake them beneath the mount.]

[and Moses' anger waxed hot, and he cast the tables out of his hands] = [I beseech thee, my life from me; for it is better for me to die than to live.]

It is a paradox. On one hand a being who applies the remedy fully never ever gives up ever in explaining the remedy and on the other hand they are fully aware they cannot stop the spread of the curse on a species wide level. Jonah convinced this one city to apply the remedy but he was fully aware there were many cities he could not convince so this victory in this city was a failure because if one cannot convince everyone, the ones who are not convinced will continue to put the "curse" on the children but because of this never being able to win aspect one becomes better at concentration and in turn betters their self or they implode as a being and destroys their self. Simply put after you apply this remedy because of this narrow we live in, you will either focus on the log in your eye and become a Master of concentration or you will seek death because you cannot stand the heat in this kitchen. Perhaps you have seen far too many fantasy fairy tale endings, this reality is no such thing at all.

[Jonah 4:4 Then said the LORD, Doest thou well to be angry?]

This comment is really saying focus on the log in your eye. Jonah's anger is waxing and he is pondering it and realizing is anger is not going to change anything. He is asking himself "Is getting upset assisting you to concentrate so you can better yourself or it is only making you become more angry?" But again this is not fantasy land. Many allow their anger to get the better of them once they apply the remedy because the heightened awareness is just too great. It is best related to by imagining looking outside your window and see many children being abused to unimaginable levels and you are frozen and unable to do anything about it so your mind is screaming to assist the little ones but you cannot move and cannot do anything for them and freeze that image in your mind for infinity and one can understand what this is [and Moses' anger waxed hot]. That is why it is very important to be mindful of focus on the log in your eye because no matter what happens many beings who get this education are fatalities relative to the fact they simply cannot escape that mindful place they have been put in or fallen to. For example even if every leader in the world said "it is important to apply this remedy because you got written education." That does not mean much of anything at all because at the end of the day the remedy is mental suicide. Only the meek, the depressed, the suicidal have a chance to apply the remedy and the world does not have six billion suicidal people relatively speaking so it is a very dark reality relative to our chances as a species escaping this written education induced neurosis.

[Ecclesiastes 1:18 For in much wisdom is much grief: and he that increaseth knowledge increaseth sorrow.] = [I beseech thee, (take)my life from me; for it is better for me to die than to live (in this grief).] = For in much wisdom(awareness) is much grief. So this cerebral giant is realizing all the cerebral power in the universe is no match for the neurosis or curse this written education causes on the mind. Jonah was wiser than any human being this planet will ever know yet in the face of the curse he was defeated swiftly. Jonah applied the remedy so he had no sense of time so he was in infinity and realized he could not defeat the curse on the species and he had all infinity to live with that reality so he was begging for death because in infinity one day is like a thousand years. This of course in not to be confused with depression, it is a cerebral sensation, and this is just a passing sensation, a moment of doubt. I wake up every day and start the battle again and by the end of the day I am defeated and then I go to sleep and wake up and I am ready for another day of getting annihilated by the heightened awareness but I never stop and I never sense I lost the day before, I only know I can better myself today and then I am defeated again into infinity. I do not have time for vacations or fun because I am far too busy getting annihilated. I am mindful I never stop writing and I never take a break and I do this until I can no longer do that and that is as good as it gets and I am pleased for the opportunity. I am in the machine state and the program has been initiated.

[Jonah 4:6 And the LORD God prepared a gourd, and made it to come up over Jonah, that it might be a shadow over his head, to deliver him from his grief. So Jonah was exceeding glad of the gourd.]

[to deliver him from his grief] Relative to [For in much wisdom(awareness) is much grief]. This is simply saying because right brain is random access, ones thoughts change swiftly. One second a being is thinking they are defeated by the curse and then the next moment they see a new angle to take and so they have hope and then they swiftly go back to a moment of doubt and so ones overall mind set is neutral, so one is reduced to just doing. They never maintain a state of hope or depression they just do, they are in a machine state. There is no other purpose in life but to stop the curse and it perhaps cannot be stopped so one has a great purpose or much purpose. If one cannot stop the curse the whole species is doomed to this mental suffering so any other purpose outside of stopping the curse is vanity, yet the curse is on a species wide level and can perhaps never be stopped. If you doubt that call the board of education and ask them if they warn the parents or children of the potential mental side effects of written education on the mind of a young child and ask them if they suggest the fear not remedy after one gets the education and you will understand any optimism you have is simply a symptom of your blindness. So in the above comment the gourd was a moment where Jonah was relieved of his grief from his extreme awareness that he could not stop the curse. The gourd means Jonah was pondering a new strategy and preparing to jump back into the battle so he could get his teeth kicked in again. The gourd is a moment of clarity and an escape from the grief but both are of course short lived due to the random access aspect of right brain. I am certain your cult leader of course explained all of this to you when they told you the tree of knowledge is written education and math.

[Jonah 4:7 But God prepared a worm when the morning rose the next day, and it smote the gourd that it withered.]

This is very accurate. Jonah got some sleep and in the morning he was ready for the battle again. I call sleep regenerating because one can sense when they need to rest because their mental clarity starts to diminish and that means one starts to become very docile and starts having this sensation that they can win the battle so one becomes complacent so to speak, and that means they must rest and when they wake up they are fully rejuvenated and understand there is no beginning and there is no end to the battle. Sometimes it is the opposite also, when one gets docile they become very defeated. One can look at the infinite battle as job security.

[and it smote the gourd that it withered.] So Jonahs moment of rest with gourd = [the LORD God prepared a gourd, and made it to come up over Jonah, that it might be a shadow over his head, to deliver him from his grief] , was over and now he was back to the battle.

[Jonah 4:8 And it came to pass, when the sun did arise, that God prepared a vehement east wind; and the sun beat upon the head of Jonah, that he fainted, and wished in himself to die, and said, It is better for me to die than to live.]

[the sun did arise] Simply means Jonah had a rest and woke up and he saw with full heightened awareness again and realized he could not win this battle against the curse, the ones that sense time and he wanted to die again. It is an interesting cycle that is happening but it is suggesting the same day over and over. It is an infinite cycle that our species is trapped in this curse. A long time ago someone got written education and then they taught their child and both of them got their right brain veiled and could not even tell and so they taught it to their children and here we are 5000 years later and we are fruits of that event of 5000 years ago and once in a while someone figures out a way to escape that curse and attempts to explain it to the rest of the species and the rest of the species, the ones that sense time, only sees the explanation as insanity because they are insane and thus see sanity as insanity. I am under no obligation to prove anything to anyone the last I checked. I am only obligated to give my testimony to the best of my ability and that is it. I do not detect anything is going to happen to anyone after they die if they do not apply this remedy because I am not a sorcerer. I am explaining the remedy to the tree of knowledge so one can return to sound mind and if you do not wish to restore your mind that is none of my business because I am in infinity no matter what you do. I am not going to use scare tactics on you like the scribes use on you. It is very difficult to apply this remedy so the proper way to look at it is , no pressure because to apply this remedy one needs their full mental power relative to the fact if one senses time they only have 10% mental power.

[Jonah 4:9 And God said to Jonah, Doest thou well to be angry for the gourd? And he said, I do well to be angry, even unto death.]

Jonah is understanding his anger and grief is a gift.[I do well to be angry, even unto death.] He is understanding although he may not be able to convince anyone to apply the full measure remedy so if he does not look at his grief and anger caused by his heightened awareness of that reality as a blessing it will kill him. He is saying I prefer the hottest coals because the hottest coals are all he has, denoting the extreme heightened awareness. Any happiness you have is nothing but a symptom of your ignorance and a symptom your right brain is veiled because when you unveil the machine it is so powerful your awareness is so great and in this narrow, grief will be your only happiness but quite often a nice gourd comes along and takes the edge off and that is as good as it gets. Your level of happiness in this narrow is relative to your level of ignorance about this narrow so pray for grief, a symptom of awareness.

[Jonah 4:10 Then said the LORD, Thou hast had pity on the gourd, for the which thou hast not laboured, neither madest it grow; which came up in a night, and perished in a night:]

This is saying although when you wake up after sleep the heightened awareness is very strong and causes much grief you will become tired again and get to sleep and the heightened awareness will be reduced and so you get some rest. Of course with no sense of time a day lasts a thousand years so it is complex. Freud or Jung said something along the lines of "My battle is mine." This means a being that applies this remedy is still a student because they have to learn how to be a sound minded human being and there is no one that can assist them or tell them or train them, they have to learn on their own. This is the unspoken reality of ones who apply the remedy, once one applies the remedy they are on their own. There are no teachers for the ones who have applied the remedy, they are only teachers who assist the ones that sense time to apply the remedy. What this means is once you apply the remedy you know exactly what I know so we have nothing to discuss, we just go about our purpose. This is why Jesus told the ones who did apply the "deny yourself" remedy, go unto the world and spread the news, because Jesus could no longer teach them for they had applied the remedy and become teachers. This teacher student relationship ends when the student applies the remedy and the teacher is no longer of value to that student because that student becomes the teacher. All teachers relative to this remedy are saying the exact same thing in many variations "seek the shadow of death and fear not". "Seek the shadow of death and then lose your life mindfully (let go) to preserve your mind."

[Jonah 4:11 And should not I spare Nineveh, that great city, wherein are more than sixscore thousand persons that cannot discern between their right hand and their left hand; and also much cattle?]

[And should not I spare Nineveh, that great city, wherein are more than sixscore thousand persons that cannot discern between their right hand and their left hand] Jonah ends his testimony with a question.

[persons that cannot discern between their right hand and their left hand] Left and right hand is left and right hemisphere. He is asking himself "Should I just attack that city and kill six thousand people to stop the curse because they are too mentally far gone to even tell the difference between a being in neurosis and a being that is of sound mind? This question is a symptom of right brain traits , it is very questioning or very curious just like little children are. Little children ask lots of questions almost to the point a being that senses time cannot even figure out what the point is of the questions at all, but right brain is just very curious or likes to ponder. The answer to the question gives right brain more data to ponder and thus it can ask more questions and so the final answer is not even important , right brain just likes its pondering. Like scientists and experimenters are not really as interested in the results of the experiments as much as the answers to the experiments lead them to more questions and that is an infinite cycle.

This is relative to the "book" Apology of Socrates written by Plato:

"But far more dangerous are these, who began when you were children, and took possession of your minds with their falsehoods, telling of one Socrates, a wise man, who speculated about the heaven above, and searched into the earth beneath, and made the worse appear the better cause."

[But far more dangerous are these, who began when you were children, and took possession of your minds with their falsehoods]

[But far more dangerous are these] = the ones that sense time, the scribes.

[who began when you were children, and took possession of your minds with their falsehoods] = How did the scribes take possession of your mind as a child?

[[we have been traditionally taught to master the 3 R's: reading, writing and arithmetic -- the domain and strength of the left brain.]

234

Simply put, the education favors left brain and after years of this it alters ones perception and if another being alters your perception they alter your mind so they have brain washed you or controlled your thoughts because all of your thoughts are relative to your perception. Whether a being knowingly or unknowingly alters another beings perception using this left brain favoring education is not important at all, the fact is ones perception is altered and thus ones thoughts are altered and thus ones thoughts are controlled.

[telling of one Socrates, a wise man, who speculated about the heaven above, and searched into the earth beneath,] This comment is an indication Socrates was a curious man, he asked a lot of questions. Questioning things is relative to right brain traits it has lots of ambiguity so it asks lots of questions. Contrast that concept with this comment by Buddha " Do not take the word of a blind man ask questions." In a tyranny there is one thing a tyrant will not stand for and that is a person that asks a lot of questions. Thus the comment by Freud "Neurosis is the inability to tolerate ambiguity (questions)" Left brain dislikes questions and right brain is based on questions and that is why children ask so many questions and parents says "Stop asking so many questions." Parents are the ones with the inability to stand the questions of the children. Parents get the education and become left brain influenced and then the children ask them questions and they cannot stand that and seek to make the children like they are so the children stop asking so many questions. I apologize I am beyond your understanding.

"If one does not understand a person, one tends to regard him as a fool."- Carl Jung

The last thing Socrates said relative to his trial and trail was a deep pondering.

[The hour of departure has arrived, and we go our ways - I to die, and you to live. Which is better God only knows.]

[I to die, and you to live. Which is better God only knows.] Socrates was saying if you kill me at least I do not have to be around you mental abominations any more, and although I die I get to get out of this narrow and you get to live but your living is death and my death is relief. The ones that sense time did not kill Socrates they freed him they just thought they killed him. And that is the same with all of these wise beings. The ones that sense time never killed them they freed them from this narrow. [I to die, and you to live. Which is better God only knows.]

.[Genesis 3:6 And when the woman saw ... a tree to be desired to make one wise..]

"When your lost in deep despair you just ask the lonely" - Ask the lonely – Journey

The lonely are the ones with no sense of time because they have this burden to convince the world about the tree of knowledge and the ones that sense time hate them and spit on them so they are lonely like Moses who went off alone in the end, up on the mountain because he was defeated by the cursed. Moses was: [I do well to be angry, even unto death.] Grief is a gift.

Greif : the cause of intense, deep, and profound sorrow(not sorrow, grief), especially a specific event or[situation](the curse caused by the tree of knowledge and the inability to stop it)

Sorrow is being unable to think or "see" clearly, grief is being able to think and thus "see" clearly. Sorrow is the result of being mentally hindered and grief is the result of being conscious and aware of what is happening in this narrow.

[Ecclesiastes 1:18 For in much wisdom(one that applies the fear not remedy) is much grief: and he that increaseth knowledge(tree of knowledge) increaseth sorrow.] The more of that wisdom education ones gets the more veiled their right brain becomes and thus the more sorrow they experience because they cannot think clearly with an unsound mind. Silly pattern detection.

6:58:35 PM – Jonah applied the remedy the full measure on his second attempt. He then became so wise or a better way to look at it is he unveiled right brain so well he walked right into a city and said "let me speak to the King" and he spoke to the King and convinced that King to apply the remedy and ensured everyone in that city applies the remedy and then Jonah realized after he did this, that was not good enough because written education is such an attractive golden calf even if he convinced the entire world to apply the remedy eventually one person would teach another person the written education and the curse would start all over again. But Jonah summed this entire reality up in four chapters and small chapters at that. He applied the remedy to a degree and then realized he still had the spirit of fear and applied the remedy the full measure and then went out and attempted to convince the Rulers of the need to apply the remedy after getting the education and did that with no problem and then realized that was not good enough to stop this curse caused by the written education on the species. He ended his testimony with a question . [Jonah 4:11 And should not I spare Nineveh, that great city, wherein are more than sixscore thousand persons that cannot discern between their right hand and their left hand; and also much cattle?]

He is saying perhaps Noah's solution is the only solution. What that means is, civilization today cannot survive without written education and math therefore we are doomed to remain in this curse forever and ever as a species. It is the age old reality that you can sell your soul for a luxury or you can choose not to sell your soul(mind) for some luxury but on a species level we sold our soul for some luxury called written language and math 5400 years ago and there is perhaps no possible way to stop it on a species level because there is always going to be someone that is going to teach it and then not suggest the remedy or even be aware of the remedy so the curse will revive and spread again. We sold our soul as a species for this written education and math and we cannot take that back as a species but on an individual level one can apply the remedy, but on species level we are permanently mentally hindered as a result of this invention we created. The Quran 37:139 – 37:148 speaks about the book of Jonah so certainly Mohammed read this question posed by Jonah [Jonah 4:11 And should not I spare Nineveh, that great city...?] This is the end enlightenment question. One applies the remedy and unveils right brain and if they go the full measure right brain sifts through all the data and comes to this final question. Everything relative to the species of mankind comes down to these options.

Option 1: Do everything in ones power to defend the children from having their right brain veiled by the written education because they are the life spring of the species.

Option 2: Focus on the log in your eye and face the reality you have no sense of time so you are going to spend infinity watching the children being mentally harmed and thus observing the fruits of that for infinity. For example:

S. W. (29) allegedly committed suicide by overdose

K. H. (25) allegedly committed suicide at his home

D. G. P. (15) committed suicide by gunshot

One being in these texts gave his opinion.

[John 15:13 Greater love hath no man than this, that a man lay down his life for his friends(the children).]

When one applies the remedy they restore their right brain so they revert back to how they were mentally as a child relative to mental harmony so their friends are the children.

Another being answered the end enlightenment question:

[Genesis 6:7 And the LORD said, I will destroy man(ones that sense time, the ones who veil the children's right brain using written education) whom I have created from the face of the earth; both man, and beast, and the creeping thing, and the fowls of the air; for it repenteth me that I have made them.]

It is regrettable as a species we have yet to understand pushing left brain favoring education on a child of seven, whose mind does not even develop until the age of twenty, has devastating mental side effects on the mental development of that child's mind and thus affects that child's entire life and thus that child's "fruits" thereafter.

Other beings answered:

[Genesis 19:13 For we will destroy this place, because the cry of them(the ones that sense time) is waxen great before the face of the LORD; and the LORD hath sent us to destroy it.]

One may be thinking there is a proper answer or a correct answer to this question but the reality is once a person applies the remedy they are "ministered" to and they are the only one that can answer this question for their self. There is no absolute correct answer because no matter which answer one chooses the species has fallen from grace mentally because of this tree of knowledge invention. There are beings that have applied the remedy to a degree that have gone mad attempting to decide what to do about the [persons that cannot discern between their right hand and their left hand], the ones that sense time. I perceive I will be far more effective writing books but so far I am only writing poorly disguised thick pamphlet diaries. I am blessed no one can understand anything I say ever, into infinity.

[Jonah 4:11 And should not I spare Nineveh, that great city, wherein are more than sixscore thousand persons that cannot discern between their right hand and their left hand; and also much cattle?]

[And should not I] is out of sequence so it is a sign post of authenticity. It should be [And should I not]

To sum up the book of Jonah, he unveiled right brain so well that he reduced the entire situation and eliminated all details and went to every conclusion possible and ended with a question. "Should we just start all over as a species?" And that is an indication of impossibility. It is as simple as this. We can get rid of this curse but we have to get rid of all forms of written education and since that is never ever going to happen we are trapped in this pit forever as a species. Because of that reality what is the point of all this control and rules and locking people in jail for stupid reasons and wars and pitting country against country and all this economic competition crap? We already killed ourselves off mentally as a species with this wisdom education many years ago so what is your point with all of your control structures? Perhaps respect everyone's life, liberty, and pursuit of happiness and that includes giving everyone a choice about what kind of mind they wish to have and that is relative to what kind of education they wish to have is the only logical or required rule on this planet since we are already mentally ruined as a species anyway. There is perhaps only one line in these texts that is of any value to our species at this point in time. [Genesis 2:17 But of the tree of the knowledge of good and evil, thou shalt not eat of it: for in the day that thou eatest thereof thou shalt surely die.] The deeper reality is right brain does not bother with anything but impossibility because possibility situations are left to left brain. Left brain wilts in impossible situations and right brain thrives.

[1 Corinthians 4:20 For the kingdom of God is not in word, but in power.] This means the kingdom is veiled by written education, written "word", script. The power of right brain is hindered by learning written education math and script. The comment seek the kingdom first simply means in this life you can have a sound mind or you can have written education and math and all the education in the universe is not going to make up for the fact it veils your right brain. The beings in these texts were saying thousands of years ago "Wake up and think about what you are doing with that new invention you have, demotic script." and our species missed that boat and now our boat is sunk. No need to panic it is just impossibility.

Please be mindful the ones that sense time are in deep neurosis and mentally hinder the children with their "brand" of written education because they have no conscience, right brain intuition, and thus they know not what they do.

It takes courage to see the emptiness and fearlessness to understand the sorrow in it.

This is not an opinion:

X ="In humans, the frontal lobe reaches full maturity around only after the 20s, marking the cognitive maturity associated with adulthood"

This is not an opinion:

Y = [we have been traditionally taught to master the 3 R's: reading, writing and arithmetic -- the domain and strength of the left brain.]

This is not an opinion:

Z = "What it comes down to is that modern society discriminates against the right hemisphere." - Roger Sperry (1973) - neuropsychologist, Nobel laureate

Modern society is civilization.

Because of X , Y mentally hinders the right brain which is what Z is suggesting.
I accidentally negated that neurosis or mental hindering and restored right hemisphere traits and I understand how anyone can do the same.
 Any human being on the planet that gets this [reading, writing and arithmetic] as a child becomes mentally hindered. I am not suggesting ghosts, lizard men or aliens I am suggesting elementary cause and effect relationships.
The remedy to this is education induced neurosis is simply one has to seek a situation their hypothalamus gives them a "death" signal and then one ignores it and the amygdala remembers that and then the right brain aspect unveils in about a month. I am mindful you grasp the concept of this remedy so the important thing is to experiment with that concept.

"Don't find fault, find(apply) a(the) remedy." - Henry Ford = focus on the log in your eye.
Simply put after ones right brain intuition is veiled ones has to be told what to do and what to think, so one is just a sheep, and to boot ones fear is through the roof and thus they are easy to control.
Perhaps I will clarify these clarifications clarifyingly in the next clarification, perhaps.
Everyone is doing the best they can based on their perception, understanding and influence.As awareness and comprehension of a situation decreases hope increases. - 2/20/2010 7:16:56 PM